Philosophy, Politics and Citizenship

Philosophy, Politics and Citizenship

The Life and Thought of the British Idealists

ANDREW VINCENT
and
RAYMOND PLANT

Basil Blackwell

© A. Vincent and R. Plant, 1984

First published in 1984 by Basil Blackwell Publishers Limited
108 Cowley Road, Oxford OX4 1JF

British Library Cataloguing in Publication Data

Plant, Raymond
   Philosophy, politics and citizenship.
   1. Political science
   I. Title   II. Vincent, Andrew
   320'.01 JA66
   ISBN 0-85520-693-4

Typeset by Katerprint Co Ltd, Oxford
Printed and bound in Great Britain at
The Camelot Press Ltd, Southampton

T. H. Green tried to inaugurate a new concept of citizenship which would link men of different social classes. The concept was based upon the notion that there was a good common to members of all classes, a goal the existence of which could be established from German Idealist metaphysics and which could be made visible in actual measures of educational reform and social welfare.

A. MacIntyre, *Secularisation and Moral Change*

Contents

Preface

This book has had a long period of gestation. In the late 1960s, Raymond Plant initially began work on a book on the British Idealists which was a natural outgrowth of his interests in Hegel and the politics of the welfare state. In 1974 he published *Community and Ideology*, in the Preface to which he suggested that he might shortly be in a position to publish a book on the issues dealt with in the present volume. In the same year Andrew Vincent came to study for a doctorate in the Philosophy Department at Manchester University where Plant then was. This marked the beginning of a long period of fruitful collaboration and the present book is the long-delayed result of this process. Changes of job, growing families, a diversifying of interests, have all played their part in making the process of writing the book more protracted than we expected. This has, however, had its compensations. In the intervening period important studies on topics and figures relating to the issues raised in the book have been published by Collini, Clarke and Freeden, among others, and as a result there is today much more interest in Idealism and its relation to political and social movements than there was ten or fifteen years ago.

We hope that this book will make a useful contribution to this debate. During the period covered by this book, roughly 1880–1914, the foundations of the welfare state were being laid and the present work can be seen in some respects as a contribution to the history of the idea of the welfare state and the role of voluntary agencies within it. As such we hope that the book will appeal to students of social policy and administration as much as to political theorists. At a time when the role and purpose of the welfare state is being subjected to a scrutiny which it has not had for over a generation, it is a good thing to go back and look at aspects of the origin of the view that the state has a responsibility for welfare and for the character of the citizenship to be exercised within the welfare state, and the moral and political values which made these considerations appear to be imperatives to an important group of thinkers at the time.

Andrew Vincent
Raymond Plant

1 The State, Citizenship and Idealism

We who were reformers from the beginning always said that the enfranchisement of the people was an end in itself. We said, and we were much derided for saying so, that only citizenship makes the moral man; that only citizenship gives that self respect which is the true basis of respect for others, and without which there is no lasting social order or real morality.

T. H. Green

Britain was . . . the home of idealist political philosophy in the late 19th century, a philosophy that put up barriers against any realistic examination of politics.

J. M. Buchanan

In an age in which it is frequently argued by critics of the Left and Right that there is a fundamental crisis affecting the role of the state in welfare capitalist societies, it is worthwhile turning to a reassessment of some of the intellectual roots of the welfare state and its attendant political forms, particularly Liberalism and social democracy.

In this book we shall be concerned to describe and evaluate the political theories of the Idealists, a group of philosophers centred around the pivotal figure of Thomas Hill Green[1] in Oxford in the last three decades of the nineteenth century, whose influence was crucial in the early years of this century when the foundations of the welfare state were being laid. These thinkers, including Sir Henry Jones,[2] Bernard Bosanquet,[3] D. G. Ritchie,[4] William Wallace,[5] E. Caird,[6] and Lord Haldane,[7] fundamentally changed the conception of the role of the state within the Liberal tradition of political thought. They developed a theory of the state which was a long way removed from the rational calculative tendencies of utilitarianism and provided a justification for the role of the state in the spheres of economic life and welfare which went beyond what has usually been countenanced within Liberalism, whether based upon utilitarianism or Lockean theory. The Idealists achieved this by means of a complex theory which gave the state a particular moral significance. They saw the role of the state not merely as a set of instrumentalities for securing material welfare but as the focus of a sense of community and citizenship, an institution in which a good common to all classes and recognizable by all interest groups could be articulated. The purpose of the state was to promote the good life of its citizens and to develop the moral nature of man. Unlike subsequent social democratic thinkers such as Durbin, Jay, Gaitskell and Crosland, the Idealists were 'moral' rather than 'mechanical' reformers, in terms of the distinction developed by Peter Clarke in his *Liberalism and Social Democrats*,[8] believing that the transformation of society depends upon changes of moral attitude among citizens as much as changes inaugurated by central governments.[9]

Obviously such an exalted view of the possibilities and purposes of political action, of removing 'all obstructions which the law can remove to the free development of English citizens' could not be achieved without a considerable reinterpretation of some of the central concepts of political thought: the individual, rights, duties, liberty, property and community, concepts which in their turn required a conception of the nature of man as their undergirding. In so doing the Idealists sought to state in a richer and more complex form a variety of Liberalism which would give more stress to the role of the state and to the place of community within the polity than had been characteristic of 'old' *laissez-faire* 'night watchman' state Liberalism. To do this they turned away from the tradition of empiricism which had been at the heart of English Liberal thought from the time of Locke, and which the Idealist saw as allied to a calculative individualism, and turned for inspiration to Aristotle, Plato, Kant, Baur and, above all, to Hegel.

In the light of this, it might be thought that while the Idealists may have changed the intellectual categories in terms of which politics was conceived, the change was purely academic with no impact outside small groups of academic philosophers and political theorists. However, this would be a mistake and this judgement is supported not just by historians of ideas who might be thought to be biased on the importance of the role of ideas in practical politics, but also by political historians. Some examples from relatively recent literature may serve to make this point. In his book *Marxism* George Lichtheim argues:

in England, where Marxism was without influence before 1918, and indeed had scarcely any competent spokesman, philosophical idealism in some cases underpinned a radical critique of existing institutions. Neo-Hegelian emphasis upon the state and the collectivity became fashionable, via the universities, among members of the governing elite who prided themselves upon their emancipation from oldfashioned laissez faire liberalism . . . The common denominator was contempt for laissez faire and an altogether novel readiness to employ political coercion – the state – for the purpose of remoulding society.[10]

In the most recent general study of British politics during this period, Martin Pugh argues for a recognition of the importance of the influence of Idealism in the field of practical politics.

Aware of the strains of their society, adherents of Liberalism tended to reaffirm their basic object of maximising liberty as a means of individual moral improvement. T. H. Green, the Oxford philosopher, urged greater and more purposeful use of social intervention. What is important here is that by the 1900s it was those who thought along Green's lines who were to come to typify active political liberals.[11]

Echoing this theme in his extensive survey of *The State Tradition in Western Europe*, Kenneth Dyson argues:

During the period from about 1880 to about 1910 philosophical Idealism enjoyed considerable success within technical philosophy (principally at Oxford) and had an influence upon political leaders like Herbert Asquith, R. B. Haldane and Alfred Milner, social reformers like William Beveridge and Arnold Toynbee, and public servants many of whom were educated in Oxford liberalism.[12]

The aim of this book is not only to describe and assess Idealism as a form of political theory but also as a 'practical creed' in Sir Henry Jones's phrase, looking at its influence upon the development of 'New Liberalism' and thus on the foundations of social democracy and upon various forms and agencies of social reform such as social work, community work and education. A political theory which placed such emphasis upon the moral vocation of citizenship and the value of community organized around a common good could not be indifferent to the activities and agencies whereby individuals are integrated into society and given a sense of membership, whether these agencies be political or located in the sphere of voluntary action and charity rather than the coercive apparatus of the state. The moral basis of the political community had to be made intelligible to and have relevance for not only the Oxford undergraduates, enthused by

Green's teaching and destined for service in politics and administration but also to Green's deracinated 'denizen of the London yard'. In this sense Idealism had to be a practical creed, giving a sense of moral purpose to efforts, both political and charitable to transform the lives, and not just the material conditions, of the citizens of the modern state.

However, the argument of the book is not wholly historical. There is a widespread sense of crisis about the role of the state in modern society. Its involvement with welfare is seen as immoral and inefficient by critics of the Right, such as Hayek,[13] Friedman,[14] and Nozick,[15] while on the neo-Marxist Left, the social democratic consensus as represented in the institutions of the welfare state is seen as inherently unstable by commentators such as O'Connor and Habermas. The Liberal/Idealist view of the state has contributed a very great deal to the moral undergirding of the social democratic state, and to examine it more closely will enable us to perceive more clearly some of the intellectual pressures which led to the state being understood in this modestly collectivist way. Indeed, to talk about the social democratic state in the context of Idealism is not wholly anachronistic. A number of recent books have stressed in some cases the actual influence of Idealism on the development of social democratic thought – for example R. Terrill's study of R. H. Tawney,[16] whereas others have pointed out affinities with social democratic arguments. Alan Warde for example in his recent book on the Labour party since 1945, *Consensus and Beyond*[17] has pointed out that there is a clear link in language (in some respects) and concern (in most respects) between the Idealists such as Green, and the social democratic tradition in British politics, as exemplified in the writings of Tawney, Marshall and Crosland. Indeed, in his recent book, *Radical Earnestness,*[18] Fred Inglis has argued that there are intriguing similarities between Green and Crosland in terms of social origins, character and moral concerns. This general thesis about the connection between Idealism and social democracy is not new – in 1951 Adam Ulam published his *Philosophical Foundations of English Socialism*[19] in which the point is stressed.

What is very marked about Idealism, however, in contrast to more recent social democratic and Liberal political thought, at least before the publication of Rawls', *Theory of Justice*[20] is the amount of effort which they put into developing ideas about state intervention and collectivism in the context of a fully developed moral and political theory. In his Introduction to *Parliament and Social Democracy*[21] David Marquand argues that one of the major gaps in modern social democratic thought is the lack of a theory of the state. It is instructive to turn to the very beginnings of the development of the tradition to see how such a theory was developed and how it came to be abandoned. In an important sense therefore the Idealists' stress upon the role of the state, citizenship and political community also raises questions for modern political theory, and indeed political science.

It is a central irony of the intellectual life of our times that one of the effects of the enormous growth of political science has been the displacement of the concept of citizenship, and the theory of the state, from the centre of political theory. This is true even of recent works such as Rawls' *Theory of Justice* and Nozick's *Anarchy State and Utopia,* which seek to recapture some of the systematic character of earlier forms of political philosophy. The Idealists offered their contemporaries and us a theory of the state and citizenship; but do we need one? After examining the Idealist view of citizenship we shall need to explain the demise of the concept in political thinking and to assess whether we are in need of a constructive theory of citizenship today.

The argument of this book falls into two parts. Chapters 2 and 3 depict the general character of Idealist political theory. This involves looking closely at the Idealists' metaphysical and religious views, since their conception of politics is very clearly derived from metaphysics. Chapter 2 deals with the way in which Green's views on the nature and purposes of man arise out of, and are a rationalization of, his basically Hegelian view of religion; the subsequent chapter looks at the systematic exposition of this theory in *The Prolegomena to Ethics.* The second part of the book is concerned primarily to examine the way in which the Idealists' conception of citizenship influence political practice, in the narrow sense, and also the non-political agencies which they regarded as important to citizenship: social work, community work and education. In order to reduce a vast amount of material to manageable proportions we have in this second part looked at the influence of Green on Liberal thought; at Bosanquet on social work; at Toynbee on community work; and at Haldane on education. They are all Idealists sharing the same cast of mind and approaching issues within the same broad perspective.

Finally, we consider that although Idealist arguments are mistaken and embody assumptions which we can no longer share, nevertheless they do confront issues within the Liberal/social democratic tradition in political theory which are beginning to be raised again.

2 'The Word is Nigh Thee': The Religious Context of Idealism

The word is nigh thee even in thy mouth and in thy heart: that is the word of faith.

Romans 10.8

At a time when every thoughtful man accustomed to call himself a Christian, is asking the faith which he professes for some account of its origin and authority, it is a pity that the answer should be confused by the habit of identifying Christianity with the collection of propositions which constitute the written New Testament.

T. H. Green

Philosophy on its part is seen to be effort towards self recognition of that spiritual life which fulfils itself in many ways but most completely in the Christian religion and is related to religion as flowers to a leaf.

T. H. Green

Religion was a critical aspect of the metaphysical basis of Idealist theories of politics, and paradoxically it is religion which provided the Idealists with the link between metaphysics and politics. The Idealists situated their view of collective action, the common good and freedom within a metaphysical theory which claimed to state, in a more rational form, the real essence of Christianity and to do this in a way which largely by-passed the historical basis of that religion – a basis which was being increasingly contested during the second half of the nineteenth century. The wedding together of social and political theory with a powerful defence of Christianity, which at the same time drew upon but transformed some of the sources of contemporary doubt gave to Idealism a force which it might not otherwise have had. It did this not only by its philosophical defence of Christianity and its willingness to face up to the historical critique of the Bible, important though that was, but also by being able to claim that the vision of man and society which Idealism articulated was in fact present in a pictorial form in the religious conceptions of ordinary Christian people. As Green argued: 'Philosophy does but interpret with full consciousness and in system, the powers already working in the spiritual life of mankind.'[1] In this sense Idealism could present itself not as some abstract political theory which sought an entry into the social and political conceptions of ordinary citizens, *but rather it claimed both to make articulate and defensible the central elements of that consciousness as it already existed.*

In the second half of the nineteenth century Christianity was in a very weak intellectual and moral position to offer a radical critique of capitalist society largely because its own basis had become so contested and the intellectual doubts about both the philosophical and historical basis of Christian belief spread very widely. Arguments which purported to prove the existence of a personal God had been subjected to radical criticism by Hume and Kant and both the evidence for, and religious importance of, miracles had been rejected by Hume. The historical basis of Christian belief had come under fire from the Hegelian-inspired biblical critics of the so-called Tübingen School, particularly F. C. Baur and D. F. Strauss. In addition, evolutionary theories tended to undermine the biblical account of creation and in particular its dating of 4004 BC by Archbishop Ussher, while at the very same time theories of evolution were widely held to provide a scientific underpinning to *laissez-faire.*

The reaction of Christians to this intellectual onslaught on their faith was of course varied. Many conservatives both on the Tractarian and evangelical wings of the established church resolutely turned their backs on these problems, the Tractarians such as Keble, Newman and Liddon insisting upon the authority of the Church as opposed to human reason in these matters, the evangelicals, insisting, on the contrary, upon the authority of the conscience of each individual Christian. When defences were offered they were frequently feeble.[2]

However, bland and ineffective replies were not sufficient for many influential Victorians. George Eliot for example lost her evangelical faith as a result of reading Hennells' *An Enquiry Concerning the Origins of Christianity,* and indeed went on to translate two of the major critical works on Christianity: Strauss's *Das Leben Jesu,* and Feuerbach's *Das Wesen des Christentums.*

Benjamin Jowett, the Master of Balliol, Green's college, was deeply influenced by continental researches, as evidenced by his comment-aries on the Epistles to the *Thessalonians, Galatians* and *Romans*, and his influential essay on 'The Interpretation of Holy Scripture' published in *Essays and Reviews*. Jowett was indicted for heresy for the publication of this essay and the whole volume scandalized the orthodox. This mood of religious questioning and uncertainty was profoundly unsettling at least to those who felt the need for secure discursive foundations for their faith whether these were derived from history, philosophy or science, and it was perhaps Tennyson in *In Memoriam* who encapsulated most poignantly his profound intellectual uncertainty in his well known lines in a poem which Green regarded as reflecting many of the anxieties of the age:

> I falter where I firmly trod,
> And falling with my weight of cares,
> Upon the great world's altar stairs
> That slope through darkness up to God
> . . . I stretch lame hands of faith and grope
> And gather dust and chaff.

Thomas Green addressed himself directly to this problem. Going back to some of the major sources of contemporary doubt in the ambiguous theological legacy of Hegel, Strauss and Baur, he used their work to fashion Christian belief into a metaphysical system, the truth of which could be demonstrated independently of contested evidence whether derived from history or the natural sciences. At the same time this rational form of Christian belief was held by Green to illuminate and render perspicuous and actual religious beliefs which Christian people had, but which were represented in both a misleading and contested idiom within the life of actual religious discipleship. In addition, this developed and transformed Christian-ity would for Green provide the basis within the consciousness of individual citizens for the appeal of a common good within society to make itself felt. It will be argued later that Green's political and social philosophy, and indeed the work of those who followed him, spoke to the condition of many radicals not just because it developed a theory of the common good and human freedom which made them able to make sense of their collectivist tendencies within a recogniz-ably Liberal pattern of thought, but also because it did so in terms of a metaphysical system drawn from German Idealism which claimed to make Christianity at once rational and defensible. As Arnold

Toynbee was to claim later, this religious-based metaphysic fulfilled a very clear need for many radicals of the period:

Earnest and thoughtful people are willing to encounter the difficulty of mastering some unfamiliar phrases of technical language when they find that they are in possession of a sharply defined intellectual position on which their religious faith can rest.[3]

Alasdair MacIntyre in *Secularisation and Moral Change* points out in a sceptical way that the common good in society was to be demonstrated by 'proofs drawn from German Idealist metaphysics'; he goes on to argue that few philosophers today would regard metaphysics as having an appropriate role in this kind of context.[4] The implication is clearly that the common good established as a result of these seemingly esoteric arguments would be abstract and academic and not part of people's everyday social and moral experience. However, put in this way the criticism misses the crucial point that German Idealism and Green's version of it, claims not to be a philosophical position independent of other human activities, but rather is an attempt to bring out in a conscious and systematic way what is already implied in those activities and particularly the highest form, namely religion. *Religion is the link between political philosophy and social practice.* It is because Green's metaphysic is based securely in and provides a defence for Christian belief that it has an entrenched position within the moral and religious beliefs of the ordinary citizen. The point is exactly as Arnold Toynbee, Green's pupil argued: 'Christian dogma thus must be retained in its completeness, but it must be transformed into a philosophy. Other thinkers have assailed the orthodox foundations of religion to overthrow it. Mr Green assailed it to save it.'[5]

To save Christianity, Green turned to the work of Hegel. Hegel was profoundly concerned with religion but treated it in a highly ambiguous manner. In his early theological writings, which remained unpublished during his lifetime, Hegel was very much concerned about the bad effects that he thought orthodox Christian belief had upon contemporary society. He considered that the emphasis in Christianity, inherited from the Judaic tradition, upon the transcendence and 'otherness' of God tended to encourage a citizen to look outside and beyond his community for his moral ideals and for his sense of self-realization. The ends of human life and the springs of human morality were seen within orthodox Christianity in terms of the obedience of the individual to the will of a remote and transcendent God, rather than encouraging a man to find his self-fulfilment in the morality to hand in the activities, institutions and relationships within his own society. Christianity in addition, emphasized the privacy of the relationship between man and God and this equally led to a dislocation between man and his community. It was thus no accident in Hegel's view that Christianity began to flourish during the post-Augustinian era of the Roman Empire when public involvement and participatory citizenship were on the decline. Orthodox Christianity signalled a retreat from *res publica* into the privacy of personal devotion which fitted in very closely with the development of the social and political structure of the Roman Empire. As Green was later to argue: 'it [Christianity] would convey the idea of inward peace for which the self introspective spirit of the later Empire debarred from outward activities was painfully seeking.'[6]

Orthodox Christianity had deleterious social effects which were very largely, in Hegel's view, the result of a faulty conception of God, a conception of God as utterly transcendent. Such a conception of God, deeply embedded within orthodox Christian theology and indebted to both the Jewish and Aristotelian conceptions, was not adequate in Hegel's view because it could not account for creation. If God is self-sufficient, completely perfect, fully self-conscious and totally transcendent, how could such a God come to create a world in which both the act of creation and nature so created are to be seen as manifestations of the purposes of God?[7] God in a sense requires nature for his own self-completion and thus he realizes himself in creation and in human history.[8] On this view human history and human institutions are, as it were, epiphanies of God and they stand to individuals in an almost sacramental manner.[9]

Not only does such a revised view of God enable creation to be made intelligible, it also yields a revised acount of the incarnation and Christology within the Christian tradition.[10] It is Hegel's view that his revised concept of God and of Christology is a case of transforming a muddled, mythical and pictorial account into a rational exoteric account of Christian doctrine. In traditional theology Christ was the *one* incarnation of God within history, the one person and the one time at which the divine and human were united. This is presented as a claim based upon history that at a particular point in time an individual had been the incarnation of the divine, and it was just this claim which was becoming widely attacked in the nineteenth century. It was attacked as a claim based on history in terms of the view developed by Strauss and Baur that the biblical data purporting to reveal the facts of the life of Jesus were extremely problematic, and as a theological point in terms of the argument that there could be no logical basis for the construction of a theological conception of Jesus as the God–Man on the basis of the historical evidence about the life of Jesus even assuming that the evidence is unproblematic. There is a logical gap between claims about the Jesus of history, which can be contested on historical grounds, and the Christ of faith which can be contested on theological/philosophical grounds.

Hegel argues that what is required is a speculative or philosophical view of the figure of Christ, one which is unencumbered by either contested historical evidence or contested theological doctrine. The figure of Christ marks the point in human history at which men began to realize the inter-relationship between the divine and human, the finite and the infinite. This unity of the finite and the infinite can now be demonstrated philosophically. The figure of Jesus Christ is a kind of symbol for the general identification of God or Spirit and the world; he is not to be seen as the one unique incarnation. The figure of Jesus is by way of a general symbol of God's involvement and self realization within human history and institutions. Indeed, on this view all men are incarnations of God and institutions reveal the divine presence in history. As Green states eloquently in the penultimate paragraph of his *Essay on Christian Dogma*; 'God has died and been buried, and risen again, and realized himself in all the particularities of a moral life.' The task of the philosopher parallels that of the Christian community, to grasp the whole world and its development as part of the self realization of God. Such a vision of the human situation of course has profound implications for the understanding of politics and human history: it means that history has a rational structure, and the modes of human experience, including the practical realms of politics and morality have a part in this structure. A metaphysic grounded in, but transforming the Christian vision, will teach the immanence of God, the rationality of human life and history and the continuity of human purposes as part of the development of the Absolute. Green summarizes and endorses this position in his review of John Caird's Hegelian *Introduction to the Philosophy of Religion*:

That there is one spiritual self conscious being of which all that is real is the activity and the expression; that we are related to this spiritual being not merely as parts of the world which is its expression but as partakers in some inchoate measure of the self consciousness through which it at once constitutes and distinguishes itself from the world: that this participation is the source of morality and religion; this we take to be the vital truth which Hegel had to teach. It still remains to be presented in a form which will command some general acceptance among serious and scientific men.[11]

This was to be the basis of Green's own philosophy of which his political philosophy was an integral part, and he sought to state this vision in a less esoteric way than Hegel had managed, so that it would 'command some general acceptance among serious and scientific men'.

In the work of David Strauss, who produced his monumental *Das Leben Jesu* within four years of Hegel's death in 1831, the historical basis of Christianity, which is shown by Hegel to be ultimately irrelevant, is shown by Strauss to be without foundation. In a book of half a million words, written at the age of twenty-seven, Strauss subjects the gospels to searching internal criticism and finds them desperately wanting; at the same time though, Strauss, like Hegel, sees the essence of Christianity to lie beyond the reach of historical criticism: 'the recognition of God as Spirit implies that God does not remain as a fixed and immutable Infinite encompassing the Finite, but enters into it, produces the Finite, Nature and the Human mind merely as a limited manifestation of himself.'[12] Again we see the propensity to lift religion from the mythical, allegorical imaginative level of *Vorstellung* to the conceptual exoteric level of *Begriff*.[13]

Aside from Hegel and Strauss, the other philosopher/theologian who influenced Green was F. C. Baur. In fact Green was for a time engaged in making a translation of Baur's *Geschichte der Christlichen Kirche* and in Green's estimation he was 'nearly the most instructive writer I have ever met with'. *The Essay on Dogma* which Green wrote as a result of his researches into Baur's work testifies to the strength of his influence on Green. The crucial idea which Green seems to have derived from Baur, and which was to play an important role in making his political philosophy more critical than that of Hegel, was that the self-realization of God in human history is never a finished process. Whereas Hegel seems to have thought that the Absolute or God has come to full self-consciousness and full self-realization in the early nineteenth century, Green following Baur, takes a different view. Commenting upon Baur's progressive view of the Christian revelation set out in *Geschichte der Christlichen Kirche* he argues:

The revelation therefore is not made in a day, or a generation, or a century. The divine mind touches, modifies, becomes the mind of man, through a process which mere intellectual conception is only the beginning but of which the gradual complement is an *unexhausted* series of spiritual discipline through all the agencies of social life.[14]

The idea of revelation of the divine as a progressive way through human history is crucial for Green. And yet he is not committed, as was Hegel, to the view that the present culture and political structure of Western Europe is the final form which the Absolute's self-realization will take; at the same time it enables Green to deal after a fashion with evolutionary theories. He is not committed to the view that man was created fully formed with all his capacities and powers fully developed; rather their development through history are themselves part of the way in which God is immanently at work in the guidance of human history. Nor does Green believe that man has now assumed his final form – there will always be room for the development and the transformation of human capacities. The future is open, and the past is explicable in teleological terms, in terms of the progessive development of the characteristic human qualities, including those which are involved in the formation of social and political relationships.

The figure of St Paul was crucial to Green and Baur, it enabled them to explain the progressive development of Christianity from a narrow Judaic basis to a universal one, embracing as Green was later to say, the whole of humanity 'for whom Christ died'. Indeed Green's moral philosophy could be described as Pauline. St Paul's Christianity is, in Green's view, independent of knowledge of the detail of the 'historical' life of Jesus and this lack of acquaintance with historical evidence did not impair St Paul's discipleship. Of course, St Paul was given a revelation on the Damascus Road and this might be thought to compensate for his lack of acquaintance with the historical Jesus,[15] and for the conviction which presence at his miracles might be thought to have conferred, but in fact Green even argues that such a revelation is not necessary to come to understand the essential vision of Christianity.[16]

It is in some of Green's earlier reviews and 'lay sermons' given in Balliol Hall that the link between humanized, rational and non-historical Christianity on the one hand, and metaphysics on the other, comes out particularly clearly. Observing this connection we are able to appreciate the religious dimension[17] to Green's metaphysical thinking, and from that to understand some of his most characteristic metaphysical concepts such as self-consciousness, and the real or best self – concepts which are of crucial importance for his political thought. At the same time to see Green's metaphysic in this light enables us to see its force in the context of late Victorian Britain: it provided a theory of politics which sought to show that there is good to be attained in society which could be the aim of all men, and not just of a particular group or class in terms of a developmental metaphysic – thus fitting loosely into ideas about evolution – and trading upon a philosophical understanding of religion which aimed at saving the essence of Christianity while making it immune from the historical critique which had threatened to destroy it.

The problem posed by the transcendence of God lies at the heart of Green's metaphysic much as it did in that of Hegel. Green in fact went a very long way in these early writings to connect the revelation of God in history with some of the central themes of his political thinking. One of the basic sources for this view is to be found in the lay sermon 'The Word is Nigh Thee':

If there is an essence within the essence of Christianity, it is the thought embodied in the text that I have read; the thought of God not as 'far off' but as 'nigh', not as master but as father, not as terrible outward power forcing us we know not whither, but as one of whom we may say that we are reason of his reason, and spirit of his spirit, who lives in our moral life and for whom we live in living for the brethren, even as in so living we live freely.[18]

The fulfilment of the duties of citizenship are seen by Green to be involved in 'living for the brethren' and the basis of this conception of citizenship is, as we shall see, deeply imbued with theological understanding. However, it is important to notice at this point in the argument that the immanence of God is not being established by theological or philosophical argument, it is rather being regarded as being implicit in the actual practice of religion. Nevertheless, we can see some of the central motifs of Green's mature metaphysical views present in this lay sermon: the self-revelation of God in and through human life, morality as living in accordance with this spiritual principle, living thus involves living for others because we are all part of this developing spiritual process, and, because there is no fundamental discrepancy between the spirit of God and our own moral actions, to live morally and religiously is not a diminution of freedom, it is not obeying a positive law outside of oneself, but rather a law which is constitutive of our character as rational agents and moral beings.

Indeed, for Green the relationship between God and the individual is to be found in moral endeavour. Moral activity is determined by an ideal which the agent presents to himself. In pursuing this end which is not actually present in reality I identify myself with it and so desire to be something which I am not but which I conceive myself as capable of becoming. Moral endeavour thus reveals for Green a duality in the self: my actual self, my interests, desires, prejudices, etc., and my possible self, that which I could become by a redirection or a transformation of my desires, interests, passions, etc. Morality is a matter of self-realization in the sense of continually attempting to bring into being this possible and desirable self. This possible self, the telos of moral endeavour is identified by Green with God.[19] He grants that this has the effect of making man identical with God, but Green has two ways of dealing with this paradox. If God is regarded as being so totally other, so utterly transcendent then, Green argues, he would be irrelevant for man; the other argument goes back to what, as we saw, Green took from Baur and rejected from Hegel, namely that there is no actual state in history or within the life of an individual in which all moral possibilities are fully achieved, and thus there is no stage in which God is actually identical with human life. The possibilities of self-realization, the achievement of the possible self and the actualization of the moral ideal are always open:

Our formula then is that God is identical with the self of every man in the sense of being the realisation of its determinate possibilities . . . that is being conscious of himself man is conscious of God, and thus knows that God is but knows what he is only in so far as he knows what he himself really is.[20]

Again this is linked up with the views of St Paul in the essay 'The Witness of God':

A death unto life, a life out of death, must in some way be the essence of the divine nature, must be an act which though exhibited once for all in the crucifixion and resurrection of Christ was yet eternal – the act of God himself. For that very reason however it was one perpetually enacted and to be renacted by man . . .[21]

In other words God constitutes in us a new intellectual consciousness which transforms the will and is the source of the moral life.

Green argued that a glorified life was basically the growing completion of this process. This glorified life was a progessive realization of God in the moral life and the possible self. Moral activity is therefore based on the contrast between the possible self and the actual self. Theology, ethics and other such systematic expositions of the human ideals represented objects that the individual could present to himself. The possible self or higher interest was seen as a desire to be something that the agent was not, yet which he conceived that he could become. The contrast established the terms of the actual and possible. The impulse was to make the possible actual. In this process the self, as the higher entity, was to be realized through the ends which were worthwhile.

Religion, for Green, was giving expression to God in the moral life. It was also imagining God in his most adequate and fulfilled revelation. This could only be done by imagining a man in whom the end of moral discipline and progress had been fully attained, which Green called 'A union of the will of God, perfect unselfishness, the direction of desire to ends which one rational being can consciously share with all other rational beings.' We could never wholly know this man in our present condition, thus its image had become glorified in Christ, who though put to death in the flesh, lived still in the spirit. Green's aim was to draw distinction between the man who works for himself alone, and the man who works 'as from the God that worketh in him'. In this indwelling God, represented in Christ, we find a bridge between the finite and infinite, heaven and earth, and religion and social life. Christ died for all men. Until each individually had reincarnated him in himself, his daily work and citizenship, perfection and the common rational good would not be realized.

Sin was thus an attempt to actualize those selfish possibilities of one's own which could not be actualized universally. Redemption was, after a period of self-reproach and consciousness of alienation, the overcoming of the barrier between God and man through good works. Faith was thus a state of mind, based on consciousness of God, in which the agent was enabled to actualize the ideal in works of citizenship 'in living for the brethren'. Sin was in a sense a prerequisite to faith, since unless we were conscious of our possibilities and our failure to live up to them, we would not be driven to have faith in the task of overcoming our alienation from our real possibilities. Men needed, in Edward Caird's favourite phrase to 'die in order to live'. In this path lay freedom. Green identified God with all the determinate possibilities of ourselves, the realization of which was the realization of divinity and freedom. God was no longer divided from man or the world. God was realizable in the mind of man and consequently in the agencies of social life.

The importance of Green's theological and philosophical thought on religion cannot be overstated. Virtually all the Idealist school, contemporaries with Green, and following him, accepted the essence of his theology. The pursuit of a life greater than our own, to find the best that we know, to try to see the ideal in all our everyday activities, civic and personal, to unite the infinite with the finite, these were the basic views of religion shared by the Idealist philosophers. Bernard Bosanquet's *What Religion Is,* Edward Caird's *Lay Sermons,* and Henry Jones's *The Faith that Enquires,* all expressed similar theological sentiments to Green. This philosophical interpretation of ordinary religious consciousness enabled Green, Jones, Caird and others to claim that their philosophy, though metaphysical, was a reconstruction of ordinary consciousness. As such, philosophy itself was part of the divine service.

3   A Metaphysical Theory of Politics

Bear ye one another's burdens and so fulfil the law of Christ.

Galatians 6.2

No longer members of a single class, but fellow citizens of one great people: no longer poor recipients of a class tradition but heirs of a nation's history.

Toynbee

However unconsciously, the effort for social amelioration implies what we commonly call a religious faith.

D. G. Ritchie

So far we have been concerned with the religious roots of Green's metaphysical theory because only the link between the two is able to provide a plausible explanation of the hold which his philosophy came to have over the minds of so many involved in politics and social reform. However, in the present chapter we shall turn to his philosophical works proper, and particularly to the *Prolegomena to Ethics* and the *Lectures on the Principles of Political Obligation*. Both of these works are deeply indebted to the religious conception which we have already discussed, but their arguments bear much more concretely upon practical morality and the social and institutional setting within which moral endeavour – man's making the best of himself – can take place.

The aim of the *Prolegomena to Ethics* is to attempt to prove on philosophical grounds what we have already seen Green regards as the correct understanding of religion and the place and purposes of human life within this religious framework. The work constitutes an extended discussion of the nature of human life in an attempt to show that a naturalistic understanding of the person is impossible, that there are aspects of human existence which cannot be made a subject for science. Green makes short work of the assumption that there can be a naturalistic theory of morals on the grounds that such a theory would be forced to regard the sense of obligation which we feel to be illusion; he considers that this is itself sufficient to make us pause and pose the fundamental question in this area, namely: whether a being that was merely the result of natural forces could form a theory of those forces explaining himself.[1] For Green this is the central question of metaphysics: whether the experience of connected matters of fact which are represented in science does not presuppose a principle which is not itself any one of these connected matters of fact. Green's answer to this question is, in some ways, similar to that of Kant, in other ways very different. Green, like Kant, counters naturalism by arguing that experience is not of a chaotic manifold, but at all times an awareness by an enduring subject of a unified, related world of objects. He differs from Kant in arguing that far from the manifold of experience being supplied outside of us, being constituted into a unified world via the operation of the mind through the categories and the forms of intuition, the 'objectivity' of objects has to be considered in terms of the necessary relations in which objects stand to one another: 'the idea of an object is that which is always the same in the same relations.' This enables Green to say that the manifold cannot be provided independently of the activity of the human mind because only minds or consciousness can make relationships and this is just what objectivity *means*. The self is the author of the world which it knows. 'Experience in the sense of consciousness of events as a related series . . . cannot be explained by any natural history so called. It is not a product of a series of events.'[2] At the same time Green argues that such a conception of objectivity in terms of relationships presupposes an order of nature – an unalterable order of relationships which is a presupposition of all inter-subjective[3] enquiry and activity, and that this requires the operation of a spiritual principle:

An eternal intelligence realised in the related facts of the world, or as a system of related facts rendered possible by such an intelligence, partially and gradually reproduces itself in us, communicating piecemeal, but in inseparable correlation, understanding and the facts understood, experience and the experienced world.[4].

The unifying power of the individual's mind reveals and reproduces, or mirrors, the absolute unifying power of the spiritual principle which Green of course identified as God.[5] At the same time this eternal intelligence does not reproduce itself fully in any human consciousness and because of this our knowledge of relationship and therefore of objectivity is always piecemeal and never fully completed. The existence of such an individual transcending mind is central to escaping the solipsism of subjective idealism. If the objectivity of experience is a product of mind, then there can only be a sense of *intersubjective* reality in so far as the operations of individual minds reproduce the operations of a mind or spirit in which we all share. In this sense Green has combined aspects of both Kant and Hegel and his eternal principle, so central to an objectivist epistemology is clearly similar in function to Hegel's *Geist* which plays the same unifying and objectifying role in his own philosophy. Green thus dismisses naturalism and seeks by metaphysical argument to demonstrate what had been central in his conception of religion: that we are all part of the divine life which reproduces itself in us progressively but never finally, and that the growing realization of the Absolute in human life must be seen as something necessary to make sense of our pursuit of objective knowledge. This is something for which Green is prepared to give a metaphysical justification but never something that is actually achieved in a particular generation as, for example, Hegel thought that it was.

However, at this stage the argument is exclusively concerned with cognition and although, as we have seen, Green had a central *moral* purpose in seeking to refute naturalism, he has yet to put his own metaphysic to work in moral thinking. The connection is made, however, in an argument about the nature of moral action. Green had argued earlier that if man is a creature driven by impulse and instinct, explicable in terms of natural physical laws, then morality becomes redundant. However, having refuted this suggestion by the use of the argument that the human mind, reproducing the eternal mind produces the world which it knows, Green suggests that it is in the activity of the individual mind, reproducing the divine mind, that morality is to be found. Human beings are not merely creatures of want and instinct, rather there is in each individual this spiritual principle which stands over and above the organic and natural aspect of an individual's life. The conscious mind pursues purposes and its ends are not *caused* but *posited*. A motive is not some physiologically explicable causal factor but an idea of an end which a self conscious subject presents to itself and which it strives to realize. Natural instincts and wants are transformed by these purposes and ends. In so far as they are transformed and made to serve self consciously posited purposes then man is acting in accordance with his real self, his self-conscious spiritual self. In its turn, of course, this struggle for the self-conscious transformation of natural instincts to serve rational purposes is an aspect of the eternal spiritual principle. To echo Green's more religious terminology in *The Witness of God*: 'God constitutes in us a new intellectual self consciousness which transforms the will and is the source of the new moral life.'[6] An end of the sort in question, posed for the self by our rational and deliberative faculties is always good: 'The motive in every imputable act for which the agent is conscious on reflection that he is answerable is a desire for personal good in some form or other.'[7] Moral activity is therefore the pursuit of an ideal set by ourselves and to which we aspire, a possible self which we could become and this is again the manifestation of the spiritual principle seeking to unify the actual and the possible, the natural and the ideal, in just the same way as in the case of cognition it is operative in securing the congruence between experience and an intersubjective reality. For the moral sphere, however, this is a matter of constant endeavour and we have no knowledge of its actual realization.[8]

On such a view of human nature and the structure of moral action, freedom cannot consist of the 'negative' freedom of being able to satisfy one's immediate wants, desires and impulses because it is just these that are capable of naturalistic causal explanation. Freedom consists of motivated actions, that is to say those actions which involve the transformation of impulses to serve those ends and purposes with which one has identified oneself. Freedom is positive in the sense that it is related to self realization, to the actualization and development of one's possible self, and of course involves the constant struggle to transform instincts and desires into such a form that they will serve the overall trajectory and purposes of a person's deliberative life. The idea of freedom as being the ability and power to make the best of one's self, and as such being part of divine disclosure in the human person,[9] is clearly crucial to Green's political theory and to the problems within liberal political and social theory to which Idealists addressed themselves.

The moral ideal which is the object of free endeavour is thus the realization of the unconditioned will or the goodwill, that is to say the will which transforms and transfigures the passions and instincts. However, it is clearly necessary to specify this ideal in more detail, but at the same time there are some difficulties in doing this because self realization is never finally attained.[10] However, Green does try in general terms to indicate the form which human self realization necessarily takes; its substance though depends on circumstances and the particular historical situation in which persons find themselves. In the first place, Green did not allow there to be a fundamental dichotomy between personal and public good, not because he was a collectivist as such, but rather because he saw a non-contingent relationship between persons and society so that an individual's possible self has an intrinsic social dimension. This position and the arguments which he used to support it is crucial for his overall political philosophy and for his conception of Liberalism. The argument seeks to establish the metaphysical basis of the view that between classes, hierarchies and groups in a society there is still a common good which all men share, whatever their differences in natural powers and social circumstances, and which is the basis for community life linking all persons in society into one harmonious whole. Those who argued that all interests were either personal or sectional, related to the material conditions of life were to be confounded by an argument designed to show that there is a common good shared by all, the existence of which could be demonstrated by argument and which could manifest itself through the political process in measures of social and political reform. At a personal level, the attempt to achieve the realization of one's capacities must always be restricted by the position in which one finds oneself and the function which one fulfils in society:

Human society presupposes persons in capacity – subjects capable each of conceiving himself and the bettering of his life as an end to himself – but it is only in the intercourse of men each recognised by each as an end not merely a means and each as having reciprocal claims that the capacity is actualised and we really live as persons.[11]

He concludes that society is 'the condition of the development of our personality'.[12]

The basis of Green's position here seems to be derived from Hegel's view that mutual recognition is necessary to one's own consciousness of self. We learn to regard ourselves as persons among other persons in certain sorts of social situations: in family life, in society and in the political life of the community, in which there are reciprocal rights and obligations which give formal recognition to persons and their relationships. Education in both the narrow sense and in the wider sense of socialization has as its presupposition the development of personality beyond the level of our conditioned animal nature. Society in Green's view 'supplies all the higher content to this conception, all those objects of a man's personal interests in living for which he lives for his own satisfaction.'[13] Human nature then has an intrinsic social aspect so that the achievement of our best selves and therefore the exercise of freedom requires a society in which persons are recognized as ends in themselves. Many Idealists followed Green's view of society and the individual, supporting him with the above and other arguments, Bradley, in chapter 6 of *Ethical Studies,* stresses the extent to which the individual is a product of a particular culture only acquiring values and ideals within a particular cultural setting; Sir Henry Jones in 'The Social Organism' in *Essays in Philosophical Criticism,* the memorial volume to Green, argued the same thesis.[14] Free action, as we have seen, consists of the intentional pursuit of ideals in an attempt to make the best of oneself, but the content of these ideals, what self realization is thought to be, is derived from the context in which one lives. Again this conception of the individual and his relation to society underpins Green's argument that the individual's moral capacities are linked up with the possibilities inherent in the social order. The social order, the community, are the spheres within which our characters develop. Such character-developing social environments are possible only under conditions in which individuals are prepared to accept one another as persons and to treat one another as ends in themselves.[15] Beneath the tensions and bifurcations between persons which seem to be such a part of social and political life there is a common good, the mutual recognition of personality, without which there will not be the social possibilities required for personal growth, granted that our conceptions of our own good are so deeply influenced by the society in which we live. This 'Kingdom of Ends' may vary in scope depending on time and place, the form of communal life and the types of experience it encompasses. It may appear in tribal organizations in which the rights of personality extend only as far as other members of the tribe, it may be restricted in certain contexts to family ties; in the present age the nation state is primarily the sphere in which personality is recognized and invested with rights and duties, and its fullest articulation, in Green's terms of universal citizenship is as wide as the humanity for which Christ died.[16] In fact history reveals in Green's view a gradual process of rational breaking down of the barriers to reciprocal recognition. In the same way, according to Baur and Green, as St Paul made the saving work of Christ available for all and not just Jews, so the same is true of the task of politics, to secure a broader and broader basis in society for citizenship – the recognition of persons as persons and the development of those conditions which will enable persons to pursue their ends.

Granted the way in which Green ties the pursuit of the common good to the particularity of social circumstance it might be thought that there is very little that could be said about what the common good requires in particular circumstances. However, Green does argue that there are formal criteria for determining whether a particular piece of legislation or a particular social policy serves the common good. Whatever a society may recognize as its barriers in terms of the recognition of persons, whether it be as narrow as a tribe or as wide as a nation state, respecting persons and building up a social environment in which they may pursue their ends will require that policies should be:

(1) good for all men;
(2) no one should gain by another's loss;
(3) loss and gain is to be estimated on the same principle for each person in society.

What, in particular circumstances, will meet these criteria cannot be determined in advance. There may be circumstances so pressing in which, according to Green, the moral demands of the common good require that you look no further than your family to keep them alive; at the opposite extreme it may express itself in working for some social reform which will enable individuals to find within themselves the mental and physical resources for their own self-development.[17] The common good is therefore to be seen in terms of the mutual development of character and the realization among persons in society, however broad or narrow that society may be, of their mutual status as persons and the recognition of this status in all the spheres − political, legal and economic of that society. However, understood in this way the common good becomes something much more intangible than, for example, the distribution of material resources in society as it became in subsequent social democratic formulations. Indeed Green goes so far as to say that because the common good is the mutual facilitation of self realization it should not be looked for in the economic sphere, at least beyond a certain basic level of the distribution of resources:

Civil society may be and is founded upon the idea of there being a common good but that idea in relation to the less favoured members of society is in effect being unrealised and it is unrealised because the good is being sought in objects which admit of being competed for. They are of a kind that they cannot be equally attained by all. The success of some in attaining them is incompatible with the success of others. Until the object generally thought as good comes to be a state of mind or character of which the approach to attainment by each itself is itself a contribution to its attainment by everyone else, social life must continue to be one of war . . .[18]

Green believed in and vigorously defended an extensive right to the accumulation and free transfer of property, and clearly, granted such a view, the common good was not to be cast in terms of some kind of equal ownership of resources or equal distribution of goods and services. He provides an extensive theoretical justification for this view in *Prolegomena to Ethics*. Having argued that the Divine principle can only realize itself through persons in society, Green goes on to argue that society is inevitably differentiated into distinctions of social position and power[19] and he argues that these distinctions are necessary to the development of personality. There can be no development of the personality 'without a recognised power of appropriating material things' and this power of appropriation will vary in its effects 'according to talent and opportunity' with the result that there will be differences in 'the form which personality takes in different men'. The common good is achieved by each person within his differentiated function[20] which makes some 'contribution to human perfection'; he argues that it is only as far as this development and direction of personality 'is obtained for all who are capable of it (as presumably everyone who says "I" is capable), that human society . . . can be held to fulfil its function, to realise its idea as it is in God.'[21]

The recovery of community and a sense of common life depends, as we have seen, on there being a sense of a common good between persons, but if it is seen in material terms it cannot be achieved; rather it must be something which can be found broadly within the structure of existing inequalities. The mutual recognition of persons and their self realization does not require any *fundamental* change in the present distribution of goods in society although it *will* require certain kinds of social services to be provided which were not in Green's time widely thought to be necessary, those which bring a relief from the pressure of animal wants. Such a supply of the means of living will allow room for the consideration of the ends of living.[22] But this provision was not thought to be such as to fundamentally alter property relationships in society. Mutual respect and citizenship did not require a radical revision of inequalities. The common good cannot consist in the pursuit of objects which can be competed for and thus leaves only one good in Green's view: 'The only good which is really common to all who pursue it, is that which consists in the universal will to be good – in the settled disposition on each man's part to make the most and best of humanity in his own person and the persons of others.'[23]

In order to do this, relief from basic wants is necessary, but that is all. Community does not depend upon greater equalization of the conditions of life, but rather in a settled disposition of each person to make the best of himself and improve his character in his particular calling and to seek to enable others to do the same. Cetainly Green's views were not idiosyncratic among the Idealists and possibly it is in Hegel's work that we can see the original form of such tensions at work. Hegel well recognized social inequalities, the unequal distribution of wealth and the role of poverty in modern society[24] but he too wished to argue that the recovery of community did not require the fundamental restructuring of social and political inequalities, but rather was to be based upon a common understanding of these social relationships and their ultimate rationality, coupled with a legal system which guaranteed the rights of the individual person before the law. Among British Idealists it was perhaps Sir Henry Jones who faced squarely the implications of Green's defence of the common good and of inequality:

the essence of society is moral. It is only on moral grounds that we can determine the nature and limits of its functions. And the social reformer who comprehends this fact, so far from either welcoming or resisting the increase in social enterprises as a matter of course will seek only the supreme moral innovation namely the *moralising of our social relationships as they stand.*[25]

This sentiment is echoed by Toynbee, a disciple of Green, when he says that the Idealists were after 'differentiation of function and not differentiation of spirit'.[26]

The perfection and moral condition of a state is dependent upon the degree of citizenship in its membership.[27] As Henry Jones remarked in his work *The Principles of Citizenship*: 'The power of the good state empowers the citizen, and the power of the good citizen empowers the state.'[28] The citizen and the state grew together. In the citizen's consciousness and personality, as Jones wrote, the purposes of the state were formed. Thus, the concept of citizenship represented a co-ordination and subordination of individual actions towards some common good. It also represented a respect and realization of the moral worth of each person, which for the Idealist, John MacCunn, issued in civil and political equality although not economic. Citizenship was a prerequisite of true democracy based on respect. As MacCunn argued in his work *The Ethics of Citizenship*:

'To the great mass of mankind respect for men will not come home as conviction till they see worth looking at them out of the eyes of their fellow men.'[29] Civil and political equality are central to the common good, but they were not objects of competition.[30]

Clearly a conception of this sort poses problems for the nature of the individual. The Idealists identified different types of individuality. They did not exclude the atomic view of individuality, which they saw as present in the theories of Spencer and Bentham and the utilitarians generally, but a view of society as an aggregate of isolated atoms was seen as inadequate and abstract. Society was not just a sphere of individual self-interest. It was an organism for the realization of common purposes. The natural instinctual self was isolated to a large degree. It did not depend upon education and culture. The development through consciousness to self consciousness, however, represented a growth towards wholeness. Seeing oneself as a whole, integrating aspects of one's personality, and pursuing one's own ends were stages of individuality, as also was the development of seeing oneself as a co-agent with the world. Paradoxically the supreme achievement of the pursuit of individuality was a willed control of oneself in terms of rational purposes common to all men. In this sense individuality became co-extensive with the individuality of others. Thus if the state provisionally represented the common purposes of all individuals, it could be seen figuratively as a single individual being the representation of the common purposes of all men within it.

Again, most of the Idealists identified true individuality, citizenship and self-development with freedom. Real freedom was not the absence of compulsion but the maximum of power for all members of society to make the best of themselves. Rational activity was determined by choices. The decision of the rational agent was a free choice by the agent in terms of the higher common interests. The 'Law of liberty', as Edward Caird put it, 'is to retain permanently the consciousness of the better self in subjection to which alone we can be truly free.'[31] A problem arose as to how far the respect for the individual and his endowments could proceed before it could be said to conflict with the social purpose of citizenship. It seemed that in Green there was an assumed automatic relationship between fulfilling one's capacities and taking on a responsible role in the society. This would be so, once the metaphysical axiom was accepted that capacities are God-given and thus moral.

The theory of freedom put forward by Idealists was a positive notion, which although critical of the more negative notion in the utilitarian tradition, has itself come in for radical criticism this century. The variance between the Idealists' account and the utilitarians' was not as great as had often been maintained. Green had argued that the negative notion was perfectly comprehensible, but not manifestly the whole story. The positive conception argued that freedom was seen in terms of the performance of actions in the common interest, although the fact that an agent was positively directing his activity and using his powers was a negative contribution to the common interest in itself. The common interest, for Bosanquet, could be expressed from a man's 'groove' or station in society. He defined true freedom at one point as making the best of what we have. For Green, this groove might not be adequate for having a power, or expressing a common interest, and it would seem that he was not prepared to accept as much suffering as part of the universal order as was Bosanquet. Green's theories, by direct implication, contained an adequate defence of state intervention in the name of human freedom, to secure that freedom from want without which the moral life could not be lived.

The Idealist attitude to institutions represented a mid-way position between Burkean traditionalism and a dynamic reformism. J. H. Muirhead, in a preface to *Lectures on Birmingham Institutions*, wrote that 'institutions are not men. On the other hand living institutions . . . represent the past efforts and the present cooperation of many individuals directed to a single and continuous purpose, and in this account may claim an individuality of their own of even a higher kind than of any single person.'[32] In his own lecture in this book, Muirhead saw institutions as stable purposes as opposed to passing individual desires. In *Social Purpose* he described institutions as 'objectified purposes'. The family, trade unions, universities, social clubs and eventually the state, are an outcome of the mind and will of men.[33] This will was most often a common will which was prior to desires and aspirations. Men grew and were nurtured within institutions. Their modes of action, their ends, their rights, duties and obligations were prescribed by institutions. The vitality of the institutions was seen as proportional to the recognition of their purpose.

The ideal purpose of life lay in the secular world and institutions around us.[34] Our task was to try to realize these ideals and their significance. Salvation lay in a deeper understanding of *this* world, and not in another. Edward Caird stated the point with deep conviction: 'To believe that we can, here and now, make our lives ideal, that the round of duties that seem commonplace and secular

– these family ties, this college companionship ... furnish the very environment that is needed for the realisation of the highest.'[35] In 'The Kingdom of God on Earth', Bosanquet stated 'All that we mean by the kingdom of God on earth is the society of human beings who have a common life and are working for a common social good.'[36]

It was in this light that the state was viewed by the Idealists as an institution embodying the mind and purpose of its members, not members or parts as in a machine, but living, independent, rational and organic members. The state was the most important institution, since it united all the range of voluntary and statutory associations and groups embodying more limited purposes within them.

As we have seen, the common good did not presuppose identity of interests. The state as an institution representing this common purpose did not demand an absolute conformity. Yet it tended to overcome, insofar as it approached any perfection, the separation of interests. As Green argued: 'in other words, just so far as there is a state, interests are no longer merely separate.' Separation of interests in the state represented one aspect of its reality, yet for Green these were neutralized by the other factor, namely the common interest. As he wrote: 'neither would be what it is without the other but in the state neither retains any separate reality.'

For Green the common good existed in a partial sense. While competition, hardship and class divisions remain, the common good remains essentially a counsel of perfection, potentially present as the purpose of the perfect state. Green's admiration for John Bright and William Cobden, and his acceptance of some of the ideas of non-interference with unearned increment and property accumulation,[37] his views on the origins of the proletariat in the ownership of land in feudal times[38] and his idea that any man could compete for capital,[39] and his defence of full rights of inheritance,[40] rest uneasily with his ideas of the common good and freedom. This is especially true in relation to his lecture 'Liberal Legislation and Freedom of Contract'. If men could not achieve a common good in the competitive sphere, and yet the attempt to alleviate this competitive hardship through intervention in property rights or the unearned increment was also denied, on the grounds of freedom, surely this led to a paradox. There were reasons here for state action and reasons to deny action. Green seemed to uphold the sanctity of contract, so dear to the Manchester School, and yet to deny its sanctity in one of his most popular lectures. He accepted the value and necessity of property to each man and then denied its possibility for each man.[41] He recognized competition as valuable and yet admitted that only a few could acquire freedom through it. The common good was thus present, for Green, in the very fact of having a state and community, in the possibility of making the best of oneself in one's social function and seeking for the same for others. However, as we have seen, competition is both necessary for the development of the personality but also incapable of providing the arena within which the common good could be found.

Rights too were based on the common good. The moral capacity in each man was to Green 'a consciousness on the part of the subject of the capacity that its realization is an end desirable in itself, and rights are the condition of realizing it.'[42] It is through rights that the power of the individual came freely to make the common good his own. Thus, they were, in a sense, 'the negative realization of power'. They were not an arbitrary creation, neither were they antecedent to society, but were created in a social situation and needed to be recognized by others in order to become rights. Green dealt summarily with natural right. Rights apart from society were a contradiction. To ask why I accept rights prescribed in society, or in fact to the power of the state, would be like asking why I allowed my life to be ruled by a complex of institutions without which I should literally have no life to call my own.

Rights were therefore defined by John MacCunn as 'advantageous conditions of social well-being indispensable to the true development of the citizen, enjoyable by all members of the community, and which we are prepared to say that respect for them ought (in one way or another) to be enforced.'[43] The advantage of rights should be, for MacCunn, the opportunities they bring. Fullness of life, and not just freedom from aggression, should be the test. MacCunn saw the full life as that of an adequate livelihood, health, a chance to have a family life, to partake in tasks of citizenship, education, and religion.

A similarly based analysis was put by William Wallace in his essay on 'Natural Rights': rights, he argued, were not carried from birth, but were recognized claims in a community, presupposing a common standpoint. The controlling authority was the logical antecedent to the individual man. The authority and its attendant institutions made the man what he was. The mere individual, to Wallace, had no rights as such. He had rights 'only as a person, [i.e. as a member of society] as embodying in himself . . . the larger aggregate'.[44]

Green's theory of property was based on the principle that all should have the means to develop themselves and the use of their powers. Property was a right based upon the common good. It was thus distinguishable from mere possession on the count that it was dependent on recognition by others. In a sense property was possession, recognized as legitimate by others. Property needed to be initially appropriated. The man takes and fashions certain external objects as a permanent object of his satisfaction and expression. As rights, for Green, rested on the common will, so property rested on will understood as a constant principle operative in all men. The power to utilize property was secured to individuals irrespective of their use, so long as that use did not interfere with a like power by others. Everyone should labour for their property and respect similar appropriation by others. Property enables the self to develop as a will and also to develop responsibilities. It was inevitable, to Green, that in trade, inheritance, and ability, property would be unequal. As long as the inequality did not affect or prevent the right of others to become owners of property, it was justifiable.

Green wished to justify a system of responsible private enterprise, ultimately a form of humanized capitalism. The individual, if he was to be able to make choices, decisions and to pursue moral ends, must have the conditions whereby he can perform these. In other words, he cannot be coerced by a government into moral ends. Green seemed to envisage that society, industry and culture could be transformed only from within men's hearts. As long as the state provided basic conditions, and, more or less, an equality of opportunity, it was promoting common ends, namely, the equal chance of 'getting and keeping the means of realizing a will which in possibility is a will directed to social good.'[45] A man must be given a sphere of responsible action in order to exercise his moral faculties.

Later Idealists took up Green's theme. J. S. MacKenzie, writing in the 1890s, argued that 'the right of property may almost be regarded as part of the right of freedom.'[46] Nearly all men's ends and desires needed instruments to achieve them. If men did not possess these instruments their powers were rendered void. Use of instruments was of course limited by supply and demand, but, Mackenzie continued, their distribution could not be limited to the few. Property, as instrumental to freedom, implied a far wider distributive framework on the ethical grounds of self-development. However, we see here the distinction between the sphere of the common good and the sphere of competition and inequality, which Green insisted upon in breaking down.

Green's theory could easily be developed in different directions. With ideas of property as a basis to freedom and self-development, and with rights based upon the common good, it was open to interpretation by collectivists. The state, in ensuring individual development, could theoretically introduce a wide range of social measures, and only needed to ignore the aberrations of Green's arguments on the inviolability of unearned increment and inheritance. On the other count, if self-development were based upon a free market there was no precise limit to the acquisition of property. Property was in this case a reflection of the self-maintenance of the individual. In this case, state intervention necessarily took a back seat. Bosanquet, for example, who claimed to base his position on property on Green, argued that no property ought to come 'miraculously', i.e. in the form of pensions or state doles.[47] Failure to achieve adequate property reflected more on the individual's competence, than society or economics, and it was not the function of the state to bolster up incompetence.

The Idealists overall had an ambiguous view of property, competition and capitalism. It was as if they wanted to achieve a unity of the competitive instinct with the moral and rational good, within a moralized form of competition, yet all the time realizing that the two were exclusive, and providing no detailed account of an institutional resolution of the conflict.

For many of the Idealists the competitive struggle was inevitable. It was seen as the arena of soul-moulding and hardship by Bosanquet. Suffering and pain, the difficulties of acquiring property, reflected the moral condition of man. It was up to individuals to work themselves out of their condition, with qualified forms of help. Green, as has been shown, vacillated and gave out many hostages to fortune on both sides of the political fence. Many took him to imply that in order to create conditions for the development of individuals, it was necessary to make property ownership more equal and lessen the stress of capitalism by state intervention. Certainly, this was the impression of his justly famous lecture 'Liberal Legislation and Freedom of Contract'. Other Idealists, like Henry Jones, went back to the roots of the problem and objected to Hegel's views. Jones thought that 'it was Hegel's cardinal error . . . to hold that economic activity must always be the sphere of otherness' and thus exempt from ethical considerations. Hence, Jones looked towards an 'increasing ordering of economic organization by the conscience of the community, and a great extension of public control in the use of private property and in industrial relations'.[48] But he held that control need not necessarily and would not most effectively be exercised by the state itself.

This quotation from Henry Jones's biography encapsulates the uncertainly felt by many Idealists. He did not want the field of economic activity to be an area of pain and stress, and therefore suggested an ordering of the economic field. Yet, this control, which he envisaged to combat the ravages of an unimpeded market, was through the conscience of the community. Jones, in fact, was very keen on education in ethics and citizenship as a mode of training the community conscience. So, although he objected to Hegel's view of economic life, he was not prepared to take very far some of the implications of Green's theories. So the paradoxical solution to the destructive side of the economic process on self-development, morality and citizenship was essentially training in self-development, morality and citizenship, but without any really detailed discussion of how they would moralize the market.

The Idealist theory of property rights was in fact open to criticism from many sides. C. B. Macpherson in his book *Democratic Theory*[49] attacked Green for his failure to recognize that the individual's property on which he insisted meant a denial to most men of equitable access to the means of life and the means of labour. Green's theory was the kind of justification needed for a capitalist market economy. In a later essay Macpherson spelt out his objection in detail. Green had connected free development with unlimited property, through the market mechanism, and even justified full inheritance. Green had recognized that the existence of a proletariat was inconsistent with the rationale of private property, but he had so little insight, that he attributed the existence of the proletariat not to capitalism, but to the effect of an original forcible seizure of land in feudal times and unrestricted landlordism. In Green's view we are still suffering from the legacy. Thus, capitalism was exempt from responsibility.[50] Idealism overall, although recognizing the value of individual self-development, failed, in Macpherson's view, to see the class basis to politics, and hid themselves in an anachronistic Greek city state doctrine based on rational citizenship.[51]

On the other side of the political spectrum, especially on the issue of property rights being based on the common good, as being socially created and limited to the extent of interference with others possessions, Green could be open to criticism from a natural right point of view. If my rights are pre-social and individual, and my acquisition of property is related, for example, to whether I have mixed my labour with an object, then my entitlement to property bears no relation to a common good or social life *per se*. This theory which is associated with theorists like Locke, and most recently Robert Nozick,[52] would reject Green's theory from such a natural rights basis.

However, the theory of the Idealists entailed a wide range of moral duties, responsibilities and obligations. These moral notions were conceived of as binding on the state and the individual. The state was ultimately a moral institution which aimed at a common good. It, thus, had certain basic responsibilities and obligations to its citizens, to provide the conditions for the self-realization of individuals. On the same count, the individual, although having rights, also had a corresponding range of correlative duties to seek the common good. The state could, however, only provide the conditions for the exercise of rights, it could not coerce the individual to exercise them. The responsible citizen was one who was conscious of the nature of his actions. He was presumed to be capable of self-control and also had some knowledge concerning the general principles of human conduct. The obligation of the citizen was to conform to an external legal order and to conform, if possible, internally to universal moral laws. As the Hegelian, William Wallace wrote, 'It is because and insofar as we live thus not for ourselves, but in a common life, the general work, of some portion of the world, that we are moral beings. To be moral is to be raised out of our selfish isolation.'[53] However, the Idealist position was not just seen as academic theory about the nature of morality and the state. It was seen as having a practical interest, and the conception of citizenship which it embodied as having implications for practice – for direct political practice through an attempt to provide at least one theoretical basis for developments in British Liberalism, and indirect practice through an attempt to illustrate the moral demands of citizenship in the fields of education and welfare.

In the following chapters an attempt will be made to illustrate some of the practical effects which Idealists thought would flow from the moral demands of citizenship. In the first instance we shall consider the role of Idealist political thought in providing a basis for developments within the tradition of Liberal thought and practice. Green and the other Idealists are often referred to by historians in the growth of 'New Liberalism' but there have been very few attempts to pin down precisely the role, if any, which Idealism played in the development of New Liberal thinking.

4 Freedom in a More Subtle Sense: The Political Context of Idealism

I am fundamentally a dead man; one fundamentally a Peel, Cobden man.

Gladstone to Bryce, December 1896

The Liberal Party has accomplished the main part of what it has to do in the way of establishing more freedom from interference for the individual. It has now to win him the condition of freedom in a more subtle and far reaching sense of freedom.

R. B. Haldane

Early in 1882, Arnold Toynbee, a disciple of T. H. Green, who carried out in a practical way many of the teachings of Green, made a speech to an audience of workers and employers in Newcastle. In it he managed to put his finger on one of the main problems in political understanding of his day, and one to which Idealist political philosophy was of crucial importance:

The times are troubled, old political faiths are shaken, and the overwhelming exigencies of the moment leave but small breathing space for statesmen to examine their principles on which they found their practice. The result has been that startling legislative measures, dictated by necessity – with which no compact can be made – have been defended by arguments in sharp contradiction to the ancient principles of those who have pressed these arguments into their service. I think this contradiction is undeniable. It is asserted in connexion with the support given by Radicals to recent Acts of Parliament not only by enraged political opponents but by adherents of the Radical and Liberal Party who have refused to abandon their allegiance to their former principles. The gravest of these charges brought against Radicals is the charge of Socialism; a system which in the past they strained every nerve to oppose.[1]

Toynbee had in mind the fact that during the previous few years a good deal of interventionist legislation had been passed by the House of Commons, much of it by Liberal governments, which could not be squared very easily with the Liberals' supposed historical attachment to *laissez-faire* principles and the so-called 'night watchman' view of the role of the state. Examples of such legislation would be the Irish Land Bill of 1881; The Ground Game Act; the Employers' Liability Act; the Education Act of 1870; and various sets of regulations and legislation relating to public health and sanitation. Such legislation may look minimal today but in the late nineteenth century such 'constructive' legislation, as Gladstone was apt to call it, appeared to many to present a severe ideological cleavage within the Liberal tradition of political thought and practice. It seemed to involve a degree of state intervention not sanctioned by the view of the role of the state supposedly central to Liberal political understanding. Not only this, such pieces of legislation were thought by many to pose a threat to individual freedom: a problem for a tradition which set very high value, if not supreme value, on the emancipation of the individual from the chains of the state. Indeed, the radical movement in British politics out of which the Liberal party emerged might be seen as having its roots in its opposition to the intervention of the state in the economic life of the country as embodied in the regressive Corn Laws. Earlier in the nineteenth century the repeal of the Corn Laws had been the touchstone of radicalism, and the reactionary consequences which the existence of the Corn Laws were supposed to have for the economy were taken to be an object lesson in the baneful consequences which followed from the state's attempt to constrain the free market. However, the growth of constructivist legislation and the so-called New Liberalism seemed to involve some kind of break in the political tradition of Liberalism, and this break was frequently seen as such by both wings of Liberalism: New Liberals self-consciously arguing for the modernity and innovatory nature of their proposals; Old Liberals seeing their tradition becoming perverted into socialism.

In dealing with the relationship between the Idealist social theory and the New Liberalism, an account needs to be given of the doctrine to which they were reacting. A simplistic characterization of the situation would be that the New Liberals in the early 1900s, were reacting to notions like *laissez-faire*, anarchic individualism and also governmental complacency. They were attempting, through this reaction, to build up some kind of collectivist theory of the state, and a theory of state responsibility which would enable them to justify wide-ranging welfare policies. These policies were consequently in direct opposition to the tenets of the Old Liberalism.

Radicalism can be divided into three fairly fluid stages throughout the nineteenth century, as Green himself argued in his lecture 'Liberal Legislation and Freedom of Contract'. The first stage, from 1830 to the 1860s, was characterized by the activity of Peel, Cobden and Bright, the Anti-Corn Law League, and exemplified in the Manchester school. The second stage was dominated by what might be called Chamberlainite radicalism, the 'unauthorized programme', and the founding of the National Liberal Federation in 1877. The 1870s and 1880s saw the development of an advanced programme of social domestic reform, including proposals for free primary education, extensive municipalization of local government, and a number of other measures. The final stage followed the Home Rule split and the secession of many Whigs and also Chamberlain. This period of radicalism through the 1890s, although stultified by the inactivity and rivalry of leaders like Harcourt, Morley and Rosebery, was characterized by the New Liberal radicalism of young politicians like Acland, Asquith, Haldane and Grey, and other figures like Tom Ellis and Munro Ferguson.[2] This stage, which was slowed in momentum by the Boer War and the Imperialism issue, eventually reached fruition in the reforming administrations between 1906 and 1914. It was this final stage that really saw the revision of the social theories and a full perception of the nature of the Liberalism practised in the previous decades. Thus the crisis was apparently solved, at least for New Liberals like Hobhouse, Samuel, Haldane and Asquith.

The crisis of identity was due to a number of elements within the radical movement. The radicalism of Bright and Cobden was a middle-class doctrine, which found its most active expression in the Anti-Corn Law League in the 1840s. Both men represented manufacturing interests and a strong non-conformist ethos. The Corn Law agitation was seen in the context of a struggle against restrictive government. On a deeper level it represented a clash of interests between landed Whig and Tory interests as against those of the industrial classes.[3] The landed interests, accustomed to political power and influence, showed only contempt for the Manchester Radicals' aim of buying on the cheapest market, and selling on the dearest. This contempt for the ark of free trade, coupled with the manufacturers' pride and hard-headedness, caused a mutual contempt for the landed class as the parasitic drones of government and society. T. H. Green, a deep admirer of Bright, shared the radicals' distaste for the landed aristocracy. As we have seen, he attributed many of the problems of the industrial proletariat to the ownership of large tracts of land by these semi-feudal magnates.[4]

The triumph of the Anti-Corn Law League led to the growth of the Manchester school, which aimed to build up the commercial strength of England on the basis of free trade. Ultimately their view of legislation was simple enough. It was based on the principle that the removal of an obstruction to trade or commercial activity was good government. This removal led to freedom and progress. After the repeal of the Corn Laws and Navigation Laws, and Gladstone's budgets, it was felt that there were no more legislative worlds to conquer. This view of legislation was thus limited and negative.[5] As Green argued in 'Liberal Legislation and Freedom of Contract', there had been no exchangeable commodity in England except land – no doubt a large exception – of which the exchange has not become perfectly free. The realization of complete freedom of contract was the special effort of this reforming work. It was to set men at liberty to dispose of what they had made their own that the free trader worked. The Anti-Corn Law League and Manchester radicalism still had certain basic preconceptions about society. The great objects were the security of property, the individual's freedom, sanctity of contracts, and the right to the possession and retention of one's appropriations. The free economy and the rights of the individual were a fundamental belief. This ebullient confidence in the ability of the private enterprise society to surmount all difficulties contributed to the contempt for the aristocratic landed class. Thrift and parsimony were reflected as much in government, as Gladstone demonstrated, as in personal life. Ultimately, as one writer has put it, the party in the 1840s, stripped of its top dressing of Whigs, was one of middle-class industrialists, espousing an aggressive view of individualism.[6] Legislation which tried to extend state intervention was resisted, especially that which affected manufacturing interests, as factory legislation did. As Green stated in 'Liberal Legislation and Freedom of Contract' the workman should be left to take care of himself by the terms of his agreement with the employer. This was partly self-interest, and partly a belief that the extension of municipal or central control was merely an extension of corrupt paternalistic government.

The natural harmony of interests and progress of society expected by the Manchester radicals did not, however, materialize. Gladstone's ambiguous politics, which encompassed and outlasted Chamberlain, exposed many of the general anomalies of the radical position. Gladstone seemed to harness many of the potential forces at that time, maintaining a precarious unity of innate Toryism, moral radicalism, Whig fears of new trends, Manchester radicalism, and the Chamberlain group.[7] Since the two Reform Acts of 1867 and 1884 destroyed effectively the monopoly of the upper and middle classes on the franchise, political success came to depend on an appeal to the working-class vote. As Green noted in 'Liberal Legislation and Freedom of Contract', these developments became very pronounced after the election of a more democratic parliament. In addition the decades of the 1870s and 1880s also saw a depression in the economy which partially broke down the Manchester radicals' vision. Gladstone, however, seemed to be able to stand astride all these movements.

Gladstone's second ministry (1880–85) was characterized by 'constructionism', as the 'Grand Old Man' derogatively referred to interventionist legislation. Legislation such as the Ground Game Act transferred important rights from landlords to occupiers. The Irish Land Act of 1881 ensured the right of the Irish tenant to a fair rent fixed by a judicial tribunal. This Act, as one recent scholar has put it, provided 'clear proof that Gladstone did not hesitate to depart from orthodox principles and press forward vigorously with revolutionary projects.'[8] Arnold Toynbee, who had pinpointed the crisis in identity of Liberalism, discussed the Irish Land Act in his speech 'Are Radicals Socialists?'[9] He pointed out that many of the arguments used by government members in defence of the Act paralleled those formerly used by the defenders of factory laws. They even, Toynbee pointed out with alacrity, 'used some of the illustrations employed in discussing the Poor Laws, dwelling upon the fundamental principle that there is no freedom of contract between men who are unequal.'[10] The radicals, Toynbee maintained, were now using arguments akin to those of Sadler in 1832, which Bright or Cobden would have vilified. Yet, Toynbee claimed, the Act was progressive and not retrogressive. The Act demonstrated the commitment of the radical cause to socialism, not Owenite or Tory socialism, but the socialism which recognized that between men of unequal wealth there was no freedom of contract.

This, of course, was the key point made by T. H. Green in the 1880s, in his famous lecture 'Liberal Legislation and Freedom of Contract'.[11] Green saw this lecture as a conscious intervention in the dispute about the identity of Liberalism. The Liberals had outgrown the fight for parliamentary and civil freedom and freedom of trade. The issue now was the freedom of each man to develop his capabilities and to realize himself. Unequal contracts did not enable this freedom to be achieved. The state needed to ensure certain basic conditions in which the morality and self-realization of each man could be made possible, morality consisting in the disinterested performance of self-imposed duties. Law thus contributed to the realization of the moral vocation of humanity.[12]

This type of intervention did not diminish self-help and character. As Toynbee drily remarked, 'I am not aware that the Merchant Shipping Act had diminished the self-reliance of the British sailor.'[13] The same theme and argument held true of the Agricultural Holdings Act, the Employer's Liability Act, and much local government reform. The Agricultural Holdings Act of 1883 in fact constituted a fairly extensive encroachment of state paternalism. Similar measures were contemplated in other spheres, as in Gladstone's plan to equalize duties payable at death on real and personal property. Again, graduated tax on landed estates, and measures to protect vulnerable classes from exploitation, extended government interference. The city corporation of London was threatened by Liberal proposals to deprive it of ancient privileges and endowments. Wealthy vestries and Poor Law Boards had to argue against the attempt to equalize rates and the subsidizing of the needy authorities. As Michael Barker has effectively argued in his book *Gladstone and Radicalism*: 'Gladstone, who earnestly wished to "purge" Liberalism of "centralizing tendencies", defended, in the name of local enfranchisement and local autonomy, what Radicals frankly demanded in the interests of social justice.'[14] By 1885 it seemed that Gladstone and others, consciously or not, through social necessity or the logic of argument, countenanced the extension of constructivist politics.

This, in summary, was the crisis of identity which Idealists like T. H. Green and Arnold Toynbee pointed to and tried to resolve theoretically. The ancient theoretical principles, in the perception of many Liberals, were being challenged and undermined by the actual practices. The situation was only exacerbated by Chamberlain's Radical Programme and its disseminating body, the National Liberal Federation. Their advocacy of land reform by multiplication of ownership, revisions in the taxation system, and free primary education, produced a split in the Liberal ranks which eventually, coupled with the Home Rule Bill, led to the defection of Chamberlain and his Whig opponents. Chamberlain's course was seen as a further testimony of the drift from true Liberalism towards socialism.

After the loss of Chamberlain and Whigs like Goschen, Lord Hartington, and Sir Henry James, a new generation of Liberals arose, who only confirmed the tendency towards constructionism. Men like Sir Edward Grey, Sidney Buxton and Arthur Acland, from important Liberal families, joined with professional men like Asquith, R. B. Haldane and Frank Lockwood. Many of these figures like Acland, Grey and Asquith were pupils of T. H. Green at Oxford. Haldane though not a pupil, was an editor of a memorial volume to Green and an Idealist philosopher of note. They worked through the Eighty Club, the Articles Club, and through personal contact with leaders like Morley and Rosebery, aiming to extend the Radical programme into many new fields. The 1890s were characterized by an increasing theoretical and practical emphasis on social problems, which Gladstone seemed either to ignore or at least unofficially countenance. Although showing antipathy to social reform, and criticizing Harcourt's budget in 1894 as too revolutionary, especially the composite estate duty, Gladstone was obliquely in sympathy with the old age pensions movement, and that of the limitation of working hours.

Gladstone's hesitancy was probably symptomatic of many Liberals even in the 1890s. He found himself supporting measures with which theoretically he was in disagreement. Yet conversely the new ideas did not demand a complete revision of views, as Green, Toynbee, and later D. G. Ritchie were all at pains to insist. In the views of these Idealists the newer claims meant progess within Liberalism. Legislation especially in the 1880s, was increasingly seen as simply the inevitable response to facts. Legislation still aimed at the old radical demands of liberty, justice and self-help, but with the added structure, as Arnold Toynbee put it, 'that under certain conditions the people cannot help themselves, and that then they should be helped by the state representing directly the whole people.'[15] However, the very fact of the flexibility of the old Liberalism allowed a fluid reinterpretation by the Idealists like T. H. Green and Arnold Toynbee. These Liberal philosophers precipitated in many minds a reassessment of some of the key terms of Liberalism, which was carried through the 1890s into the 1900s by the new Liberals like R. B. Haldane, Asquith, and later Samuel and others. Some Liberals claimed that the older views did not have to be overcome but rather brought to fruition. As Green put the argument in 'Liberal Legislation and Freedom of Contract':

The immediate object of reformers and the form of persuasion by which they seek to advance them, vary much in different generations. To the hasty observer they might even seem contradictory, and to justify the notion that nothing better than a desire for change selfish or perverse is at the bottom of all reforming movements. Only those who think a little longer about it can discern the same old cause of social good against class interests, for which under altered names, liberals are fighting now as they were fifty years ago.[16]

Green's message was concerned with an internal reform of the Liberal tradition; it was not his aim to create a breach within Liberalism. In the next chapter we shall discuss this view in more detail.

5 The New Liberalism and Radical Philosophical Idealism

There is an environment favourable to a good life and an environment unfavourable ... this the statesman can affect, making it easier for his people to be good or bad ... the State does not directly enforce morality ... it establishes rights, defines duties and creates opportunities for a better life.

Sir Henry Jones

The teaching of T. H. Green was penetrating deeply ... there was earnestness about State intervention everywhere.

R. B. Haldane

We shall not understand liberalism unless we recognise that it was always a moral doctrine ... For a philosopher like T. H. Green, seeking to restate liberalism in a form which could mend poverty and slums, the Christian background of ideas, or at least of moral impetus, provided the intellectual drive. Once the aim of liberal theory was negative, to get rid of the clutter, obsolete law, interference, privilege restriction. Now it became positive – to accept restriction for the ends of morality and justice.

O. Chadwick

The aim of the present chapter is to consider the main aspects of New Liberal theory and practice, especially between 1906 and 1914, in relation to some of the major concepts of the social and moral philosophy of Idealism. The argument is concerned to demonstrate that many of the ideas and assumptions which came into the forefront of politics through the New Liberalism bear directly upon those arguments produced by the Idealists. This situation came about partly because many of the New Liberals were educated at Oxford[1] in the heyday of Idealism and also, more significantly, because Idealism provided a context of political discourse which appealed to many intellectuals and politicians during the 1890s and early 1900s. This is not to say that we think there is a clear causal relationship, but we do seek to demonstrate a clear convergence of views.

The New Liberalism was an extremely complex phenomenon which, as argued in an earlier chapter, had its roots in the 1880s. The crisis of identity in the Liberal party was resolved by the New Liberals. Liberal political theory was realigned with the actual legislative practices. This is not to argue that there were not many Liberals who still felt disquiet at Liberal interventionist legislation between 1906 and 1914.[2] However, it was not so marked as in the 1880s and 1890s. The 1890s prepared the ground for the reforms of the 1900s. Men like Haldane, Asquith, Acland and Grey, who argued strongly for closer attention to social problems in the 1890s, found a far wider and at times more radical basis after 1906, with men like C. F. G. Masterman, Herbert Samuel and L. T. Hobhouse, among others. The New Liberals considered that there were good grounds for the interventionist legislation and a consequent reinterpretation of Liberal theory. Their activity in justifying and promoting the Education (Provision of School Meals) Act of 1906, the budget of 1909, the Trade Boards Act of 1909, the National Insurance Act of 1911 and a number of other measures, was bound up intrinsically with the change of attitudes and theoretical commitments. It is important to understand these Acts in terms of the attitudes or theories which they embody. These attitudes and commitments relate to a context of argument and discourse which was partly provided by Idealism.

There have been a number of interpretations of the reforming legislation and New Liberalism between 1906 and 1914.[3] The development of New Liberalism, for example, could be seen as one reason amongst many for the actual legislative practice.[4] However, this is manifestly inadequate since the legislation was pushed through by those who espoused the New Liberalism; therefore, to understand the legislation is to understand the New Liberalism. Other more formidable accounts have been offered to explain the New Liberalism and interventionist legislation, and these can be summarized under a number of headings. The first explanation claims that the legislation was due to the work of a paternalistic elite of politicians, civil servants and journalists; the second, that it was the result of pressure, in some manner, from socialist forces and the working class or, more obscurely, economic and social forces. Finally, it is also suggested the legislation was a pursuit of social justice.[5] All of these accounts can be split up in a number of ways. The reforms themselves have also been divided by some writers, for example, between those reforms which were merely regulatory, like education and housing, and those which were economically limiting, as in progressive taxation and insurance.[6] B. B. Gilbert, in his work on *The Evolution of National Insurance*, divides the reforms up between those of specifically nineteenth-century origin in the true Liberal tradition, and those introduced from abroad without precedent in Britain, for instance, the National Insurance Act of 1911.[7] However, the dividing line between the various distinctions is at times so fine as to be meaningless. Many of the minor economic incursions, for example, on wealth and the market, could be justified as merely helping to regulate the economy and society through ensuring the health and safety of the work-force. Also, Acts like those dealing with insurance were largely self-financing and basically traditional answers to the social problem. However, even if the distinctions are accepted, the regulatory reforms were as disturbing to Whigs and Conservatives as the economically limiting ones, since they were all interventionist, and it was intervention which basically characterized the New Liberalism.

This intervention can be seen as the work of an elite of paternalistic politicians. The 'heavenly twins' of social reform, namely, Lloyd George and Winston Churchill, are often cited here, partly because they were seen to have been associated with some of the most radical measures, like the 1909 budget and the creation of labour exchanges and minimum wages, and partly because they collaborated closely during the Liberal administrations between 1906 and 1914. Scholarship has weighted their contributions differently.[8] Asquith commented that both men tended to think with their mouths, C. F. G. Masterman that Churchill was a 'Johnny-come-lately' to social reform.[9] A slightly stronger view of elitism argues that it was the 'anonymous empire' of civil servants working behind the scenes, like R. B. Morant, Llewellyn Smith, George Askwith and Ernest Aves,[10] who really engineered the legislation. These were the men who constructed and piloted the legislation of the reform period, although, as others have pointed out, the civil service had as much of a reactionary effect on government in other spheres like the Local Government Board.[11] An even more extensive view justifiably encompasses the journalistic world. Some, like W. H. Beveridge and C. F. G. Masterman, passed from the journalistic world to work on the Liberal reforms. Others, like C. P. Scott,

L. T. Hobhouse, J. A. Hobson and William Clarke, remained in journalism and writing, yet promoted considerable interest in social reform through their work on journals such as the *Manchester Guardian, Nation, Speaker,* and *Progressive Review.*

Overall, whether the focus is on politicians, the press, or civil servants, the reforms can be seen as being imposed on the population.[12] A less sympathetic reading could maintain that none of these professional groups understood the real needs or values of the working masses, and that reform was an exogenous and alien import.[13] However, a more sympathetic assessment might maintain that although the reforms were paternalistic and imposed from the values of an elite, nonetheless they were genuinely beneficial. It is still probable, in the latter view, that many of the reforms were resisted by the working people, as has been pointed out, yet this was probably due to an adherence to ideas of self-help.[14]

A second line of interpretation is that the Liberal reforms were due to the pressure of socialism and the working classes.[15] This argument takes a number of different forms. First, on a crude level, that the Liberals were frightened or coerced into welfare reforms by the militancy and activity of the socialist groups and working class. Thus the real significance of the legislation was the rising force of the proletariat. This kind of argument, which was somewhat flippantly advanced by historians like G. Dangerfield in the 1930s, has now been bankrupted, although many vestiges of it still tirelessly haunt historians' minds.[16] A second line more subtly advocates the view that the New Liberalism was really identical with socialism.[17] The New Liberalism was in other words a 'socialistic Idealism', which had noiselessly slipped away from the true Liberalism into socialistic concerns with intervention in the economy. This argument presupposes some kind of essential core of meaning to socialism and Liberalism, which is, to say the least, debatable. It also seems to avoid the New Liberals' own perceptions, which in most cases were manifestly non-socialist, rather than anti-socialist. In addition, a third approach has been to associate the New Liberalism with Fabianism.[18] This is a view favoured and advanced by Fabians themselves, especially by G. B. Shaw, with the famous doctrine of permeation. Again it is arguable that this myth has been exploded now by modern scholarship on the Fabian Society.[19] However, it is ironical that if the Fabians had predominated, the end result would have been no less elitist and distinct from the working people than the Liberals were themselves. A final argument, which could be offered here, is that the New Liberals were desperately trying to offer a radical alternative to socialism.[20] It was thus not a reaction of fear of the working class, but more an attempt to catch the working-class vote and to undercut socialist claims. This last notion again seems to ignore the major concerns of the New Liberals themselves, which were not interested in providing an alternative to socialism. In fact, socialists in the Independent Labour Party did not really provide any dramatic challenge, politically, till much later.

A final point of interpretation is that the New Liberalism was concerned with pursuing a theory of social justice. This can again be approached in a number of different ways. The concern with social justice could be said to be a response to the large-scale statistical studies, conducted by Booth and Rowntree and government bodies like the Inter-Departmental Committee on Physical Deterioration, and the Royal Commission on Physical Deterioration (Scotland).[21] Also, popularized statistics on, for example, the low standards of health in the Boer War recruitment programme, can be said to have convinced some Liberals of the need for basic reforms.[22] Again, the need for more social justice could be said to derive from a new view of economics, in that the market system was no longer regarded as a fair adjudicator and self-sufficient entity.[23] In other words, commutative justice in the free market needed to be tempered by distributive justice, to rectify the latent injustices of the system.

The present account is not concerned to dispute the other types of interpretation, apart from those which try to argue that the reforms were wholly the result of economic or structural forces. An understanding of the reforms can be gained through an understanding of the perceptions of the New Liberals themselves. It is probably true that the legislation was paternalistic and promulgated by an intellectual elite. It is through understanding the intellectual concerns of the elite that we can understand the New Liberalism. Further, it is indisputable that socialism had some role to play in relation to the New Liberalism, although it remains a very ambiguous one. Much of the Fabian notoriety can be seen as the result of a similar rendering of the collectivist philosophy, so it was not so much a direct influence as a similarity of basic principles. The socialism that many New Liberals were concerned with was not a revolutionary socialism or Tory collectivism but a distinctive Liberal or radical socialism. This New Liberalism or radical socialism was concerned, as Arnold Toynbee had stated in 1880, with equalizing the conditions of contract between men, and with promoting the common good.[24] As argued in a previous chapter, this entailed interventionist legislation.

It is no surprise that this radical Liberalism should find some theoretical support in philosophical Idealism.

A parallel movement, although less politically successful, had developed in Germany through the 1880s up to 1900. German Liberal philosophers and revisionist socialists, for example, Albert Lange, R. Stammler, K. Vorländer and even Max Weber, and later most notably Eduard Berstein, developed a social democratic Liberal position critical of Imperial and authoritarian government. This new Liberalism found its theroetical basis in philosophical Idealism and the revival of Kantianism. As George Lichtheim has pointed out: 'By the 1890s the process was sufficiently advanced to make it possible for leading neo-Kantians – who were also full-fledged university professors – to draw radical conclusions from Kant's ethics, and even to suggest a thoroughgoing synthesis of socialism and philosophical idealism'.[25]

The English New Liberalism was less concerned with a direct synthesis of socialism and philosophical Idealism. Nonetheless, its main theoretical commitments, which underpinned its activities, were concerned with many notions central to the moral and political philosophy of Idealism. Some leading Liberal lights, like R. B. Haldane, Herbert Samuel, L. T. Hobhouse and to an extent H. H. Asquith, had a theoretical grasp of the relation. Others took hold of the theories more or less unconsciously as part of the context of discussion. In this chapter we will show that the concerns with socialism, intervention, the new economics, the results of statistical enquiries and social justice, can be explained more effectively if they are viewed within the context of the argument and discourse that characterized the period from approximately 1870 until after the Great War. The New Liberals were the heirs of this tradition of discourse in the first decade of this century.

CONSCIENCE AND OUTRAGE: THE ETHICAL STANDPOINT IN POLITICS

One of the predominant concerns of the New Liberal writers was the notion of social morality. Their writings were enmeshed in a sense of moral outrage, conscience, sympathy with the destitute, and the consequent moral function of the state and law to rectify these disorders. One of the leading political and journalistic lights of the movement, C. F. G. Masterman, writing in the *Contemporary Review*, stated that in London a social reformer found an imbedded poverty a kind of colossal ant heap of stunted life.[26] The disgust and outrage with the social abyss came out more forcibly in his book *The Condition of England,* where he maintained that poverty was literally the foundation of the industrial order.[27] National distinctions were less estranging, he claimed, than the fissure between the summit and the base of society. The reason for this moral outrage was, as Masterman retrospectively put it in 1920: 'the continuance of civilization is incompatible with the continuance of poverty.'[28]

The force of this position was directed against what Masterman saw as the older creed of Liberalism. In his own essay in the book *The Heart of the Empire,* he characterized the older creed as an astonishing doctrine which, he maintained, encouraged each man to asiduously pursue his own advantage and interest.[29] Somehow, by some divinely ordered interconnection, the progress of society was assured. This creed, he contended, should be cast into the limbo of forgotten illusions. The atomic view of society on which it was based, and the selfish commercial philosophy that it espoused, only led to the degradation of a large number of people. This was not compatible with civilization. The moral task of Liberalism was to raise the population to a civilized level of existence. Tranquillity at home and abroad, as a later essayist in the *Heart of the Empire* put it, lay in recognition, in theory and practice, of the supreme claim of the moral ideal.[30] In a later work, Masterman described this higher state of civilization at which Liberalism aimed, as a kingdom of righteousness, where, if merit was rewarded, poverty was unknown.[31]

This kind of moral language was not just picturesque and uplifting, it was conversely the nub of the argument directed against the older economic and political concerns. This was especially true of the work of the New Liberal economist, J. A. Hobson, whose thought was a distinct influence on Masterman, through their joint efforts on the *Nation* newspaper. The orthodox economists, vaguely associated with the Manchester radicals and classical economics, could not really be opposed effectively on a purely abstract economic level, for this would have been admitting that moral or 'ideal-regarding criteria' were not applicable to the 'want-regarding criteria' of the economic man, attempting to maximize his utilities. The economic order had to be made subject to a moral critique, based on the premise that the political and economic life of man were shot through with ethical concerns. The rigtous, civilized order that Masterman demanded made economics subordinate to moral ideals.

The moral theme can be illustrated in a number of New Liberal writings. For example, in the collection of articles by journalists from the Liberal *Speaker,* entitled *Towards a Social Policy,* one essayist attacked the unearned increment in town land, claiming that new measures had 'sufficient ethical justification'.[32] Another writer maintained that the state ought to intervene in the unemployment situation to arrest the moral decay that issued from it. The New Liberal journalist, H. W. Massingham, also gave many examples of this moral theme. A biographical account by H. N. Bailsford maintained that Massingham's predominantly ethical outlook made him reluctant to face the facts of a class struggle.[33] His editorship of the *Chronicle,* and later the *Nation* was characterized by his striving for a 'humane civilization'.[34] In a famous introduction to a collection of Winston Churchill's speeches, Massingham spelt out his principles.[35] There were, he maintained, two fundamental propositions to the New Liberalism. One of these was the claim that the state ought to intervene in areas previously regarded as sacrosanct and hopeless. It was not a question of relief or just increasing the power of the state, but conversely a method of humanity and a demand to raise the morale and character of the citizen body. The second proposition was the practical proposal of changing the taxation system to enable the state to achieve a more humane civilization. This he saw, as the aim of the 1909 Budget, which he described as a proposal of 'practical Christianity.'[36] Liberalism, he concluded, was a mission and a moral concern, wherein the party was aiming at the practical service of the existing society.[37]

Massingham was a distinctive and influential figure in the New Liberal circles. His sketch of parliamentary life which appeared night by night in the *Nation* was read avidly in Westminster. His weekly editorial meetings in the National Liberal Club attracted notable theorists and political figures like C. F. G. Masterman, J. A. Hobson and L. T. Hobhouse. Masterman wrote of him in the *Nation*: 'His influence was certainly greater than that of most of the ministers and ex-cabinet ministers of the time. Indeed, quite a number of these used to solicit policy or praise; he was making the reputation of the new men, such as Mr Lloyd George and Mr Winston Churchill.'[38]

Certainly, both Lloyd George and Churchill reflected Massingham's general theme in politics. Churchill, despite his altercation with Llewellyn Smith on unemployment insurance, on not mixing 'moralities with mathematics', based his Liberal position on ethical concerns. The aim of fiscal policy was, he claimed, to create conditions favourable to the moral and social welfare of the citizen body.[39] Property was not to be interfered with unless it was associated with ideas of wrong and unfairness.[40] In Churchill's view, Liberalism was the higher impulse which advanced social evolution. The 1909 Budget encapsulated this 'faith' in Liberalism. This faith was involved in a 'spirit of social service ... of a conscious and concerted effort towards a better state of things'.[41]

Lloyd George also described his work on the Budget and national insurance, somewhat rhetorically, as 'doing the work of Nazareth'.[42] Although undeniably a confusing and enigmatic man, Lloyd George had one undoubted consistency in his career, and that was his concern for the 'underdog', the destitute and poor. His concern, through legislation, was to find an ethical and civilized base to society. This same principle was present in Churchill, Masterman and Massingham and most other New Liberals. The premise of New Liberal legislation was the moral criterion whereby the state helps to provide the conditions for civilized life. The state, in other words, ought to exist for providing a better life for its citizen body.

L. T. Hobhouse, in his work *Liberalism,* claimed on a more theoretical level that the crux of modern Liberalism was a moral one. He viewed Liberalism as based upon the self-directing power of the human personality. He wrote of this personality, that 'in realising his capacities of feeling, of living, of mental and physical energy ... in Green's phrase, he finds his own good in the common good.'[43] The aim of the common good was concerned to show a possible ethical harmony, which would come about partly through self-discipline and partly through the improvement of social conditions. The justification of this process, Hobhouse felt, led to philosophical first principles and a theory of ethics. Yet, he claimed, the movement towards ethical harmony, which Liberals should be aiming at, was the persistent impulse of the rational being.[44] The application of ethical principles to the social structure was merely the effort to carry one step further that guidance of life by rational principles.[45] This application led him to claim that the living wage, the social minimum and related issues embodied ethical demands.

Thus, in Hobhouse's estimation, it was morality and ethics which were supreme in social life. The state was a moral agent concerned with the realization of the common good in the various personalities which constituted it. Hobhouse's views were underpinned by a reconstructed Kantianism and philosophical Idealism, which in many ways resembled Green's ideas. These factors probably led Melvin Richter to maintain that it was Hobhouse who claimed Green for the New Liberals.[46]

The moral function of law, rights and the state was the fundamental concern of T. H. Green's political philosophy. As he argued in the beginning of his *Lectures on the Principles of Political Obligation*: 'My purpose is to consider the moral function or object served by law, or by the system of rights and obligations which the state enforces.'[47] Green wished to consider the permanent moral value of institutions, and the manner in which they contributed to the possibility of morality in the citizen body. The important point to note here was that the law and the state were not solely seen as separate and distinct from individuals. The state and its component institutions were viewed as moral entities which existed for moral purposes. The institutions, though built on customs and habits, were nevertheless seen as repositories of man's ideas of the social good, and at their worst, only hardened and outgrown purposes. As an individual man's moral activity was based upon the idea of a true absolute good, consisting in the full realization of the capabilities of the human soul, so the state acted according to common purposes on the same foundation.[48] The aim of the law was to provide conditions for the development of man's capacities and powers towards a moral end of self-realization. The capacity of institutions to achieve this end was the criterion of their moral development and progress. Civic institutions were therefore, in a sense, the outward expression of morality.[49] In this sense, as one of the older commentators put it:

Political and social life is merely the concrete shape which moral ideas take when they are translated into actuality. Through civic institutions alone is it possible for the idea of moral perfection to be realised by human beings. In criticising such institutions, in asking them to justify themselves, we have to consider what permanent moral value they possess; in other words, how far and in what way do they contribute to the possibility of the moral life.[50]

Canon Scott Holland, an ex-pupil of Green's at Balliol, contributed an article to the New Liberal journal, the *Progressive Review*, in 1897, where he argued that the Church needed to assert the necessity that Liberal legislation should witness to the corporate brotherhood of man and moral aims and needs, as against the mechanical and instrumental view of social life. Society, he argued, existed for the humane life, which was the moral end of legislation.[51] Later that year, writing to the Liberal Whip, Thomas Ellis, Scott Holland complained that parliamentary tactics alone were not enough. These, he wrote, 'cannot replace the moral force and religious spirit that have, before now, given life to the Liberal creed.'[52] Similar sentiments were echoed by other Idealists; for example Henry Jones, a close friend of Lloyd George, in his work *The Principles of Citizenship*, maintained fervently that the solution to the problem of the nature of the state lay in the recognition that it was a moral agent, and that its service was, in consequence, for the better life of its citizens.[53] Thus the state as the repository of man's idea of the good, reflected the moral consciousness of all men. It was in this vein that L. T. Hobhouse wrote that no welfare or legislative action could be final, in which the spontaneous, deep-lying and constantly recurring claims of the moral consciousness do not find a legitimate satisfaction.[54] Severe poverty, destitution and political apathy did not lead to this satisfaction. Admittedly, some drew the conclusion that poverty reflected largely personal failure and moral ineptitude. However, to others this was an inadequate analysis. Poverty reflected as much a condition of society as an individual's character. If the state was not just an impartial umpire of a market-based society, but was conversely a moral institution providing the conditions for the self-realization of all citizens, then it was the duty of politicians to rectify this intolerable situation of mass poverty.

J. A. Hobson, the New Liberal economist and friend of L. T. Hobhouse, developed a similar theme in his own writings. He admired Hobhouse's theory of the moral personality, and also constructed a notably organic theory of the state, which he felt negated the old democratic idea of political equality.[55] He described the state as a moral organism which displayed a psychical and spiritual unity. The general will or common good embodied the wisdom of society and therefore was the determining criterion of legislation. In fact, Hobson admitted in his autobiography that ethics, as human valuation, continually held sway over his views on politics and economics.

Herbert Samuel, a Liberal MP and leading figure in the New Liberal Rainbow Circle, also argued in the first chapter of his book, *Liberalism*, that the state was governed by the moral law. This morality taught, he maintained, that the primary function of the state was to help man. The trunk of the tree of Liberalism, he wrote, is rooted in the soil of ethics.[56] This ethic of Liberalism was concerned to achieve the best life for all citizens. In this sense it was no wonder that the journal, the *Progressive Review*, which had Samuel as one of its editors, should have argued that it was seeking to realize 'the moral foundation of democracy'.[57] Samuel's own New Liberal views had their foundation in his student days at Balliol. As his biographer recorded: 'Against current theories of political relativism and *realpolitik*, Samuel always affirmed that politics should and can be governed by morality. The principles stated in the first chapter of his book on Liberalism, derived from T. H. Green and the Liberal humanist tradition.'[58]

The moral and ethical concerns of New Liberal theory sometimes waxed hotter in terms of a positive religious conception. Samuel in his work *Liberalism* had argued that the principles that permeated a true secular Liberalism were nothing else but the application to public affairs of a religious spirit.[59] Masterman also, in an essay included in *The Heart of the Empire*, claimed that Liberalism needed to give a background to life, a common bond or spiritual force, to combat the divisiveness of industrial society.[60] His wife, Lucy Masterman, described her husband's view as the attempt to realize a spiritual democracy, which was a similar assessment to H. W. Massingham's summary of the New Liberalism as a practical Christianity. B. B. Gilbert, a recent scholar, has classed Masterman and his New Liberal colleagues as Christian humanists, which is probably closest to the mark.[61] L. T. Hobhouse also saw the essence of New Liberal collectivism as summed up in the Sermon on the Mount. Liberalism, he maintained in another work, was a liberation of living spirituality.[62] In endorsing mutual aid between men, he avowed that when all the world were as one family, 'the millennium' will have been reached. This spirituality that New Liberals spoke of was a particularly secular and humanistic one. Its religious nature was concerned with achieving the best for humanity, the best human personality, family or institution. The spiritual was in essence, the realization of the best secular, civilized condition for the citizens of the community.

Both J. A. Hobson and L. T. Hobhouse had probably imbibed much of their humanistic ethics from their work in the ethical societies. The ethical societies were concerned with a humanistic religion, virtually based upon Kantian ethics.[63] Many idealists like Bosanquet, Caird and Muirhead were also involved in the ethical societies, some as founder members. It was Bosanquet, for example, who regarded religion, on a very secular level, as 'something generally and obviously taken as symbolic of the best we know.'[64] Henry Jones also defined religion in a similar way. The religious life, he stated, is 'nothing but the secular devoted to the best we know.'[65] This idealization of the finite and secular was a common feature of the Idealist philosophers overall. As John S. Mackenzie argued in the *Introduction to Social Philosophy*: the atmosphere of thought which surrounds material interests veils 'the heaven in which higher

interests of our nature have their centre'.[66] Mackenzie, in similar vein
to Masterman, looked for a principle which would enable a more
'perfect connection between the parts of our society'.[67] The secular
world of institutions, laws, families and customs needed to be seen as
bound up with the moral personality. It was the task of Liberalism to
serve this moral personality, enabling him to achieve the spiritual end
of the good life or 'best that we know'.

The theory that lay behind this in the Idealists was connected with
a specific attitude to religion, as examined earlier in this book.
Religion became, for many, virtually synonymous with civic service
and citizenship.[68] Many of the New Liberals were probably not
precisely aware of the background. Yet for Idealists like Henry Jones,
the moment religious faith was made to rely upon anything super-
natural, the moment the divine did not express itself in the ordinary
world and life of men, religion became indistinguishable from mere
superstition. Religion and living spirituality were thus characterized
in the actual institutional, social and moral life of man.[69] There was
therefore no sense in looking beyond the social and political life
which confronted the individual. Spirituality and the moral good
were central to the present reality. If institutions were not living up to
their moral function, they could be changed for the common good.
Morality was, therefore, central to the economic and political life of
man.

INDIVIDUAL AND COLLECTIVE RESPONSIBILITY

An article in the *Nation* in July 1908, questioning the treatment of
children and the old, argued:

In many cases the whole theory of responsibility is at present misapplied . . .
By punishing the parents through the child . . . (that is to say the ill-fed or ill-
clothed child) . . . the state is guilty of a confusion of ideas. The true line of
advance here is not to diminish, but to raise the standard of parental
responsibility. The parent ought not any longer to be content with saying so
and then passing on to its other business. It is true to say that the parent
ought to feed the child and the state ought to see that it is fed.[70]

T. H. Green argued 'on similar lines in a public lecture in 1878.
Speaking specifically of children, he stated that in an ideal society
their education might be left completely to the parents. However, in
the actual state of English society, no one pretended that children
could be so left. 'It is doubtful', Green continued, 'whether under the

modern system of labour in great masses . . . the fate of children can ever be left solely in the hands of parents. For individual action in such matters, however, the proper substitute is not the casual action of charitable persons, but the collective action of the state.'[71] The ideal situation, for Green, was where a balance could be struck between collective and individual responsibility. The state, he acknowledged, must take the best security it can for the young citizens growing up in such health and with so much knowledge as is necessary for their real freedom.[72] However, in so doing it need not interfere with the independence or self-reliance of an individual. Over-legislation and too much responsibility were as dangerous as under-legislation and too little responsibility. As L. T. Hobhouse also argued in his book *Liberalism,* all cases of restraint ought to be justified on the ground of yielding more effective freedom.[73]

Hobhouse in fact, on the question of responsibility, propounded an argument extremely similar to Green's, although oddly, more tentative. He claimed responsibility, as in the *Nation* article and Green's account, to be a compromise between individual and collective responsibility. He went on, by way of example, to argue:

When children are in question, the principle of responsibility cuts two ways; for, if we take the responsibility off the parent by saving the child, we neglect a common responsibility if we leave the child to its fate. And if one course impairs the character of the parent, how does the other affect our own? What it would finally throw upon the society, and what it would leave to the individual, is a matter which collectivism has to thrash out in each case upon its own merits.[74]

H. H. Asquith, another of Green's pupils at Balliol, took a similar line through the 1890s and early 1900s. In a speech in 1895, defending the Factories and Workshop Bill, he argued that it was the duty of the Government to intervene where the public conscience had been quickened.[75] Where it was seen to be necessary for health and safety to intervene in conditions of the working people, the Government had a definite duty to do so.[76] In another speech in 1906, he reaffirmed that the state had a responsible role to play in providing for the effective working and living conditions of its citizens.[77] Where over-crowding, intemperance, defective nutrition, or the question of the training of the young, or the care of the old arose, the state had a responsible supervisory role to play. Asquith's close friend in the 1890s, R. B. Haldane, also described the progressive social policy of the New Liberalism as the attempt to emancipate the population from conditions which denied fair play to the collective energy for the good of society as a whole.[78] This enlightened attitude and earnestness toward state intervention he attributed in his *Autobiography* to the influence and teaching of men like T. H. Green.[79]

Herbert Samuel, in a retrospective lecture in 1954, looking back on his early years, maintained that it was men like Asquith, Haldane and Grey, who had worked out and devised a broader Liberalism to meet the needs of the time. They recognized that it was necessary to bring the power of the state into play to rescue people from evil social conditions. He continued that 'most of us younger generation who were then coming into the political field supported these views; we went about the country advocating what we called "the New Liberalism".'[80]

The essence of this theory of responsibility and duty, which was present in the social theory of Idealism and the New Liberalism, was two-fold. The state must ensure that the individual has sufficient conditions, 'without which a free exercise of the human faculties',[81] could not occur. Yet in so doing it should not overstep its role and try to force citizens into particular moral paths, or, in other words, replace or supersede the individual's capacity for self-betterment. It was a duty of the state and the individual to aim at the best life. In this 'best life' the two facets ought to correspond, namely, the individual good and the common good. As Asquith wrote in 1910: 'popular government is the best means in the long-run of securing the subordination of particular interests to the common good.'[82] Herbert Samuel echoed this sentiment in his work *Liberalism*, where he argued it was the duty of the individual and the state to seek the 'best'.[83] He qualified this later, by noting that law and reform also need the self-reform and responsibility of the individual citizen through his thrift and self-reliance. An essayist in the volume *Towards a Social Policy* summarized this point succinctly, when he stated that the state had a responsibility and duty to protect the citizen from the 'blows and buffets of outrageous fortune', only where 'national self-help is more efficacious than the self-help of isolated individuals.'[84]

This complex interplay between collective and individual action was a common and distinctive theme of New Liberalism. In the directly economic sphere its result was, as H. W. Massingham put it, to forbid the elimination of private enterprise and the assumption by the state of all the instruments of production.[85] The state, in giving its protection to some, must also allow free play to the individual. This was a central theme: a concern for a Liberalism which integrated both individualism and collectivism, that is to say a collectivism which organized for corporate ends, while retaining individual initiative.

Many of the New Liberal legislative ventures and schemes can be seen through this double principle of individual and collective responsibility. W. H. Beveridge's classic work, *Unemployment: A Problem of Industry*, was based on a principle that 'unemployment is not to be explained away as the idleness of the unemployable. As little can it be treated as a collection of accidents to individual . . . people.'[86] In other words, unemployment was not solely due to economic fluctuations. Individual responsibility did have a role to play.[87] Where it was shown adequately that economic conditions, outside the control of the individual, had been the cause of the unemployment, then the state had a duty and a responsibility to intervene. It was this notion which lay at the root of the ideas for labour exchanges and unemployment insurance proposals. Many measures like these and the Old Age Pensions Act were a conjunction of individual and state responsibility.

J. A. Hobson's economic theories can also be interpreted in the same light, on the ground of individual and collective responsibility. The basis of his views was that individual responsibility, character and development could not be secured without corporate action.[88] The state provides the secure conditions and viable base for the ethical development of individual character. This theory did not enunciate a total break with the Liberalism of the nineteenth century. As Idealists like Green and Toynbee pointed out, as well as New Liberals like Hobson, the state was not being given a totally free rein at the cost of individual self-reliance. Conversely, the New Liberalism extolled the virtues of true individuality. However, this was tempered by the argument that social welfare and not individual self-interest, was the end of organization. Freedom was not just the lack of compulsion or hindrances. Contracts were not sacrosanct. Alternatively, freedom was an exercise of power and responsibility by an individual, and this could only be achieved in a situation of equal contracting partners. The exercise of individual power, responsibility and ultimately, character, and the enforcement of equal contracts, demanded that the state take on a responsible, interventionary role to provide the grounds and conditions for individual responsibility.

THE MINIMAL CONDITIONS OF CIVILIZED LIFE

One of the main inferences from the doctrine of collective responsibility was that the state had a duty to supply and maintain certain minimal conditions, as in health, sanitation, working conditions and education. As Herbert Samuel wrote:

Whoever admits that the duty of the state is to secure, so far as it is able, the fullest opportunities to lead the best life, cannot refuse to accept this further proposition, that to lessen the causes of poverty and to lighten its effect are essential parts of the right policy of state action.[89]

The real question here was, what kind of policy and minimal conditions would the state affirm? The problem was to fix the boundaries of individual and collective responsibility. The necessity for some minimal provisions by the state can be seen to be a necessary outcome of some aspects of the Idealist social theory. Certainly, men like Samuel interpreted Green in this way.[90] Where it was maintained, as in Green's *Prolegomena to Ethics,* that the function of society was concerned with the development of persons, 'then the realisation of the human spirit in society can only be attained according to the measure in which that function is fulfilled.'[91] If this function was to be fulfilled it was necessary that the state enabled its citizens to develop. Those citizens below normal conditions of health or subsistence would not be able to develop. As T. H. Green argued in another work: 'left to itself, or to the operation of casual benevolence, a degraded population perpetuates and increases itself.'[92] Green went on to claim that a certain standard of material and moral well-being ought to be maintained. Each man, in other words, must have certain conditions of life in which he can realize his powers and capabilities, and can strive towards his 'possible self'. This is a central moral claim on other citizens and a condition of citizenship for deprived individuals.

Green himself approached the problem of the minimal conditions of civilized life somewhat circuitously. In his *Prolegomena to Ethics,* he argued that while a man was continually borne down by animal wants and mere demands for sustenance, he could not be concerned with 'living well' or 'well being', as distinct from 'merely living'. The primitive organization of life for merely living was still rational and not instinctive, yet it did not allow man to envisage ends to which life ultimately was a means. 'Until some relief', Green continued, 'had been won from the constant care of providing for that welfare in material forms, he would have no time to think of any intrinsic value in persons.'[93] Ultimately, Green was aiming at the principle of self-realization, where the individual has a conception of good and thinks of the soul as having a value distinct from and independent of the body. This value distinct from the body was ultimately a state of mind and character, which until attained by every citizen would mean that social life could be nothing but a state of war.

There was, however, a serious equivocation in Green's views, which threw many hostages to fortune. Green drew a distinction between 'merely living', presumably at subsistence level, and 'living well' – in Green's sense, appreciating the higher values of mind and character. He went on to admit that the latter lay implicitly in the former, yet once realized, was wholly distinct. 'Mere living', was not just being alive yet unaware of higher values, but was related to irregular relief of natural needs. Until regular relief of animal needs was gained, the possibility of 'living well' did not arise. In the higher values lay unity and mutual service, while in the lower, competition and war. The question was though, what were the natural needs, and what exactly did regular relief of their needs imply? The implication, for Green, was that 'enough' state intervention was required to ensure health, security and sustenance necessary for self-development, and this was not incompatible with personal responsibility.[94] Yet the further question arose, what was the necessary requirement, and when precisely was intervention not compatible with personal responsibility? Was it to be judged individually? Legislatively, this made little sense. The corollary of accepting collective responsibility for the regular relief of basic needs entailed a policy of minimal subsistence guaranteed by the state. To justify this position, one could retreat, on the issue of 'living well', to saying that intervention entailed a policy of minimal conditions which did not interfere with moral development but gave it a firmer basis. However, the problem arose again of discerning the dividing line between meeting mere natural needs and providing for human well-being above these. How much help ought to be given by the state in this situation? When and how was the collective responsibility for the civilized conditions controlled?

The answers of various political groups in the 1900s to this dilemma differed. Many New Liberals, including J. A. Hobson, argued that it was the moral duty of the state to ensure a living wage, and conditions which would allow the development of higher interests. Yet when and how was it to be known that this standard had been reached? The broader policy of the social minimum carried with it the idea of the higher ends and values of life. Therefore, it referred to a particular optimal level rather than that of mere subsistence. That is to say, the concern was with wages that were adequate for the maintenance of life and comfort, and hours of work which were compatible with self-improvement. As Masterman put it in his work *The New Liberalism*: 'There is no reason in the future why the home of, for example, the coalminer should not be the centre of taste and culture as was once the home of the country parson.'[95]

This is not to argue that T. H. Green promulgated directly the doctrine of the minimum. However, it is arguable that the possibility of a state-maintained minimum, together with all that this implied, was mooted in some of his views. As L. T. Hobhouse is reported to have said in reply to a student who was critical of Green, 'I think you are too hard on T. H. Green. He did not say too much in those days, and hid a lot of good thinking in poor padding.'[96] Probably even more pertinent in Ernest Barker's assessment of Green, when he argues that: 'what matters is rather his principles than his analysis of a particular policy. If his principles are true, each age can progressively interpret their meaning to suit its own needs.'[97] Many other Idealists in their writings showed an explicit awareness and sympathy for some kind of minimal guarantee of conditions by the state.[98]

The New Liberal concern with the minimum was bound up with securing basic wages, a regular labour market, the banishment or at least alleviation of unemployment, and a minimum of health and security. The aim was to alleviate the unnatural distress, and more importantly, to aim at the larger body of citizens, to create an educated, hopeful and vigorous people. Variations of this view were adopted by virtually all who espoused the New Liberalism. One of its most ardent exponents was J. A. Hobson.

The essence of Hobson's economic theory was, in his own words, that 'economic thought must . . . subordinate purely quantitative estimates of value to qualitative, the humanisation of the economic process.'[99] His view of the minimal conditions which the state ought to provide was of an economic system which formed a basis to higher personal and communal life whose value evaded strict measurement.[100] Thus, without a humanized and socialized economic system, political democracy was an empty term. Social progress was dependent primarily on the solution to the problem of poverty. Poverty was a complex and stratified phenomenon which involved housing, wages, overwork and a number of other elements. The question however remained: what role had the state to play here, and what level of conditions was it necessary to maintain, and ultimately for what purpose?

One of the key functions of the state in this situation was the expenditure on welfare from the funds of progressive taxation.

Radicalism in the 1900s was characterized by a distinction between the social and private value of wealth, the earned and the unearned increment.[101] The social origin and value of wealth was drawn distinct from the private origin, on the grounds that reward due to ability was different from an unearned increment based on a favourable market position, for example, in the exploitation of rising land values and the use of sweated labour. The unearned increment could justifiably be taxed, as in the 1909 Budget. Another platform of state activity was the guarantee of a minimum wage, as in the Trade Boards Act. Unemployment and health insurance were also grounded in the idea of providing minimal conditions. However, the question in Hobson's case was, What was the ultimate function of the minimal conditions?

Hobson's answer was, in sum, that in proportion as a community came to substitute a qualitative for a quantitative standard of living, it 'escapes the limitations imposed by matter upon man'.[102] Art, he claimed, knew no restriction. The highest forms of consumption knew no limitations. The enjoyment of the finest intellectual and spiritual goods were all open and common to all men.[103] In other words, the purpose of the minimal conditions, guaranteed through wages, insurance, housing and education, was to transcend the quantitative competitive struggle of social and economic life, by giving a physical and economic basis from which higher non-competitive intellectual and spiritual interests could be developed. It was no wonder that Hobson called for an improvement of the character of consumption, as a key to progress.

The main point that arose out of this discussion of the minimal conditions of civilized life was that the minimum was an ambiguous notion. The New Liberalism, as one recent critic has argued, was concerned that 'economic security should be the party's goal for the twentieth century'.[104] Yet the question remained, what kind of economic security was desired? The intervention in working conditions, housing and sanitation was acceptable to some. Yet the minimum wage, and security through state-maintained insurance, were seen as indispensable to New Liberals like Lloyd George and Hobson. The actual nature of the minimum also remained uncertain. Was it to be a guarantee of mere living, that is to say the relief of basic needs, or was it to be a level where the individual could follow the intellectual of qualitative pursuits of life? The close of the nineteenth century and the first decade of the twentieth century saw progressive redefinitions of the concepts of poverty, needs and state-guaranteed minimums. The New Liberal and Idealist conceptions were elements within this process. Both the New Liberals and Idealists, like Green, produced an equivocal theory of state involvement and guaranteed levels. This minimum hovered between the ideas of providing for physical sustenance, and providing enough for the individual to appreciate higher civilized ends. The problem of physical sustenance was that, apart from the difficulty of defining it, its satisfaction alone did not often provide enough to ensure higher development, therefore the state's duty was not fulfilled, although it saved the state from the charge of undue interference in personal development and responsibility. The problem of providing enough for these higher ends, apart from defining 'enough', and 'higher ends', was that it might entail overstepping corporate responsibility and encroaching on individual or personal responsibility. It might also entail undue hindrance of, for example, the market system and competition. The role of intervention, although viewed as morally necessary, carried with it for many New Liberals a range of problems which were concerned with the boundaries of state and personal action. The same problem seems to have been present in the moral and social theories of Idealism, and the question of how far individual self-development of self-interests should be coerced by the common good or interest. There remained also the question of how far competitiveness in the economic sphere ought to be allowed free rein.

RATIONAL INTERVENTION

L. T. Hobhouse wrote in his seminal work, *Liberalism*, that Liberal doctrine was:

a belief that society can be safely founded on this self-directing power of personality, that it is only on this foundation that a true community can be built . . . It rests not on the claim of A to be let alone by B, but on the duty of B to treat A as a rational being . . . The rule of liberty is just the application of rational method.[105]

In Hobhouse's view personality was something which grew from within man. It was the function of the outer conditions of life to provide the means for this growth. It was the fulfilment of personality, and the action of the state in this fulfilment, which provided the grounds to rational intervention. The rationality of intervention was, in one sense, its capacity to determine the moral good in each man. Each individual, in realizing his rational capacities and fulfilling his personality, was a positive benefit and good to society. This good was thus a common good, qualitatively and quantitatively. As Hobhouse pointed out: 'In realising his capacities of feeling, of living, of mental and physical energy . . . in Green's phrase, he finds his own good in the common good.'[106] The state, in helping men to realize themselves in their various capacities, was acting rationally in terms of moral criteria. The positive rational conception of the state was based upon the effective realization of human personality. This realization was the basis of liberty. Thus, as Hobhouse wrote, society is free 'where all minds have that fullness of scope, which can only be obtained if certain fundamental conditions of their mutual intercourse are maintained by organized effort.'[107]

The state had to retain a delicate balance between public central-ized government and the self-governing individual, the latter being basic and the former providing the rational conditions for the latter. The realization of personality and liberty were, therefore, related by Hobhouse to the function of law. Law provided the conditions for liberty. It was no longer purely compulsion or restraint. It was a means to an end, namely the positive and effective realization of freedom. As Hobhouse argued, 'Liberty and compulsion have complementary functions, and the self-governing state is at once the product and the condition of the self-governing individual.'[108] The object of compulsion was therefore to provide the most favourable conditions for inward growth. As Hobhouse's biographers noted, his ethical work may be described as an attempt 'to trace the function of reason in the sphere of practical life.'[109] The practical sphere of law and individual liberty demonstrated this facet of reason.

In one sense, Hobhouse's theory was arguably the most cogent theoretical statement of the New Liberalism.[110] Admittedly there were many differences between the views of Hobhouse and Hobson, Samuel and Asquith, yet nonetheless, all subscribed to a number of ideas which were encapsulated in Hobhouse's ethical and social theories. These ideas, which formed an essential aspect of the New Liberalism, can be identified in four basic areas. First, rational intervention was justified by the common good. Second, the aim of intervention was the realization of individual personalities and capacities. Third, intervention was based upon a delicate balance between self-government and central government, which was basically a reformulation of the dilemma between personal and collective responsibility. Finally, law and restraint could provide the conditions for the exercise of freedom, and thus liberty and freedom were not just based upon paucity of restraint but conversely, lawful restraint could be a constructive component of liberty. All these ideas, which were central to the New Liberalism, have close affinities to the Idealistic social theories. We will now explore these in greater detail.

INTERVENTION AND THE COMMON GOOD

As J. A. Hobson wrote in *The Evolution of Modern Capitalism*:

limitations upon individual freedom of industry imply a clearer recognition of the falsehood of the *laissez-faire* position. The undertaking by the state or the Municipality or other such units of social life . . . is a definite assertion that, in the supply of the common services rendered by these industries, the competition of private interests cannot be relied upon to work for the public good.[111]

Collective control aimed at the public interest or common good to deal with wastage or dangers in the system. The aim of Hobson's and Hobhouse's theories was some form of moral and social organism. To benefit or improve the standard of one element of the organism was to benefit the whole. Therefore social organization, taxation of the unearned increments for social ends, and social services, were justified in terms of the common good, namely the whole organism. Hobson's humanized economic theory was based upon the idea of distribution and consumption directed towards humane values in the common good. As he stated in his autobiography, *Confessions of an Economic Heretic*: 'Our theory demands that the human values embodied in economic goods shall be "real" in the sense that they contribute to the benefit of the individual and the community as organic wholes.'[112] This idea of organic wholes was developed by Hobson into a concept of the general will. This general will he saw as embodied in the state and determining, for example, the best use of all social property taken by taxation. Hobson, like many of his compatriots in the New Liberal camp, felt incensed against class legislation, or activity in the pursuit of selfish interests. The fundamental aim of legislation was the common good and not the good of one class alone.

Other New Liberals, like C. F. G. Masterman, concurred in this aim. Nationalization, Masterman argued must be shown to be in the public interest or welfare and not exclusively to the advantage of the shareholder or employee. Liberalism, he affirmed, must be concerned with the whole, the good will of all and not one class.[113] Herbert

Samuel and H. H. Asquith echoed this plea in their speeches and writings. Individual and particular interests were subordinate to the common welfare. Regulation of wages, the statutory control of sweated labour and the insurance of health and against unemployment, were ultimately justifiable in terms of the common interest. As Percy Alden, a university settlement warden and New Liberal, wrote in his book *Democratic England,* the Liberal reforms of 1906 onwards signalled that 'The civic conscience had been aroused ... we are not dominated so much by purely commercial interests as by our regard for the welfare of all the citizens.'[114]

Again, Winston Churchill, in justifying land and income taxes in the 1909 Budget, argued that we ought to enquire 'how' wealth was acquired, which to Churchill was bringing the processes by which it was gained 'into harmony with the general interests of the public'. Churchill's aim in his work and speeches for Liberalism was the reconciliation of private interests with the public right.[115] Liberalism, for Churchill, stood for the people's welfare against class or selfish interests. In standing for the 'left-out millions', it did not, for Churchill, advocate antagonism, but conversely a more just society based on general interests. Intervention ultimately aimed at this general interest. As J. H. Harley, a contributor to the New Liberal Rainbow Circle, wrote: 'The objective of political organization is not to accentuate or develop class-consciousness, but to combine ... all sorts and conditions of men in one great enthusiasm for the common life.'[116] Ramsey Muir also put the point in his work *Liberalism and Industry*; the state was the vehicle for the good life. It had a duty to enable all its citizens to realize this. Intervention was justified by the common good.[117]

T. H. Green, in a famous passage, also argued:

The passion for improving mankind, in its ultimate object, does not vary. But the immediate object of reformers and the forms of persuasion by which they seek to advance them, vary much in different generations ... To a hasty observer they might even seem contradictory, and to justify the notion that nothing better than a desire for change, selfish or perverse, is at the bottom of all reforming movements. Only those who will think a little longer about it discern the same old cause of social good against class interest, for which, under altered names, Liberals are fighting now as they were fifty years ago.[118]

In Green's theories, and the Idealists' social theories overall, the elements of rational intervention were unified, in that it was in the realization of the individual's capacities and powers, and through the exercise of rights, that the common good was reached. This process was concerned with a delicate balance between responsible self-government and central government, the latter point involving corporate intervention and a positive conception of law and liberty.

There was, as we have seen, a considerable ambiguity in Green's notion of the common good. The ambiguity arose through the conflicting ideas that it was impossible to realize the common good in a competitive society, and that competition was necessary. How was the common good to be realized as mutual service, when men were at odds pursuing their own selfish interests? Green seemed to wish to say that men act unconsciously through the common good. As he stated: 'The pure desire for social good does not indeed operate in human affairs unalloyed by egotistic motives, but on the other hand what we call egotistic motives do not act without direction from an involuntary reference to the social good.'[119] Thus, although the state could not realize the common good, unless all its members had a disinterested devotion to an ideal of mutual service, the common good was still an involuntary counsel. Rights could be seen as examples of this involuntary counsel. Rights were seen as beneficial features which arose only in a social situation. A right was seen as dependent on the common good, in the sense that it was a power to act for one's own good, secured to the individual by the community, 'on the supposition that its exercise contributes to the good of the community.'[120] Rights, like laws and institutions, were bound up with the realization of individuals and their needs. This foundation, in Green's view, meant that an individual exercising rights was intrinsically, or involuntarily, recognizing the common good.

The capacity for rights in individuals was a social phenomenon; it could be guided and moralized through such institutions of society as the family. The neglect of family life and its moralizing contact could affect this capacity in the agent. In the same way, unequal freedom of contract, unlicensed drink traffic, and insanitary homes, and going beyond Green's stipulations, bad wages and fluctuating and seasonal employment, could affect the individual's capacity for exercising rights. It was through the exercise of rights that a man became a true citizen. It was through rational citizenship that a man became free and served the common good. The state therefore had a duty to enable men to become citizens, without destroying their personal effort. As Green wrote: 'It is enough to point out the directions in which the state may remove obstacles to the realisation of the capacity for the beneficial exercise of rights, without defeating its own object by vitiating the spontaneous character of that capacity.'[121] To remove obstacles in this case would be to do so in terms of the common good. Many Idealists after Green followed this line of argument.[122] The state intervened for the common good. However, both New Liberals and Idealists suffered in one sense from the ambiguity of the common good or general interest, that is to say, whether it could be adequately envisaged in a competitive market society.

AIMS OF INTERVENTION

The specific goal which L. T. Hobhouse saw as the aim of intervention was the realization of the capacities of all individual personalities. This was not a particularly clear notion to many, since it could be synonymous with the concept of happiness or general well-being. Hobhouse tried to argue that J. S. Mill's distinction between self-regarding and other-regarding actions was overcome by Green's organic conception of the state.[123] Self-development and fulfilment of one's capacities was distinct from happiness, in the sense that a positive use and play of energies is distinct from a feeling of pleasure. The aggregate of pleasure could not amount to a common good or unity. It was only in the realization of personality or self and its capacities that the individual could find a correspondence and good with others. Hedonism or utilitarianism could not therefore provide an adequate account of the common good. In Hobhouse's view, self-development was built upon the foundations provided and guaranteed by the state, namely, of education, a minimum of economic and physical welfare, and leisure.[124]

J. A. Hobson produced arguments very close to this. Speaking of the state, Hobson maintained:

From the standpoint which best presents its continuity with earlier Liberalism, it appears as a fuller appreciation and realisation of individual liberty contained in the provision of equal opportunities for self-development. But to this individual standpoint must be joined a just apprehension of the social, viz, the insistence that these claims or rights of self-development to be adjusted to the sovereignty of social welfare.[125]

Hobson probably went further than Hobhouse in the organic possibilities of a common good or general will. He wrote that a man has 'no right as an individual', however he has a duty as a member of society to contribute to the administration of common property.[126] The individual, as a member of society, must organically transmit accurate stimuli, as Hobson put it, to the governing brain of the state.[127] Therefore, in order to ensure this, he argued, the state needed a wide level of intelligence and a development of individuals and their abilities. The one main asset of the state in this sense was to encourage self-development through the equal access to knowledge and culture. However, Hobson's argument contained the implication that he was not so ready to allow the free play of individual judgement. He seemed more concerned to argue that man should be directed to the common good than that he should find it in his own moral and rational personality. Yet the same demand underpins both his and Hobhouse's work: that the self-development of individuals to higher common ends was the basic aim of intervention by the state.

A similar line of argument was advanced by many other New Liberals. H. H. Asquith, in a speech to his Ladybank constituency in 1906, argued:

Just as in another sphere, the Liberal conception of Empire came to this, that by giving the fullest freedom and power of self-development to every member of the Empire they best secured the coherence, unity and mutual loyalty of the whole, so they regarded these social problems at home, while they were prepared to do nothing to uproot or undermine private ownership, individual initiative, and the freest possible field for brain, character and enterprise, yet they were resolved to reconcile with these things laws and institutions that sought, as their governing aim and purpose, to coordinate the good of each with the good of all.[128]

In another work he claimed that the determining feature of the developed Liberalism, in the field of education, better dwellings and improved social conditions, was a new and significant concept of liberty.[129] This concept of liberty was characterized by the fact that to be really free, man needed to make the best use of his faculties, opportunities and energies. Thus freedom was the power of doing something and exercising one's capabilities, based on minimal intervention, an intervention justified by the need for the reconciliation of the private self-developmental good with the common good.

This same core of argument and justification was echoed in a number of the New Liberal writings. Herbert Samuel maintained in his work *Liberalism* that real freedom included the opportunity to 'reach a high level of character and capacity'.[130] The state had a positive duty to enable all its citizens to lead the best life. W. Lyon Blease wrote in 1913 in his work *A Short History of English Liberalism* that although Liberals did not believe in equal abilities, they did believe in the equal opportunity for self-expression and self-development.[131] As Liberalism led men to refrain from interfering with the development of others, so it took 'active steps to remove the artificial barriers which impede that development'.[132] The aim of Liberalism was to enable each man to realize his highest capacities. An essayist in the book *Towards a Social Policy* described this as 'filling in the positive contents of "individual liberty" by helping to secure for all citizens a genuine equality of opportunity.'[133] Civilization, as New Liberals like Masterman tirelessly emphasized, was based on providing adequate wages, hours of work, housing and leisure, so that men could become citizens, that is to say rational human beings, no longer merely truing to exist from day to day, but rather aiming at 'living well' in the higher ends of self-development.[134] Equal opportunity for self-development, as one writer in the *Nation* maintained, meant equal access to the use of land, work and mobility. A man, the writer continued, 'is not really free for purposes of self-development in life and work who is not adequately provided in all these respects.'[135] The New Liberalism aimed at this form of equal opportunity. Self-development utilized the faculties and possibilities of the individual and community life in the pursuit of the common good.

In T. H. Green's estimation, freedom was a positive power. It was the realization of one's self in universal ends.[136] As Green maintained in his famous lecture, 'Liberal Legislation and Freedom of Contract': 'When we speak of freedom as something to be highly prized, we mean a positive power or capacity of doing or enjoying something worth doing.'[137] This enjoyment was something we experienced in common with others. Measurement of the progress of society was thus by the development and exercise of powers contributory to the common good. It was this development of the individual, based on the conditions guaranteed by the state, which led eventually to the common good. Happiness was only a by-product of the moral imperative to pursue self-development and to become a rational citizen. Most of the British Idealist school followed this line of argument, if only to avoid a utilitarian conclusion.

D. G. Ritchie claimed in his book *The Principles of State Interference*, that for Green, social expediency was determined ultimately not by the probable effect of the greatest number of pleasures of an individual, but rather by the scope it gave to the individual for exercising all his capacities for self-development; all true development implying the well-being of the community.[138] It was in active participation with each other that individuals could realize themselves. As A. C. Bradley, the editor of Green's

Prolegomena to Ethics, wrote in a footnote to Green's work, the true end of life is 'the realisation of the possibilities of human nature, and that devotion to such objects as the well-being of a family, the sanitation of a town, or the composition of a book, has been described as an unconscious pursuit of this end.'[139] The aim of intervention, as in the New Liberalism, was thus self-development of the citizen body. This constituted the liberty of the individual in the positive use of certain powers and capacities. Ultimately, the state provided the conditions for the good life.

SELF-GOVERNMENT AND CORPORATE GOVERNMENT

The notion of self-government and corporate government was a reformulation of the difficult notions of individual and collective responsibility. Another possible reformulation could be private rights and obligations and public duties. The two elements were forcibly delineated by Hobhouse in his *Metaphysical Theory of the State*, as the crux of his objections to Bernard Bosanquet's absolute Idealism. It was also a similar objection, on a more metaphysical level, to that made by Pringle Pattison against absolute Idealism in general, in his book *Hegelianism and Personality*.[140]

The essential aim of the argument in a political context was a balance. The point was to create certain minimal requirements from which the self-development and capacity for freedom could grow. This self-development was guided by the educational system and the moralizing institutions of society. It would not be in the interests of the common good if the Government were to do too little, as implied in the notion of *laissez-faire*. Yet neither must the Government do too much, as in taking over the means of production by national-ization, unless justified by the common welfare. In Green's estima-tion, interference with the unearned increment was not warranted, whereas enforcement of sanitation, housing and education were justifiable. The actual items which could be justifiably interfered with altered quite markedly for the New Liberals. Some play, however, had to be given to individual self-control and responsibility, as long as it did not interfere with others. It was' the good citizen who eventually made the good state, and the good citizen needed to govern himself responsibly. According to Herbert Samuel, the citizen did this by conforming to the moral law, a notably Kantian response.[141] Ultimately, as Samuel noted, the state – and all the other institutions that play so large a part in our daily lives – are nothing apart from the existence, the will, the actions of individual men and women.

This kind of argument underpinned claims that the state helped to develop a more distinctive form of individuality and responsibility through intervention.[142] Through helping the individual over certain hindrances, like bad wages or ill-health, the state could help an individual to develop a responsible role, this was the kind of principle that lay behind comments such as Percy Alden's that, 'as a state progresses on collectivist lines, the individual, instead of being lost, seems to stand out more clearly.'[143] The same point was true of Hobson. Michael Freeden remarked, in the introduction to Hobson's autobiography, that Hobson succeeded in establishing an apposite synthesis between the old tenets of Liberalism and the newer claims of the collectivist orientation. Freeden stated:

The organic conception of society was not used by him, as by so many of his predecessors, to assert the absolute priority of the group over the individual. It preserved a continuity with earlier Liberalism by extolling the virtues of individuality, rather than atomistic individualism. However, social, not individual welfare was now seen to be the end of social organisation.[144]

This new conception of individualism was viewed in the context of the developmental potential of the citizen, in terms of the general welfare or common good. It was conceived of as a balance between self-government and the corporate exercise of government. Probably Hobson's theory was weighted a little more to the latter principle than Hobhouse's.[145]

The balance between self-government and corporate government was also a distinctive mark of Idealist social theories. As J. H. Muirhead remarked in his autobiography, he and his fellow Idealists followed Green in believing that 'the ultimate source of social betterment lay in the individuals power of responding to improved external conditions by utilising them for self-improvement as a member of a civilised society . . . What the state could do was to remove hindrances to the free action of . . . conscience.'[146] The two main hindrances that Muirhead located were the want of educational opportunities and the improvement of conditions of home and industry. In Muirhead's view the powers of municipalities ought also to be extended, a point that he felt Green would have been in sympathy with, especially the extension of power conferred in the Local Government Act of 1888. This balance of public and private eventually enabled the application of public funds for the positive objects of welfare, which previously had not been within the ambit of government.

Arnold Toynbee, in his essay 'Are Radical Socialists?', had laid down the criteria of intervention. Toynbee maintained that for an issue to be of primary social importance, it ought to be practicable and should not in any way diminish self-reliance. The area of primary social importance was involved with those problems which were beyond individual control, for example, housing or education. Since self-development was the aim, and the individual's will was the source of this development, self-reliance had to be given a firm basis. A path being trod here was between the competitive interplay of social and economic forces, which in civil society the Idealists felt to be a necessary stage of individual growth in self-consciousness and freedom, and corporate guidance and responsibility, to lessen hardship and provide an adequate base for the concerns of citizenship. In general, Idealists, such as Green and Toynbee, had a fundamental concern for the character of the individual. It was through the self-govermnent and obedience to the moral imperatives of duty that the common good could be realized.

LAW AND LIBERTY

The final point which relates to the concept of rational interference is the relationship between law and liberty. References to this relationship proliferate in New Liberal writings. Herbert Samuel in his *Memoirs* summed up the idea. He claimed:

as more thought was given to the meaning of liberty – which Liberalism existed to serve – it was seen that liberty was not a matter only of national independence, or of constitutional democracy, or of freedom of thought and religion . . . but that there could be no true liberty if a man was confined and oppressed by poverty, by excessive hours of labour, by insecurity of livelihood . . . To be truly free he must be liberated from these things also. In many cases, it was only the power of law that could effect this. More law might often mean more liberty.[147]

Asquith stated the case similarly in his introduction to Samuel's *Liberalism*. Liberty, he declared, was a growing idea; with early reformers it was a negative conception; however with the growth of experience, matured opinion recognized that liberty 'is not only a negative but a positive conception'.[148] Freedom, he claimed, was not just a lack of restraint, it was a positive opportunity to use one's powers. A columnist in the *Nation* (May 1908) echoed this plea by Asquith, when he maintained that 'the negative conception of liberty, as a definite mission for the removal of certain political and economic shackles upon personal liberty, is not merely philosophically defective but historically false.'[149] This negative conception of restraint, he argued, tended to blur the Liberal vision of liberty based on a constructive, evolutionary idea. He contended that Liberals must insist that every enlargement of the authority of the state must be justified by an enlargement of positive liberty.

Another columnist, writing in the *Nation* (November 1908), argued that the doctrines of Mill and Bentham, and in particular the negative conception of the state associated with these theorists, were going out of date.[150] A new demand for collective action was emerging – a demand which had obtained its early practical expression in the Education Act of 1870, and which demanded a closer and more organic relation between the individual and society. The state was more than a glorified policeman. Interestingly, the writer went on to suggest that such a conception 'was found by Green and Caird, partly in the Hegelian doctrine of the state, partly in the modernised interpretation of Plato and Aristotle.'[151]

C. F. G. Masterman, in his later work the *New Liberalism* characterized the ultimate goal of Liberalism as liberty. In practical application, he affirmed, the doctrine often found difficulty in expression. A man may be politically free yet in bondage to poverty. In consequence, Liberals had waged a war on poverty. This war of legislation, according to Masterman, was in no way incompatible with a principle of freedom. Law could in this sense enhance freedom, or at least provide the conditions whereby the potential for freedom could be developed. Law and restraint therefore enable citizens to escape or overcome certain obstacles to the good life.

Most New Liberals concurred with this general approach to the question of law and liberty, if only through a somewhat vague sense of the minimal conditions for equality of opportunity. Ramsay Muir summed up the idea when he argued: 'Liberty is not merely a negative thing, mere absence of restraints; it is a positive thing. No man is really free until he possesses, in sufficient degree the material basis of liberty.'[152] He went on in this account to contend that in the great Liberal ministries of 1906 to 1914 marked advances were made in the adoption of the view that it is the duty of the state to secure for all its citizens such conditions of life as will make real liberty possible. He also claimed that the Old Age Pensions Act, the Trade Boards Act, the insurance against unemployment and sickness, and a multitude of other measures, marked the emergence of a new type of Liberalism and a more generous conception of liberty.

The idea that law or restraint could be a positive and constructive element in liberty is one which is associated specifically with the Idealism of T. H. Green. D. G. Ritchie, speaking of the development of Liberalism, in his *Principles of State Interference,* claimed that it had grown 'from the merely negative work of removing mischievous state-action to the positive task of employing the power of the government, which is now, more or less, the real representative of the 'general will', on behalf of the wellbeing of the community.'[153] Ritchie saw that it was natural and necessary that the intellectual basis for such a new creed of Liberalism should be founded in a constructive philosophy, which he associated explicitly with Idealism.

Thus law and compulsion by the state were necessary components of community life. Force was part of the 'flywheel' of the state. In Ritchie's assessment of Green's view, law was expedient in so far as it tended to promote freedom, in the sense of self-determined action to the objects of reason, inexpedient so far as it tended to interfere with this.[154] Henry Jones also wrote in his work *The Working Faith of a Social Reformer*: 'It is only the pseudo-freedom of irrational caprice which has been limited. Nor has the state invaded any rights in such action; for the liberty to do wrong is not a right, but the perversion of a right and its negation.'[155]

Positive Liberals in this period were concerned with a conception of society not simply based on an aggregate of individuals, but as an organic community or moral rational citizens. The state could intervene in the interaction of citizens so as to enhance and increase liberty, by removing obstacles and preventing undue coercion in, for example, the market situation, by introducing labour exchanges, unemployment insurance and progressive taxation. There was no contradiction in Liberals striving to remove bad restrictions and imposing new and positive ones. Both, the New Liberals contended, could enhance freedom. Municipal and state enterprise had grown markedly through the 1890s and 1900s, yet for the New Liberals this fact had not diminished freedom but enhanced it.

Nearly all the British Idealist school, apart from F. H. Bradley, were active Liberals. These included men like T. H. Green, Arnold Toynbee, Henry Jones, Bernard Bosanquet, J. H. Muirhead and J. S. Mackenzie. All held the positive theory of liberty, which claimed that free action was not merely doing as one desired, in the sense of caprice or licence, but that true freedom arose in obedience and conformity to laws, civil and moral, and it was in the increasing realization of oneself through these various laws and institutional commitments that the citizen aspired to the good life. All of these Idealists adhered to this theory, philosophically and politically. In one sense, it was virtually a secular religion, in that religion was often seen as merely the 'best that we know', this 'best' being freedom embodied in rational citizenship and the recognition of the ethical grounds to law.

In a purer metaphysical sense, the principle of the law for higher freedom was encapsulated in Edward Caird's favourite phrase of 'dying to live';[156] that is to say one died to selfish ends and passions in order to live for the higher life of reason and morality. The idea itself, in philosophy and religion, has a very ancient heritage going back through mystical and philosophical writers, such as Spinoza, to early Christian, Judaic and Greek thought. Green of course makes a great deal of the idea and, as we have seen, drew much of his inspiration from St Paul whose work he regarded as providing the kernel of morality. This alone tends to make the idea appear remote from practical politics in the early twentieth century. Yet despite these reservations the positive theory of liberty and law was strongly present in New Liberal theory and practice. It was only Idealists who had a coherent and worked-out theory of positive liberty, although of course it is compatible with other political theories and views about human capacities and powers.

THE STATE AND CITIZENSHIP

The new conception of the state is a topic which features constantly in the foregoing arguments. The state was seen no longer as a necessary evil or mere protector of property rights and the sanctity of contracts. By the 1890s and 1900s the state was beginning to be viewed as an integral part of economic and political life. It was no longer just restraining or clearing obstacles to the free economic activity of individuals, but was actively and consciously promoting a better life for all its citizens. The self-consciousness of this conception arose, for many New Liberals, through their perception of the growth of the new from the old Liberalism. As we have seen, the old Liberalism was an inchoate and complex phenomenon, yet in the perception of the New Liberals it was a doctrine which had in some way to be confronted. As the Rainbow Circle members declared in their book *Second Chambers in Practice*:

It is proposed to deal with (1) the reason why the old philosophic radicalism and the Manchester School of Economics can no longer furnish a ground of action in the political sphere; (2) the transition from this school of thought to the so-called 'New Radicalism' or Collectivist politics of today; (3) the basis, ethical, economic, and political of the newer politics.[157]

The editor of the *Progressive Review*, William Clarke, declared to his readers that the journal claimed as its adherents all those who realized the urgent need to rally the forces of progress to the 'newer and higher ground which the nineteenth century has disclosed'.[158] Most of the New Liberals like Hobson, Haldane, Hobhouse, Samuel and Churchill did not criticize the old Liberalism to destroy it, but rather to reinterpret it. They admired the heritage of Liberalism, but felt that it ought to be brought into line with the needs of the time. This led to a series of qualifications and readjustments of certain basic concepts such as responsibility, liberty and citizenship.

The notion of citizenship was bound up with the ideas of the social minimum, personal responsibility and the intrinsic worth of the personality. The duty of the state was to provide the minimal conditions and standards necessary for the exercise of freedom. Part of this freedom was the actual performance of the duties of citizenship, and actively and intelligently participating in the functions of social life. This active participation implied certain duties and obligations as well as rights, which are illustrated in the New Liberal attitude towards trade unions. As well as the state providing the preconditions for citizenship, citizenship carried certain duties to the welfare of the community. Social reform was still, in many New Liberals' estimation, connected to the general interest and an increase in productive capacity and national wealth.[159] If trade unions were conceded certain minimum wages, and rights to their own funds, they ought to demonstrate a consequent responsibility in economic terms. Thus, many of the objections by Liberals to the Trades Disputes Act of 1906 had their source in the idea of responsibilities correlated to conceded rights. Rights, as based upon the common good, entailed duties.[160]

H. C. G. Matthew, in his work *The Liberal Imperialists*, noted that the dramatic defeat that Asquith and Haldane suffered at the hands of the Labour group and Campbell-Bannerman, during the 1906 Trades Disputes Bill debate, was a rebuff to them personally as well as to their conception of Liberalism.[161] They believed that the essence of the Liberal party was that it should appeal to the national interest and not to any class. A similar idea was also put forward by

L. T. Hobhouse, who objected to trade union activity where it resorted to force to maintain its particular class interest, in the same way as he objected to the use of force against the Boers. He warned in 1898 that 'Some Socialists . . . have yet to learn that their synthesis must include all the elements of value represented by the Older Liberalism', which for Hobhouse entailed respect for individuality, and a responsibility to the whole community.[162] Hobson also echoed this concern. He could never quite see the Labour group as responsible enough. As he argued in his autobiography: 'neither section of the labour party avowedly accepts that middle course which seems to me essential to a progressive and constructive economic government.'[163] W. H. Beveridge, who had worked under Churchill as a civil servant on labour exchanges, was still espousing the same theme in 1953. He maintained, that in the Taff Vale case, unions 'should be brought within the law as responsible agents; I thought, as I think now still, that power freed from responsibility to law is wrong.'[164] Thus the root of the complaint was that unions should retain equal status under the law with other groups, to ensure responsible behaviour in the common interest.

This was, in fact, a common theme in New Liberal thought. The attitude to socialism was summed up by C. F. G. Masterman in his *Condition of England*. Socialism he maintained was largely an intellectual occupation. He claimed: 'The "socialists" who assail each other so fiercely in queer, violent little newspapers, the writers of tracts . . . the young men and women of the Universities who a generation ago would have called themselves "Radicals", and now call themselves Socialists are principally drawn from the intellectual proletariat. . .'[165] In H. G. Wells and William Morris, he claimed, we are confronted by stiff little pictures or reconstructed worlds offering little to the working people. In Marxism, he continued, we find complete illusion in the gathering together of Hyndman and Lady Warwick. Summing up, Masterman wrote that with the few 'with their ingenious devices for affecting the millennium by backdoor entrances, the many with their occasional gusts of interest . . . the observer is often discouraged.'[166]

Some took the socialist movements more seriously, and not always in the sense of seeking a coalition. Churchill, for example, was fairly expansive on the differences between socialism and the New Liberalism. Others like Hobson and Hobhouse, although deeply sympathetic to the Labour movement, as indeed were Haldane and Asquith, were so in a Liberal manner. Although in sympathy with aspirations for equal opportunity, they like Masterman, Massingham and Beveridge were suspicious of any vested interest without responsibility. The idea of a class struggle represented sectarian politics. Hobhouse continually stressed the compatibility of the public-spirited Liberalism and the socialist ideal, yet the socialism that he was looking to was a liberal or radical socialism, concerned with ethical ends and integrating the best of the old Liberalism. Hobhouse's repulsion from all extremism, and his praise for toleration and politics in the national interest, were essentially Liberalism at its best. The completely egalitarian society or the total ownership of the means of production were far too abstract for Hobhouse, and they implied bureaucratic excesses and a tyranny over individual judgement which exceeded the proper concerns of intervention.

Many Idealists followed a similar line of argument on the Labour movement. Henry Jones argued in 1911 in the *Hibbert Journal* that the mission of Labour 'stands for the interest of one class, and if it recognises any others except as secondary and subordinate, it exceeds and may even contradict its mission.'[167] He argued that Labour appeals to working men on a *class* basis and not as *citizens*. The state was consequently held up for opprobrium when it did not meet this class interest. Therefore the good of the Labour party was class struggle, its appeal was cupidity. In so doing it showed no faith in the people as a whole.

In a later number of the *Hibbert Journal,* Ramsay MacDonald answered Jones's article, arguing that Jones was using suspiciously partisan tools. He maintained that the ethics that Jones put forward were Labour ethics and that his accusations against Labour were the excrescence of the article. He continued that the Labour party was not to be moved by the scolding of 'dainty professors', and that if anybody was corrupt, it was the 'ninepence for fourpence' Liberals. It is an interesting point though that MacDonald should have claimed that Jones's Idealist ethics were also those of the Labour party.[168]

The good citizen, for most New Liberals and Idealists, entailed the good state. The state was nothing apart from the men and women who constituted it. As far as the New Liberals were concerned, the state aimed to create the honest efficient citizen by equality of opportunity and diversity of reward. Masterman expanded this theme in his book *How England is Governed*. He contended that his readership consisted of those classes who were beginning to realize what citizenship actually meant. 'Today', he argued, 'the experiment is being attempted . . . of establishing a community in which each man and woman is a citizen and every man and woman is free.'[169] Later in his book he maintained that increasingly, birth, status or wealth would matter less. The new situation would be characterized by 'service for the communal welfare'. Government would then become an expression of the popular will, 'where the interest of each is identical with the interest of all.'[170]

In citizenship we reach the heart of the political philosophy of Green and fellow-Idealists. As Melvin Richter stated:

Green was among those few English thinkers of his time who held a mystical belief in the capacities of all men, including the working classes . . . Further and better education was badly needed, but its proper goal should be preparation for full citizenship . . . He was prepared to argue that national prestige mattered much less than the standard of living of the labouring classes.[171]

To Idealists like Green, citizenship implied a noble purpose. Citizenship was active and orientated to community life. Muirhead described it as the 'consciousness of our common life and . . . the embodiment of the organic system of our social interests'.[172] He went on to argue that this was the area for the recovery of religion, as the consciousness of man's deepest interests. Citizenship was thus the consciousness of the ends of life and their origin and unity in the community as a whole. The state, by protective and developmental intervention, provided a basis from which the individual, employing his rights, could actively pursue the opportunities provided by the common life. By using his rights intelligently, a man became an active citizen. Thus, as Muirhead stated with conviction: 'To deny one's citizenship is to deny one's humanity.'[173]

If society was, in its institutions and purposes, permeated by our deepest interests, then partaking fully in these institutions, being active in mutual service, was to partake in citizenship and the common interest. To Green it was the actualization of the precepts of reason. It was bringing faith into action in good works; it was acting as the 'witness of God' (see chapter 3). The basic ideal that Green tried to popularize was democratic citizenship for all men. As J. MacCunn wrote of Green, 'the life of citizenship is a mode of divine service.'[174] Green's theory of civic Idealism was the source of his admiration for figures like Mazzini, Cromwell, Bright and Vane, who all espoused the unity of politics and religion in some form of citizenship. Citizenship endorsed the unity of the conscience of man and the public laws, of reason and authority, and of spirit and the flesh.

The Idealist Henry Jones was so keen on the idea of citizenship that he advocated a university degree in it. It was an idea that was closely bound up to the founding of the Workers' Educational Association (WEA), an organization with which Jones was closely involved. He was also closely involved in securing the Stevenson Lectureship in Citizenship in Glasgow University. 'The end of the state', Jones declared, 'is the citizen; and the state which exists for the sake of its citizens is safe in their hands.'[175] Arnold Toynbee, in one of his occasional addresses, also argued for education in citizenship.[176] He outlined a scheme for education in politics, industry and sanitation. These were to be designed for the ordinary citizen to show where duty and fulfilment lay. Any union of labour and capital, Toynbee claimed, must necessarily be preceded by such education.

The concept of citizenship had a remoteness, and a somewhat lofty ring to it, even in the 1900s. It presupposed an extensive educational background and awareness, which was in itself a severe drawback, since a large number of men and women did not possess this. However, it encapsulated a strong humanitarian and ethical spirit which lay at the base of New Liberal theory and Idealism. To many, as the Hegelian William Wallace, put it: 'civilisation is citizenship.'[177]

R. H. Tawney, a Balliol product of the heyday of Idealism, and an early WEA worker, was as Ross Terrill has stated: 'exposed to the idea of citizenship as a lofty personal performance inspired by religion, though directed towards society.'[178] Tawney, the author suggests, was probably deeply influenced by the idea of a civic religion, a conception of Christianity as immanent in society and developing through the moral progress of individuals. Terrill argued that Tawney's conception was eventually distinct from Green's, maintaining that Tawney was more concerned with a just social order. However, he later commented that the main influences on Tawney's conception of society were Matthew Arnold and Green.[179]

The essence of the idea of citizenship is also encapsulated in T. H. Marshall's study, *Citizenship and Social Class*. Speaking of his namesake Alfred Marshall, T. H. Marshall argues that the idea of citizenship was, for this theorist, a basic human equality through membership in a community. As Alfred Marshall wrote, skilled artisans were 'steadily developing independence and a manly respect for themselves and, therefore, a courteous respect for others; they are steadily accepting the private and public duties of a citizen . . . They are steadily becoming gentlemen.'[180] Alfred Marshall saw no limit to the ameliorative policies and resources which could enable each man to be a gentleman. He therefore accepted as right and proper a wide range of economic inequalities. The main conclusion was that inequality of class and income were justifiable, as long as there was equality of citizenship. T. H. Marshall continued the argument by suggesting that citizenship became the architect of legitimate inequality. He asked, however, whether this basic equality could be created without invading the freedom of the competitive market.

T. H. Marshall bases his argument on an approximate division in the historical development of citizenship, between the civil, political and social forms.[181] These roughly correspond, he says, to the eighteenth, nineteenth and twentieth centuries. their contents, he argues, were gradually realized over these periods, the first being rights of individual freedom, speech, thought and faith, the second being rights of participation in political power, and the last a right to a modicum of economic welfare and a share in the heritage of civilized life. The nineteenth century saw the foundation for the social rights of the twentieth century, the new period opening up, for T. H. Marshall, with Booth's work and the Royal Commission on the Aged Poor. The state began not just to relieve the destitute, but to remodel the whole building. The transition was characterized by a change from hereditary class privileges to one of determination by ability, based upon equality of opportunity. The final outcome, as T. H. Marshall states, 'is a structure of unequal status fairly apportioned to unequal abilities.'[182]

It is not so certain that it was solely the work of Booth or the Royal Commission on the Aged Poor which opened up the new period. T. H. Green's lecture 'Liberal Legislation and Freedom of Contract', in 1881, had argued that Liberalism had outgrown the fight for civil and political equalities. The New Liberalism was characterized by a new concept of liberty, which was the basis to Green's view of citizenship. This liberty, based on the power to do and enjoy, needed basic intervention, which for some began in the 1870 Education Act, an Act which derived from a Royal Commission on education on which Green had been a commissioner. However, the New Liberalism was duly affected by this new view of citizenship, which looked to men's abilities, status and the equality of opportunity in a competitive society. The question remained though, whether equality of citizenship could be maintained with inequality of income, and further, could social rights to citizenship exist within the nexus of a capitalistic market society?

PROPERTY AND THE MORALIZED CAPITALISM

The New Liberals, especially the economist J. A. Hobson, tried to formulate a new view of the market system. It was an attempt to resolve the discrepancy between the ideas of humanitarian reform and 'efficiency'. It was only the rounded efficient individual, the responsible freely acting citizen, who made the best and most reliable workman. This end was to be attained through humanitarian reforms. Although essentially a business proposition, it also had considerable ethical implications. The humanized or moralized capitalism was a reform within the institutional structure. The competitive instinct was not to be thwarted, but maintained within the context of certain ameliorative policies, designed to ensure standards of health and general development. The state needed to help raise up the level of the population, physically and mentally, to higher standards of qualitative consumption. This help was to be financed by the new principle of taxation based on the social value of wealth. This presupposed a new theory of property.

The middle path between collectivism and individualism, which Churchill was fond of pointing out, was one where, in Masterman's words: 'poverty will not be destroyed by revolution, nor by the diminution of "capital", nor by the abolition of "capitalism" . . . nor by the removal of incentive towards unusual effort.'[183] Masterman considered that the real need was far more effort in production, accompanied by fairer distribution of resources. This was not a war on capitalism. On the contrary, he claimed that Liberalism wanted 'everyman . . . a Capitalist'. It is difficult in this sense to see why, in the Introduction to Churchill's *The People's Rights,* Cameron Hazlehurst should argue that Churchill remained partly imprisoned in the ideas of an earlier generation, because he believed in the evolution of society through competition. Churchill, believing in competition tempered by ameliorative policies, was perfectly in accordance with most of his contemporaries. Churchill and others felt that they were giving a basis to thrift and self-reliance. New Liberals were not trying to stop competitiveness or discourage thrift, but to give them a firmer base.

The essence of Hobson's position was not an indictment of capitalism for the purpose of overthrowing it, but for the qualification and reinterpretation of its function. The divisions that Hobson made were between the industrial process, the maintenance costs of industry, the productive surplus and the unproductive surplus. The last point was the source of waste in the system. It included economic rents from land and excessive income from profits or salaries. This unproductive surplus led to massive saving by the employing class, in other words 'over-saving'. Hobson was not criticizing the factors of industry which accrued to normal maintenance and profits. His criticism was directed at over-saving by a small section of the community. This waste money, he argued, could be employed to give higher wages, and thus redistribute wealth in favour of the work-force. With more distribution and higher wages, Hobson felt that there would be more consumption, and thus depression could be avoided, depressions being the *result* of over-production, over-saving and under-consumption. Further, much of the production of wealth was to Hobson a social venture. There was no reason why some should benefit and over-save, while the majority should be subject to depression. Hobson wanted to attack the unproductive surplus, to ensure a common standard of humanity, and eventually to raise the qualitative character of consumption.

The means of this attack were higher wages, control of profits, graduated taxation and some nationalization. These were seen as the constructive improvements of the capitalist system. A writer in the *Nation*, in 1909, using a Hobsonian argument in a discussion of Lloyd George's Budget, stated:

The effect of the Budget will not be to reduce the effective capital, employment or wages, of the nation. On the contrary, if the constructive social policy of the Government for which this money is required, is faithfully pursued, the net effect will be to take certain elements of surplus wealth, representing earned income, which would have been put to unproductive expenditure or wastefully speculative investments, and to apply them to improve the conditions of labour and land, the true parents of national wealth.[184]

The attacks of Hobson, Chiozza Money and Hobhouse on the market system and competition were not therefore to stop thrift, but were an attempt on ethical grounds to make a reformed and moralized capitalism. This was to be achieved through a delicate combination of corporate and individual responsibility, a reformed capitalism tempered by social reform.

The basis of taxation, in this case, was founded on the distinction between earned and unearned increment or social and private value, that is to say, between income as a reward for ability, as a factor in the maintenance of industry, and income acquired through wasteful exploitation of the market or land prices, etc., which were factors having a social origin. As Hobhouse maintained in his work *Liberalism,* the true function of taxation was to 'secure to society the element in wealth that is of social origin, or, more broadly, all that does not own its origin to the efforts of living individuals'; the social value of wealth could validly be appropriated by the state for the common interest.[185]

The whole argument on the moralized capitalism presupposed a notion of property. The idea towards which New Liberals seemed to be striving, was brought out in a series of essays entitled *Property: Its Duties and Rights,* with a significant contribution by L. T. Hobhouse.[186] The distinction between earned and unearned increments or private and social value in wealth was nicely summarized by Hobhouse in his paper, and also by the Idealist Charles Gore, in the Introduction to the essays, as property for use and property for power. This was again reminiscent of Hobson's productive and unproductive surplus. Hobhouse and Gore saw property as a right of control over things, which was recognized by society. It was intrinsically connected to rational purpose and individual freedom and thus was essential for the development of personality. To be more explicit, as Gore argued in the Introduction, the success of civilization was not measured by the amount and character of material wealth, but rather by the degree to which it gave all members of society 'the chance of making the best of themselves, to feel that an adequate measure of free self-realisation is granted for them'.[187] Property for use was what a man needed for this freedom. Above this limited quantity it became property for power and control by the rich. Thus without property for use no man could realize himself as a personality or citizen. Since there was no valid claim for unlimited property, and property was justified by the common good, all ought to partake in property for use, which the state, as the repository of the common good, ought to guarantee.

Green's theory of property was full of a number of implications. Admittedly, he had specified that unearned increments were not to be interfered with; however, as Hastings Rashdall remarked in his essay, Green's

strong sense of the necessity of property for the building up of character led him, however, not so much to exalt the sacredness of property in the hands of the large owner, as to insist on the necessity of such legislation as would tend to the diffusion of property as widely as possible among the masses. A more socialist version of the Hegelian teaching is to be found in the writings of the late Professor Ritchie, while for a more individualistic interpretation the most conspicuous representative is Professor Bosanquet.[188]

Green, in this sense, was a seminal thinker. His theory of property could be interpreted in different ways. His doubts on the unearned increment were bound up with the difficulty of determining the exact boundary of the earned. He seemed to place greater value on a class of small proprietors and capitalists. This probably makes Bernard Bosanquet's assessment closer to Green's. Yet the rationale of property in the *Lectures on the Principles of Political Obligation* was fluid enough to be taken in quite radical directions. Each man needed property which allowed him to realize his will. Property accumulation was justifiable as long as it did not interfere with the exercise of a like power by others. If some men accumulated property and over-saved, causing general depression, the majority of citizens were consequently deprived of liberty. If it was the case that the purpose of the state was to enable individuals to acquire liberty and realize themselves, then as Hastings Rashdall and Charles Gore intimated, there was a strong basis and necessity for intervention in property rights. As Green's disciple, Toynbee, had argued in an occasional paper: 'I do not hesitate to say that this question of the distribution of wealth is the great question of our time.'[189] He demanded an increase in wealth for those who laboured with their hands, not to seize upon material enjoyments, but that 'they may enter upon a purer and higher life.'[190]

Thus despite the damaging ambiguities of Green's arguments on property, there is a case to be made out that Idealism contains a theory of property, which through the stipulations concerning citizenship, freedom and responsibility demands some redistribution of wealth. Also, ownership of property is not an individual achievement, but is relative to the common good. If ownership infringes the common good, intervention is justified.

For the Idealists and New Liberals therefore, equality of citizenship could be reconciled with inequality of income, as long as it did not affect the general standard of property for all men. The view of the New Liberals, and some of the Idealists, was a combination of social rights to some property, that was property for use, and an equality of opportunity, which implied inequality of ability and inequality of reward. Citizenship was secured through a standard of property and security. Its development was guaranteed by the opportunities of rational community life. In this sense, Stedman Jones in his work *Outcast London* was correct in his assessment of the origins of the New Liberalism, in that 'What was common to both Marshall and Green was the stress upon a moralized capitalism through which the highest potentialities of mankind were to be developed.'[191] This was essentially an optimistic claim, that in moralizing men through their participation in citizenship, their market and competitive activities could also be moralized.

The corollary of this argument was basically an equality of opportunity for all citizens. As Henry Jones had argued: 'The state provides the opportunities, the citizens use these opportunities.'[192] New Liberals expressed similar sentiments. Samuel argued in the *Progressive Review* in 1896 that 'the newer Liberal school is one that is animated by a belief that the object, and the sole object, for which society and the State exist, is to provide the fullest opportunities for every person.'[193] It could be said that the equality of opportunity argument contains the central focus of the New Liberal vision. As a columnist in the *Nation* declared in 1909: 'Is a man free who has not equal opportunity with his fellows of such access to all material and moral means of personal development and work as shall contribute to his own welfare and that of society?'[194]

The opportunity argument contained the implicit premise that all citizens had capacities and powers, not necessarily of equal amounts or types, yet each should be given an equal footing and a means to develop what they possess. The aim was to achieve the fulfilment of the largest number through their citizenship. The state, by providing the basic services, was attempting to equalize opportunities through intervention. The rationale for this was liberty and citizenship based upon a modicum of economic welfare and a share in civilization.

IMPERIALISM AND IDEALISM

The arguments concerning imperialism have passed through many distorting mirrors this century. In this case, it is intended to deal with a very limited perspective to illustrate a close affinity between the New Liberalism and Idealism, concerning the advantages and disadvantages of imperialism.

The arguments concerned with the disadvantages of imperialism have been fully articulated this century. The main one is often connected to Hobson's work. This is more commonly known as the conspiracy theory. The argument is, in sum, that landlords, squires, bankers, financiers, and ironmasters, etc., all the financial forces in the country, are drawn together in common resistance to attacks on their power, property and privileges. The attacks arise in the financial disturbance caused by social reform and public expenditure. In order to avoid this disturbance, the financial interests give their support to imperialism, which takes public attention and resources away from the social field. Thus, raucous patriotism and jingoism take the place of reform on the domestic front, and therefore, to Hobson, imperialism is an enemy of the working classes and the reactionaries' paradise.

Further problems have been raised concerning imperialism; these include the cost of administration, the increased likelihood of war, the undermining of local customs, and the degradation of native peoples through the introduction of alien diseases and alcohol. Added to this, is the moral revolt against imperialism which best expresses the 'Little England' sentiments of Lloyd George and Campbell-Bannerman. How can a doctrine of political Liberalism be reconciled with conquest and economic exploitation? If Liberalism aims at liberty, what possible justification is there for colonial rule? As Hobson pointed out, imperialism is a diversion from social reform and true Liberal concerns.

Hobson's line of argument, in its economic and radical form, was further developed by Marxists such as Hilferding, Rosa Luxemburg and Lenin. However, these theorists isolated an aspect of imperialism, which was in fact one aspect of Hobson's concern. Imperialism, like most political concepts, has a number of meanings. Certainly, violent annexation is to be drawn distinct from commercial trading, as free-trade imperialism is from neo-mercantile imperialism. Further distinctions should be made between legal hegemony working alongside local custom, and those aiming at supplanting local rulers and custom. Also a distinction should be observed concerning the aims of the imperialism, whether it is to bring civilization, in the sense of a better life as the colonists saw it, or whether it aims at simple dominance as an end in itself, that is to say legally or commercially.

The present account deals with one aspect very briefly, and this can be introduced through J. A. Hobson.[195] In his work on imperialism, Hobson felt that interference by one state in the affairs of another was justifiable on three conditions. It must be directed primarily to secure the safety and progress of the civilization of the world. It must be attended by an improvement and elevation in the character of the people. The determination of colonial conditions must proceed from an organized representation of civilized humanity. Herbert Samuel also, while listing the advantages of imperialism, summed up the case by saying that imperialism is:

a loyal determination to defend the empire we hold, ·a sentiment of close unity with the English colonists, a desire to promote the interest of the empire without injury to domestic progress, to develop its commerce while scrupulously caring for the well-being of the subject races, to maintain its sovereignty while preparing the way for an extension of native liberties.[196]

The controversy within the Liberal party, according to Samuel, was one of words. He added that 'men, united on the spirit and main principles of Imperial policy, might well differ on the questions at issue ... and one need not have been a friend of aggression to approve the war, nor a disbeliever in empire in order to think it unjust.'[197] The criteria that Samuel saw as justifying imperialism were first, that self-government ought to be extended everywhere with the development of education and political capacity, and secondly, that the empire taken as a whole should be conducive to the well-being of the rest of the world.

R. B. Haldane's thoughts on the empire represent a similar theme. He had, in fact, envisaged a fairly grandiose scheme in his lecture, 'The Higher Nationality', which had strong implications for world government. As always with Haldane, he had visions of a uniting educational base to the empire, to establish common ground on justice, religion and science. This task he saw as being accomplished through an 'Imperial University'. The same notion arose as in Samuel, of allowing liberty to develop from within each country. Contrary to what B. B. Gilbert maintained in his introduction to the reissue of the *Heart of the Empire* writings, Imperialism was not wholly incompatible with social reform. Under the moral criteria of increasing self-development and liberty, imperialism was justifiable and compatible. Conversely, under the criteria of economic exploitation, contempt for other races, and violence, imperialism was not justifiable.

L. T. Hobhouse had attempted to dismiss Idealism as generally on a par with militaristic imperialism, conservatism and anti-reform sentiments, yet he must have known that Idealists like Edward Caird and Green stood out against all of these. Both philosophers objected to violent imperialism, Green following the lead here of Bright and Cobden. Edward Caird had opposed the Boer War and also took part in the protest against honouring Cecil Rhodes with a degree at Oxford University. Yet on the other count, there were Idealists like Henry Jones and J. H. Muirhead who accepted a qualified imperialism, virtually on the same grounds as Haldane, Samuel and Asquith. As Muirhead remarked, the duty of the imperial ruler is the development 'of what is best in the instincts and traditions of these races themselves'.[198] The ruler should not destroy the customs and faiths, but should try to develop their better elements. He argued: 'Let the people then but know. Let them know through education and example what good government means, and we may leave to the spirit of all good of which government is the highest earthly expression to enlist their feeling and conscious will upon its side.'[199]

In other words, both Idealists and New Liberals saw the advantages and disadvantages of imperialism ranged on similar principles. The cardinal principle was concerned with the question: was Imperialism enhancing the self-government and liberty of the races, or was it merely exploiting them and diminishing their self-development? The argument concerned with intervention by the state is similar in many respects to that of imperialism. The object of interference domestically is to enhance liberty, that is Liberal interference. The means to this liberty is an infringement or curtailment of some negative liberty, by means of tax, rates and compulsory insurance, etc. As some New Liberals maintained, law enhanced liberty by providing positive opportunities. Thus, initial restraint in self-governance is justified by the end of more adequate self-governance. This argument runs through all the domestic pleas of the progressive New Liberals. Some of the imperialists transferred this argument from a domestic to an imperial level, as did Idealists such as Muirhead. Some felt it was misapplied or just wrong, yet these are different questions. Anarchic progressives like Hilaire Belloc or G. K. Chesterton saw this argument as misapplied in the domestic sphere. In Chesterton's words, Lloyd George's Insurance Act of 1911 was 'a step to the servile state; as legally recognising two classes of citizens; fixed as masters and servants.'[200] On the same count as some argued that imperialists interfered with other races and tried to foist alien values on to them, so some considered the domestic reforms in a similar light. Speaking of the domestic reformers, Chesterton pointed out that 'the worst of them tended to be snobs and even the best of them to be specialists.' The whole force of Belloc's *The Servile State* was directed against those who thought they best knew the interests and welfare of others.[201]

ORGANICISM AND THE NEW LIBERALISM

A final point of similarity between the New Liberalism and Idealism is on the concept of organicism. The substance of this argument is contained in a paper by Michael Freeden, entitled 'Biological and

Evolutionary Roots of the New Liberalism in England', as well as in his later book. Concluding his argument, Freeden maintains:

Advanced Liberals had arrived at an expanded and more radical expression of Green's social philosophy by means of the concepts of 'evolution' and 'organicism'. It was within this Liberal climate of ideas, with its combination of two central strands in English political thought – liberty and welfare – that the social legislation at the basis of the British Welfare State was nurtured.[202]

Freeden wishes to argue that evolution has been too much associated with the idea of the survival of the fittest, and too little attention has been paid to the way in which Green's theory has been viewed and transformed through an evolutionary perspective. This perspective consequently gave a background to notions of collectivism, community and social reform, and also seemed to corroborate the historical and philosophical assumptions of Liberal thought.

The traditional interpretation of Malthus, Spencer and Darwin was transformed by T. H. Huxley and Benjamin Kidd, who argued the merits of conjoining ethical considerations and evolutionary ones. It finally achieved a unity in Hobson and Hobhouse. These theorists posited a correlation between ethics and evolution. 'The development of mind', says Freeden, 'enabled the individual to grasp that he was acting within the framework of human society.'[203] The distinction that Hobhouse wished to affirm was between necessitarian evolution and social self-determination. Thus, the reformer and mind had a distinctive role to play. 'Mind', to Hobhouse, 'was not there merely to speed up the march of nature towards cooperation but was itself a natural phenomenon, and hence the rational self-direction of society through mind was part of the natural evolutionary process.'[204]

This theory, Freeden maintains, coalesced with 'ethical-collectivist' currents of Liberalism, by stressing the importance of society as a conscious entity and not predetermined, and second, it legitimated the role of the rational social reformer to change the environment. Thus its concern was with the will of the reformer and the recipient of the reform; that is to say it was not just a reform of conditions that was sought or envisaged, but also a change of will and consciousness. Therefore, as Freeden put it: 'Hobhouse understood collectivism to imply that human behaviour was increasingly directed by the individual consciousness that he was part of a society.'[205]

Thus society, under the criterion of organicism, became a cohesive entity with government deeply involved in the whole as the responsible repository of stimulii. Freeden contends that this argument was developed by D. G. Ritchie and Hobson into wider applications, possibly too wide for Hobhouse. As Freeden points out: 'Hobhouse posited social development as dependent on the evolution of individual minds towards harmony and collective responsibility, whereas Hobson could insist that the germ of an ethical and wholesome society existed in the psychophysical structure of any human group at all stages of development.'[206] Freeden sees this general will of Hobson's as an empirical description of Bosanquet's idea, and thus as a departure from the Idealists.

Freeden's argument concerning the transformation of Green's social philosophy through the concept of a qualified evolution is very helpful. However, it is worth pointing out that many other Idealists, after Green, explicitly used the organic conception.[207] Freeden seems to imply that in becoming empirical, historical and biological, Hobson and Ritchie were going beyond the Idealists. Hobson probably did go beyond the Idealists, but not necessarily to a more workable or better theory. He lost track of the implications of his theory of organicism, possibly through a lack of philosophical acumen, and also through a passionate dislike of alternatives. D. G. Ritchie is slightly misread by Freeden, who says that 'Ritchie welcomed the conception of organicism as helping political thinkers out of the confusions of individualism. He improved upon the Idealists in making it more than an abstract explanatory device.'[208] This misreads the point that Ritchie *was* an Idealist, as were Henry Jones and Bosanquet. He was not improving on Idealism. Secondly, the Idealists' theory of the common good and the genesis of man in social relations had already overcome the idea of individualism. In addition, Ritchie was acting under purely Hegelian principles in examining evolution. Ritchie argues 'The same dialectic movement, which had brought the human spirit to the stage at which Hegel found it and interpreted it, must urge man onwards.'[209] In other words, to be true to the Hegelian and Idealistic spirit, one must integrate all views which the *Geist* creates. Hegel interpreted his own period; the present must be reinterpreted.

Another idea worth pointing out here is that organicism still did not present a wholly coherent picture. As Ernest Barker remarked on Samuel Alexander's and Hobhouse's versions of evolution, it was doubtful whether ethics or politics would benefit by the importation of concepts from the natural world.[210] This can be approached from a philosophical angle. Associating mind and evolution with rational self-consciousness does not answer the question, if mind is an aspect of evolution, and self-consciousness is a quality of mind, why should it be distinct from its ruling principle, namely determinate evolution? Evolution is an equivocal and hard taskmaster. Once given the primaeval task of determining mind, it can appear in many guises. The theory of organicism is not adequately resolved with rational self-consciousness and ethics. However, on a fairly basic level, people of New Liberal persuasion, like Hobson and Hobhouse, were aware of and deeply sympathetic to the idea. Evolution, in these theorists, was seen as a rational rather than directly mechanical process. However evolutionary ideas themselves must be placed in a broader perspective. Much of the time these ideas were simply philosophical notions, drawn from Idealism, and dressed up in fashionable scientific clothes.

6 The Charity Organization Society: Poverty and Citizenship

Poverty in itself does not make men into a rabble; a rabble is created only when there is joined to poverty a disposition of mind, an inner indignation against the rich, against society, against the government.

Hegel

The Charity Organization Society represented the main effort of the free market society to solve the problem of poverty without government intervention.

G. V. Rimlinger

A social philosophy which places conceptions such as citizenship and the common good at the very centre of its understanding of society has to be preoccupied with those factors which weaken the integration of citizens into society. One of the major factors making for a lack of integration in modern society is poverty. Hegel, who was such a major influence upon the Idealists, regarded the problem of poverty as one of the most central in society and political theory. Poverty, in his view, was a central feature of modern civil society, and the deprivation experienced by the poor was not just to be seen as physical deprivation, however important this may be; rather poverty involves the breaking down of the various ties of citizenship – the acquisition of skill, education, access to justice and organized religion – all of which are mediating links which integrate individuals into the state.[1] The problem with poverty is how to alleviate it in a manner consistent with the principles of civil society: that is to say consistently within a privately incorporated market marked by inequalities in wealth, property ownership and income. How can a collective answer to poverty be produced in a social system marked by a strong sense of individualism? Hegel regarded the problem as insoluble and saw poverty as the main 'contradiction' of modern society. Green, Toynbee, Bosanquet, Jones and MacCunn were equally preoccupied with this issue, and in the next two chapters we shall look at two responses to the problem. One response is to be found by examining the contribution made by Bosanquet to the social theory of the Charity Organization Society (COS). This response is an individualized one which looks at the responsibility of the individual for his own deprivation and sees ways to enable him to overcome poverty through his own efforts. The other response is community-orientated: the settlement movement sought to influence and permeate the way of life of a local community so that the community could help itself to identify its problems and seek solutions to them.

In this chapter we shall discuss the individualized, casework-orientated approach to alleviating poverty; in the next we shall look at the community-orientated developments. Both of these discussions, the personal and the communitarian, are still central to our present-day understanding of and strategy towards social policy. In this chapter the initial aim will be to say something about the COS and to discuss the role which Bosanquet and Charles Loch, both Idealists, played in it.

The particular theory of casework and welfare which Bernard Bosanquet developed was explicitly Idealistic. Most scholars who have written comprehensively on the society have noted the influence of Idealism, yet it has been taken somewhat at its face value.[2] We intend to examine the relationship in detail. In the case of the COS we are dealing with self-confessed Idealists, particularly with the Bosanquets and Loch. Bernard Bosanquet was related to the founding president of the COS and it has often been seen as a family enterprise. It might also be noted that other Idealists like Edward Caird, Henry Jones and Charles Gore were involved at one time or another with the COS. Additionally, their statement on the theoretical grounds of their work express their own unequivocal belief in the relation. Finally, the brand of Idealism in this section is more limited, since it will be mainly dealing with the work of Bernard Bosanquet and occasionally T. H. Green.

As Asa Briggs has remarked, 'It is easy to caricature the outlook of the COS.'[3] In fact, much of the COS material seems to invite such a view. By co-operating with the Poor Law it appeared totally to accept the extant and faulty 1834 system. By securing thorough investigation they were likened to 'nosy' detectives. By granting only temporary relief at the last resort they were seen as mean and callous. Finally, by actively working against begging they were seen as repressive.

The aims of the early COS were clearly bound up with the ideas of the deserving and undeserving poor, the self-reliance, providence and character of individuals. They were concerned with the suppression of begging letters and indiscriminate charity. As a Charity Organization reporter maintained in 1872: 'the vagrancy and mendicity of the metropolis are attracted and developed by profuse and indiscriminate relief to vagrant and mendicants, and the absence of any control exercised over them.'[4]

C. P. B. Bosanquet argued for the importance of the contact between rich and poor. He stated that 'for a gentleman to gain influence with these men as a class, it is necessary to find common subjects of interest.'[5] These common subjects were envisaged as education, temperance and the progress of co-operative associations. Yet the primary need of the poor was religion; it was the source of morality and self-discipline. Housing, sustenance and medical care presumably took second place.

C. S. Loch was still arguing in 1910 that 'We aimed at such assistance being afforded to persons in distress as would enable them in conjunction with their own efforts and the aid of their friends to become self-supporting.'[6] This kind of remark has contributed to the somewhat stereotyped picture of the COS, which obviously has some truth to it. Yet, it must be stressed that this is not the whole picture. Many of Loch's remarks, when taken in isolation, do seem harsh and conservative, yet we shall show that they do have some deeper foundation in theory.

Many commentators have argued that the dominant ethos of the COS was extreme individualism.[7] According to Briggs, they always drew a sharp distinction between the deserving and the undeserving poor.[8] For B. B. Gilbert they disliked all government intervention and opposed all social legislation. Poverty was solely a deficiency in character.[9] In Briggs's view the COS did not accept any exact statistical statements about poverty, and their primary aim was to produce the 'liberal, economic man'.[10] To other critics, like David Owen, the COS wanted a clearly marked boundary between public and private policy.[11] Most critics seem to agree that the COS epitomized the Victorian age, in its more callous and optimistic moments.[12]

Admittedly these points may have been adhered to by some

members of the cos, yet if taken as the overall commitments of the society, the case is not so simple. On the rigid distinction between deserving and undeserving, which Briggs claims the cos adhered to, it is interesting to note what some cos members actually said. Bernard Bosanquet wrote in a paper in 1917 that the words deserving and undeserving were used by the cos up to 1878 and 1879. By 1893, Bosanquet continued, the words deserving and undeserving were 'largely passing out of use'.[13] The same point was made by his wife Helen Bosanquet in a paper in the *Charity Organization Review* of 1893 where she seriously questioned the validity of the words.[14] They both maintained that by the 1890s the cos had abandoned the terms.

Additionally, on the question of the cos dislike of government interference and social legislation, we have to bear in mind what they actually said. C. S. Loch, in a book published in 1910, argued that charity 'would intensify the spirit and feeling of members of society, and would aim at improving social conditions ... So it has consistently intervened in all kinds of ways, and, in the last century, for instance, it has initiated many movements afterwards taken up by public authorities – such as prison reform, industrial schools, child protection, housing, food reform, etc.'[15]

Bernard Bosanquet had argued in a paper that the views of the anti-interventionist theorist were not merely imperfect, but amounted to a total misapprehension.[16] In the course of the paper he continued that freedom was not to be found in the unrestrained individual. Legislative control, authority and intervention were interwoven in the social organism as necessary parts. Coercive legislation was part of the 'flywheel' of the state.[17] In yet another paper Bosanquet declared unreservedly 'I believe in the reality of the general will, and in the consequent right and duty of civilised society to exercise initiative through the state with a view to the fullest development of the life of its members.'[18] It would seem to be a misapprehension to class the Bosanquets and Loch as simple anti-government theorists or as utterly opposed to social legislation.

The idea that poverty was due to character deficiency seems to be but a half-truth, as regards the cos. In some cases the cos felt that character deficiency was the causal factor in poverty. However, the question remains, what precisely is character? We shall discuss this point later, but it should be noted here that Loch stated that 'sometimes material relief may be enough' for some; moreover, the fact that the cos did originally work with the idea of the deserving poor, implied that not all poverty was due to character deficiency, only some.[19]

In addition, it seems peculiar that Briggs should see the COS as *not* accepting exact statistical statements, bearing in mind the fact that C. S. Loch, the COS incarnate, was the Tooke Professor of Economic Science and Statistics at King's College, London (1904–08), a member of the International Statistical Institute, and the recipient of the Guy Medal by the Royal Statistical Society. Further, Loch used statistical evidence to back up his arguments in, for instance, discussion of old age pensions and disputes over the success of the old Poor Law.[20] What Briggs presumably refers to are Helen Bosanquet's objections to Seebohm Rowntree's statistics on poverty in York, which in a more contemporary sense seem perfectly valid criticism, regarding the method of data collection, and the validity of certain dietary assumptions.[21]

Furthermore, it is not clear what Briggs could mean by the liberal economic man? Anyone reading Bernard or Helen Bosanquet on the abstract one-sidedness of the economic view of man would not be able to comprehend the critic's view that development of this liberal economic man was an 'end to itself'.[22]

We should also examine David Owen's contention that the COS wanted a clear boundary between public and private policy in the light of Bernard Bosanquet's essay on 'Individual and Social Reform'. We find Bosanquet arguing: 'What has always impressed me most as the most striking feature of social progress is the inseparable identity between the two aspects of reform.'[23] He goes on to say that he wished to consider them as a 'single movement and development'. In other words, there is no rigid distinction between the public and private. This is wholly in accord with the more general Idealistic principle which Loch put simply in the phrase 'the common good is really and ultimately only individual good (not advantage) harmonized to a common end.'[24] The public and private were in this sense artificial spheres, the end of both was the same, namely the best life. The sphere of public activity was justifiable to Bosanquet and Loch as long as it created new possibilities for the self-conscious development of the individual. In this sense it had no limits if its acts were wholly in accord with the general will. However, generally a more pragmatic 'hindering of hindrances' came into play for Bosanquet.[25]

Finally, to say that the COS is a characteristic product of the Victorian age is both bland and problematic. What assumptions do we make when speaking of a Victorian age? What is it that characterizes it? Surely the age that we speak of was a plurality of things and ideas. As one scholar of Victorian times has remarked: 'While the social historian of the Victorian age, who is able to withhold opinion is for ever aware of intrinsic complexities, the critic intent upon cultural evaluation is constantly betrayed into premature judgement.'[26] There is probably another source to this problem. As W. E. Houghton argued in his work on the Victorians, we seem to imagine that we are that much better, more enlightened and generally different from our Victorian forbears.[27] Yet if we look at the range of problems that the Victorians faced: problems of religion, public and private morality, science and progress, the advance of industry, democratic growth, urban poverty, etc., they are still very much with us today, if in different forms. This is a particularly important point when dealing with the COS. Many recent scholars have confessed their difficulty in dealing objectively with the COS, since its social theories, for instance, in the view of T. H. Marshall, are 'repugnant to the modern mind'.[28] Leaving aside this modern mind, it is interesting to note the strongly evaluative bias immediately present in the historical account.

This repugnance seems due to a very basic issue. The COS can be seen as a transitional group between a conception of welfare as an indiscriminate *gift* of charity and as a *right*. Its transitional status was constituted by certain arguments relating to the destitute and incapable. It established the principle of a right to receive help, if not in many spheres, from the state, and the duty of all citizens to give help.[29] This help, it was argued, must be consistently and systematically organized. It should no longer rely on occasional sympathy, but conversely on a positive rational response, a response which at times could be from the state. Since the heyday of the COS, many of the types of help and charity have been taken over by the state, and the conditions for help have altered into statutory obligations without stigma, on the state's part. Yet it is arguable that many of the areas of state involvement or non-involvement have been progressively and hotly disputed throughout this century in theory and practice. Notions of social justice, redistribution of wealth, direct taxation, national minimums and welfare policies are still disputed academically and politically. The COS had fairly trenchant if at times flexible theories about these notions, often connected to the ideas of individualism, free enterprise and antipathy to excessive state intervention. Many of these ideas are still very much present today when theorists and political activists are concerned with, for example, the direction of public resources, the role of circumstances and character in economic misfortune. However repugnant the COS ideas may be they are not merely the hangover of a past age. The phrases about Victorian attitudes, outdated social theories and reactionary individualism perhaps point more to a polemical or ideological defensiveness and self-consciousness rather than a genuine attempt to understand the historical situation and theory of the cos.

C. L. Mowat argued in his work on the cos that they were imprisoned in a 'sternly individualist philosophy'. He quotes the twenty-first annual report of the cos, which stated that true and effective charity was concerned with the 'moral nature of the individual'. Seebohm Rowntree, in a reply to cos criticism, explained politely that his critic 'belongs to the extreme wing of the Individualistic school' and that this school magnified unduly the amelioration of social conditions through individual self-reliance and effort, and minimized state intervention.[30] A more recent argument has related the cos individualism to Spencer's evolutionary individualistic theories. The argument states boldly that 'Spencer's vigorously individualistic theories of self-help found expression in the work of the cos.'[31] Beatrice Webb had seen the individualism of the cos as associated with *laissez-faire* economic theories, and consequently having a total dislike of state intervention.[32] This corresponds, in fact, to a more recent view of the society.[33] In these accounts of the cos idea of individualism Madeleine Rooff's comes closest to their actual beliefs, when she allies their idea with that of rational citizenship. She calls this 'an essential part of the Individualist, Idealist philosophy.'[34]

Bernard Bosanquet was at pains in many places to distinguish two distinct types of individualism. These were distinguished under the ideas of atomic individualism, or 'theories of the first look', and ethical individualism, or 'higher individualism'. The distinction was illuminatingly discussed by R. L. Nettleship in his book *Philosophical Remains,* where he argued that the individuality of an atom is a minimal conception reducing man to one in a crowd, a unit or cipher. The higher individuality refers to a complete nature. A true individuality is, as Nettleship argued, 'a person in whom the universal humanity has reached a very high degree of development . . . one who concentrates in himself a great deal of human nature.'[35]

The source of this distinction probably lay in Hegel's distinction between the abstract and concrete universal. However, the point to note is that Bosanquet wishes to say the abstract atomic individualism is a one-sided understanding of individualism.[36] It takes all life and sense from the idea. It was guided, for Bosanquet, by *prima facie* theorizing, or theory guided by an impression of the separateness of human beings. This type of theorizing he associated with men like Spencer, Bentham and Mill, and with ideas of *laissez-faire*, anti-government theory and anarchic individualism. As he stated in another essay: 'Not only is anarchic individualism incompatible with liberty, but it is hopelessly opposed to that individualism which alone is an ethical good – intellectual independence and moral robustness.'[37]

In other words, although some recent scholars have seen the COS as representative of an atomic, *laissez-faire* individualism, this does not apply if the more total commitment and thought of the society is taken into account. The aim of COS members like the Bosanquets and Loch was to go beyond the physical separateness of the human unit, beyond what was seen as the cruder idea of individualism and collectivism to a concept of the ethical individual. This higher individual was characterized by a development to a high degree of humanity, being essentially self-governing and self-maintaining, and thus more complete and rounded; in Hegelian terms more concrete. Loch argued in a similar vein in many writings that the aim of charity was the self-supporting individual, the rounded rational citizen.[38] Helen Bosanquet's argument that 'The strength of a nation does not lie . . . in the uniformity of its members, but in the variety and strength of the different characters',[39] is of the same source. Bernard Bosanquet in fact took his argument on individuality much further. In his Gifford Lectures the major theme is the nature of an absolute individuality which is immanent in all finite existence and which signifies an ideal perfection.[40]

CHARACTER AND INDEPENDENCE

It may be argued that Bosanquet's higher individuality was no more than a wilful mystification of atomic individualism. This could well be so, were it not for some further qualifications that were made, concerning a more complete notion of individuality, especially through the concept of character and its close relation to the idea of independence.

The COS journals are filled with references to the idea of character. Traditionally it seemed to have been solely taken as a morally uplifting term. The condition of the poor, as Loch stated in a paper in 1904, could not be assisted unless it was assistance based on the strengthening of character.[41] To strengthen the habits of family life, to promote public measures that tended towards social and personal competence and to oppose public measures that lessened exertion and foresight; all these were avowed aims of the cos and were intimately bound up with the concept of character.

This is not to say that the paradox of the cos view of individualism is not still present. The idea of economic self-support and thrift are often seen as synonymous with economic and atomic individualism. Indeed, it is true that individuality was for the cos mutually expressed in the economic as well as the ethical sphere. However, the question was, Can economic self-support arise from anything but a sound character? – in other words an ethical character?

J. A. Hobson answered this question without hesitation. He stated: 'The Charity Organization philosophy, crystallised in the single phrase "in social reform character is the condition of conditions", represents a mischievous half-truth, the other half of which rests in the possession of the less thoughtful section of the Social Democrats.'[42] He cited Bosanquet's arguments as examples of pure monadism, and maintained that they effectively blocked economic reform on which the ethical characteristics were built. The Bosanquets replied to Hobson. They asserted that they did not ignore the crippling nature of misfortune in the economic sphere. Yet this fact could not lead the social investigator to ignore the restorative capacity of character. The function of charity in this situation, that is when individuals encountered insuperable circumstances, was to 'tide over the difficult time', and also to try to aid a positive recuperation in terms of, for example, convalescence, proper medical treatment and training, if required.[43] Bernard Bosanquet expanded the argument in one of his papers. He stated that social reformers and observers grossly underrated the power of character. To Bosanquet, even church members were blind to ethical realities in their practical daily form, which took shape in character. The particular views which predominated in the idea of social causation were the economic and the ethical. The economic view alone was inadequate, as indeed was the ethical. 'Figures and formulae', to Bosanquet, 'will no longer suffice.' What was needed was practical experience of the 'tensions and relaxations of fibre in character, to know the habits and habitats of daily life' and without this the observer was 'like a physicist without experimental knowledge'.[44] The ethical consideration for Bosanquet was no less materially based because it was ideal. He introduced the Hegelian idea that economics, which isolated certain basic, simple and definite influences, was subsumed within a more comprehensive perspective. As Bernard

Bosanquet put the point, different perspectives were to be 'criticized and adjusted by a fuller and deeper experience of man's nature and the causes which operate in his action.'[45]

The ethical aspect, when integrated with the economic view, introduces the conception of the 'greater individual', which was intrinsically the substance of character. As well as economic problems therefore, the social investigator needed to take into consideration the potentialities of the individual, that is, his or her capacity for self-development of character. It was fundamentally in this latter concern that the complete cure of poverty could be effected. The concept of character was further qualified in the idea of independence.

C. S. Loch, in a paper in 1910, argued that 'self-restraint and self-management are, it is recognised, the foundation alike of the social and individual life. ... Without them sooner or later all social intervention fails.'[46] This notion of self-restraint or self-management was the central idea within independence. To be independent was not to be purely and simply economically self-reliant. Self-reliance was a reflection of a wider faculty. This faculty was conceived in naturalistic terms by Helen Bosanquet, as she argued: 'Human nature is apt to be pretty much the same wherever we find it.'[47] For Helen Bosanquet, to utilize natural forces enabled humans to achieve success in the natural world; by analogy, to utilize moral forces should enable humans to achieve success in the moral world.

The moral faculty of self-management inherent in the idea of independence was taken by Bernard Bosanquet into the sphere of social life and evolution. Natural selection, admittedly a peculiar term for an Idealist to use, was seen to be working in society. It was a process of character formation or soul-moulding. The competitive demands of social life, the capacity for self-restraint and self-reliance were determined by a mature development of character. Evolutionary selection was described by Bernard Bosanquet as 'a severe and inevitable process, which it is both wholesome and true to regard as natural selection.' The conclusion of this selection was that survival was the 'survival of the most reasonable'. The reasonable being, in this case, the most independent.[48]

The corollary of this point in one direction was the COS attitude to the 'residuum' of society. They were mainly conceived to be social wreckage, who through lack of self-control and independence, had failed to be self-supporting. Thus Helen Bosanquet argued that character was even more evident in the resourcefulness of those in the lower wage bracket.

The idea of intellectual independence was at the heart of the issue.

It denoted a fullness and completeness in the person. 'A Man's power of endurance', Bernard Bosanquet argued, 'is measured by the depth and fullness of his life. . . .'[49] The independence of character was a material force and power which was allied to the operation of ideas in a man's life and perception. It could be seen essentially as a reinterpretation or redrawn portrait of the older ideas of self-help and self-reliance, which still figured strongly in the new moralizing. This was also true of the attitudes to economic life, thrift and even simplistic evolutionary ideas. However, through the ideas of Bosanquet and Loch, these older notions were transformed, at times almost unconsciously. Bosanquet connected the independence theory with the idea of self-government. Self-government was also integrally related to the COS view of morality, which will be discussed later. It was also the foundation to the idea of social life. As Bernard Bosanquet had argued in terms of the state's compulsion of individuals: 'Force is necessary and permissible in inverse ratio to political maturity.'[50] This maturity was determined by the individual citizen's capacity for self-government. Absolute government, for Bosanquet, becomes irrational insofar as self-government becomes possible. The idea that he wished to present was close to T. H. Green's self-realization argument. Each man was conceived of as having certain capacities and powers, it was in the development of these that a man realized himself and became unique. Yet part of this development arose in the ability to co-operate with others, as well as to compete. Institutions like the family, neighbourhood communities, trade unions and churches provided the medium for this co-operation. As co-operative ventures they involved self-restraint. Yet the impetus to their work was to contribute to the ultimate realization of each individual and his powers. As such neighbourhoods, for example, were seen as 'ethical institutions'. This process was only conceivable for Green where there was a situation of mutual respect, co-operatively, between individuals. Thus although the aim of the individual was to realize his capacities, this could only be achieved in and through others. This required respect for others and self-restraint. This strongly communitarian sentiment relied upon a delicate interplay between dependence and independence which was forged through the conception of self-government. The higher individuality formed in character and independence helped to realize the common good or common self in the social organization.[51]

The interplay was central to Bosanquet's idea of political justice, as an impartial 'development of human capacity, and to guarantee the public welfare by an efficient management, securing from individuals the necessary social performances.'[52] The individual must be allowed, through his independence, to make his own will a reality, for only through this 'it may be possible for him consciously to entertain the social purpose as a constituent of his will.'[53]

Thus the concepts of character and independence involved some important ideas whose disparate nature makes a clear understanding difficult. However, an analysis of those ideas does overcome one obstacle, and that is the accusation that character is just a superficial term or moral hypocrisy and myopia. Much of the coherence of the terms is to be found in their theoretical grounding in the Idealistic philosophy, especially as presented by Bernard Bosanquet. The ideas themselves presupposed a conception of power in the individual, which was bound up with his or her latent physical and mental capacities. These were also seen as universal and evolving through social selection. Character especially was seen as the predominance of the reasonable and intellectual faculty in man, and was the basis of his endurance and development. The idea of self-government elucidates the point further. The character which ruled itself and determined its own behaviour was essentially that of the rational citizen. This citizenship was the heart of political maturity in the state, and also the centre of any concern with justice. It was the source of the delicate balance between dependence and independence, or the common purpose and individual purpose. Character, to Bosanquet and Loch, expressed the completed human nature, in Hegel's terms a concrete universal, independent economically, ethically and politically, and consequently realizing the common self.[54]

It is in the concepts of will, mind and action that we come to the central focus of the cos vision as presented by the Bosanquets and Loch, and the idea of character must be seen in this context.

C. S. Loch stated in 1910 that charity 'has sought to transform the world by the transformation of will and the inward life of the individual.'[55] This transformation of the will was seen as a central function of charity work. At its most basic level it was a doctrine that stated that no social change could come about without a change in men's wills and minds. The aim was essentially to achieve the good will, since this was seen as the heart of character. The desire to be good, as Bernard Bosanquet argued, and the desire to be at one with the society were at the root of our life.[56] The real kingdom of heaven is within you. As we have already seen, it was the man who accepted his station and duties in society, and was responsible and responsive to his fellow men, who expressed the good character and will. This goodness Bosanquet saw as a conation towards completeness. Its aim, as in all facets of human experience, for example politics, beauty, or physical health, was a 'strong and complete self-maintenance'.[57]

The world of reality to Bosanquet is one of a scale of value. The more complete the value, that is to say the more universal, concrete and embracing, the more complete the will and character which pursued such values. This, in consequence, was a more adequate expression of reality. This idea of a more complete value and reality is the source of the distinction between the terms that Bernard Bosanquet has been often noted for, namely the real and the actual will.

The argument about the will was relatively simple in essence. The actual will can be seen in the sense of a lesser value, virtually in terms of a heteronomous impulse on a mundane level. It is the actual response that we make from moment to moment in our everyday lives, which in its immediate function only satisfies our passing desires. It is not necessarily what we might want ideally, or if we had time to reflect on outcomes, etc. Our ideal demands, if we but know it, are more embracing and universal. The will of the individual is imperfect in its actual condition, yet its existence, as far as Bernard Bosanquet was concerned, rests upon a greater whole, the greater whole constituting the true nature of will. The argument can be put in less turgid terms by maintaining that the values of an individual are relative to a wider social framework of values. This social framework is not a sociological or economic category but a moral one. It is in the external co-operation of individuals, in social practices, work, the local community, voluntary work, etc., that 'the private will finds its form and stability.'[58] In other words the private 'actual will' is seen as dependent for its continuance and expression, on the co-operative will, which being more complete is more real.

One important element of co-operation in Bosanquet's view of community was the idea of restraint, and restraint meant obedience to a law. The dilemma of law though, in Kantian terms, was that the individual was the only one who could impose a moral law. A wider body like the state could only place an external rule on the individual. If the state could only impose an external law, while morality and the real will were self-imposed, how could the state and law be moral or correspond to the real will?

Bosanquet's answer was fundamentally to say that the state could correspond to the real will and morality if, and only if, its actions were such that given an individual knew his real will, he would perform the same action that the state had forced him to do. Thus, state intrusion was justified if it corresponded to the development and growth of the individual consciousness. Law was moral when its substance corresponded to the real will of the people under its jurisdiction. This overcame the pure coerciveness of the law since it became the medium for the common good.

The problems with this argument are manifold, but we wish to deal with one important tension latent within it which had important repercussions for the COS. Melvin Richter caught some of this tension in his work on T. H. Green in the problems attached to individualism and collectivism.[59] Both Green and Bosanquet used the argument that the real will could be seen in certain laws. Since the real will entailed a conception of freedom, intervention by law could be said to enhance freedom, although it would not necessarily be the citizen's actual will. Bosanquet, in fact, seemed to equivocate on this point. Although he wanted to say that the state could only be a hindrance to hindrances, he also stepped over the line of intervention by admitting that housing, wage and educational reform could stimulate mind and will, and were, therefore, a positive contribution to freedom.[60]

The other side of the issue was the precise place accorded to character and individual self-maintenance, and its relation to freedom. One form of the argument, which is often attributed to J. S. Mill, is the dictum that an individual's actions should not be interfered with, unless those actions adversely affect another's activity. A more developed form of this argument is that law should only hinder hindrances to individual liberty, or prevent obstacles to the individual realizing certain of his powers. This argument has a close correspondence to Kant's distinction between the heteronomous phenomenal impulse and the universal, moral and rational will. This is to say, the truly moral action is self-imposed, from a noumenal perspective, and thus can not be externally imposed. In other words, individual morality is the keystone to the morality of the state. T. H. Green is in full agreement with this point. The whole could never be greater than the part. The person is sacrosanct. The essential quality of the argument is that it allowed the inferences that character, as a moral entity, must establish itself. The real will, it can be argued, more or less corresponds to the categorical imperative. It is basically the idea that self-discipline and reliance are the source of morality and the good will.

The inference from this, which Kant and T. H. Green made only with hesitation, but Bosanquet boldly, was that self-maintenance by the individual in nearly all aspects of his life was the key to morality and the real will. Bosanquet needed no Spencerian individualism or Smilesian self-help to carry his argument forward. Physical and mental self-maintenance were intimately bound up with the will. The question did not seem to arise as to whether the individual could be physically dependent, yet mentally independent, or vice versa, yet at present it is enough to point out a definite tension.

The argument about self-maintenance was a qualified and developed form of the Kantian argument that morality is a self-imposed maxim. For Bosanquet this was fundamentally bound up with character. Green and Bosanquet used this argument extensively; Bosanquet especially used it in its more extreme form. Yet this argument was also the base-line to the 'real will' argument, concerned to demonstrate that the state can interfere in law with an individual's activity, when the law corresponds with the real will or universal maxim of the individual's action. In so doing the state could contribute to individual freedom and the development of the individual consciousness. The self-maintenance argument was, and is, the core to the defence against state activity, since dependence on on the state makes the individual character weak (through doles, in cos terms). The real will and intervention argument was also utilizing the same core, especially among the more theoretical New Liberals, for the justification of interference. It was admittedly, in the latter concern, dressed up in an assortment of guises; yet none the less, it had the same core element, which was very often directly concerned with character. Muirhead put the point well in his autobiography in his discussion of the strands of Hegelianism, which moved through Ferdinand Lassalle and Marx into Socialism, and through the more conservative thinkers, into English and German Universities.[61] Green was in some ways in the same ambivalent position as Hegel. His disciples, like Hegel's, interpreted him in different ways. In the political sphere, while Bosanquet claimed him for the somewhat rightist doctrines of the cos, someone like D. G. Ritchie could claim him in support of his Fabian activities. This oscillation between emphases on character and circumstances as the basic ground of poverty was a question which dogged reform arguments from the 1880s up to 1914; possibly it still lies covertly in much political thinking. The argument is made more complex by the similar matrices to these opposing propositions. However, the concept of will, especially the real will, was a central concept in the theory of the cos view of character and independence, despite its ambivalence.

Bosanquet, in an article on the general will, argued that the will should be considered as a human mind in the form of a machine, in which ideas or groups of ideas passed into action.[62] Ideas, he maintained, were capable of being 'awakened into action by the appropriate stimulus', and the will consisted of those ideas which were guiding the attention and action.[63]

Ideas were seen as systematically organized under a dominant idea which fundamentally structures the activity. Bosanquet argued that 'This mental system with its dominant ideas in relation to external action, is the individual will.'[64] He described these ideas as marshalling the contents of consciousness. All activity was structured by them, although the actions could extend and modify the ideas. If a specific action met with success, then the idea would be reinforced, although it might thereby receive new content which it would embody necessarily. Thus, these dominant ideas, which were seen as constituting the will, were the 'inside' of activity which reflected the material action and real conditions that formed the outside.

Although Bosanquet, in this article, was building up an argument on the general will, it illustrated a central factor in his, and in many ways the COS position. This factor could be looked at in terms of the following syllogism. All circumstances and conditions were created and structured by actions. All actions were structured and comprehended by mind. The corollary of these propositions was that all conditions and circumstances were ultimately the product and structure of mind. One key inference from this conclusion was that in order to change conditions and circumstances it was necessary to change in some way the mind. To change the mind was fundamentally to change the will. The manner of doing this was to implant or substitute the dominant idea, which was marshalling the contents of consciousness. In so doing, the will would be transformed, consequently the mind and, therefore, circumstances, and ultimately the social world. What we are looking at here is a dynamic theory of the will, as part of Bosanquet's general philosophical position. Bosanquet's theory has close connections with that of T. H. Green. Green described the will as the strongest motive.[65] This motive was the 'inner side' of the act. The strong character was the consequence of the strong will and purpose. The will was the attempted realization of the idea. In fact for Green the will is simply the man.

This particular argument on the will was given a forceful psychological rendering by Helen Bosanquet in her book of essays entitled *The Standard of Life*.[66] She argued that in considering any sociological questions the appeal was to the nature of men's minds. These minds found their basis in society, so in essence it was necessary to consider both psychological and sociological questions together. However it was necessary also to consider mind in a new way. It was not an entity that is being pieced together from outside sources. This was a 'crude notion'. The mind was, conversely a growing and organic system of ideas, thoughts, feelings, beliefs and emotions. Yet from first to last it was a selective process whereby the mind determined its own content and development. This selection had a consequent effect on the circumstances and conditions of the individual. She likened the growth of mind to a plant which assimilated certain elements as nourishment and in so doing changed their form: 'What the mind sees, depends upon what it already is.'[67]

She seemed to conceive of mind in terms of a very traditional rationalistic scale of values. The higher civilization and character expressed greater reason and more control of the instinctual elements of life. She wished to say that as the mind reached higher stages of selective development, the less it consisted of trains of perceptions and ideas linked by association and contiguity, and the more it consisted of purposive controlled thought. The idea of purposive thought was developed by her from the psychological work of G. F. Stout. Stout's term, which she employed for this idea, was the 'noetic synthesis'. The noetic synthesis was the selective process whereby experience as it came to the mind 'ranges itself in subordination to the principles and purposes which are dominant and the conception of a mere stream of consciousness develops into that of a mental system.' She went on to say that we must picture this systemization as a grouping of mental elements under dominant interests and ideas. She argued that this was similar to the way in which a society was grouped in highly civilized communities: in families, clubs, unions, and religious or political sects. The higher type of mind, character, and presumably society, was seen by the greater complexity and completeness of the system, and consequently by 'its organisation according to interests and purposes'.[68]

The noetic synthesis was essentially Bernard Bosanquet's idea of the will as the dominant idea, or Green's strongest motive and inner side of the act. It cannot be grasped outside the perspectives of Idealist philosophy. It connects with two key notions in COS language, namely habit and purpose. The good social habit was that which was based on a wide social purpose. This social purpose referred to the dominant idea or will of purposive thought. As Helen Bosanquet argued in another work, the aim of much social work was to stop men's impulses being immediately transformed into action. This according to the author led to instinctual confusion. Impulses and instincts provided the drive to action, but this drive needed reflective guidance, as for instance in the family, which Helen Bosanquet described as one of 'nature's devices for drawing man out of the tyranny of instinctive life'.[69]

To weaken one of nature's devices, like the family, was tantamount to weakening the character of the individual.[70] This, in turn, was seen to weaken the whole fabric of society. This particular argument makes some sense of what now appear to be the odd manifestations of cos policy, namely the movement against free school meals. The cos felt that these free gifts would destroy the responsible role of the family for feeding the children.[71] Another example of the cure-all aspect of character was Loch's view of unemployment. He argued in 1906 that unemployment could be effectively tackled by establishing 'good social habit', that is by encouraging independence of mind in thrift, social responsibility and sound family life.[72] This point, however, was not a complete myopic dogma; public intervention was seen as necessary under specified criteria of encouraging independence. As Loch argued in 1904, charity aimed to 'strengthen habit, to strengthen the family, to promote public measures that tend to social and personal competence, to oppose public measures that tend to lessen exertion and foresight'.[73]

The essential logic to grasp is that Loch and the Bosanquets saw the human mind as being ruled by certain ideas, varying a great deal in strength. These ideas were seen as the basis of the will. The will structured, and was in turn reinforced by, the actions. These actions determined the circumstances around the individual: his total environment, work habits, housing, family life, etc. These habits had a particular interest and purpose. The aim of charity was to establish certain dominant ideas: responsibility to a family, foresight, and careful prudential behaviour. These ideas had, to the authors, real social purpose latent within them. They were capable of uniting all the disorganized, instinctual faculties of the mind into an organized systematic will, controlled by purposive thought. This social purposive thought was then seen to become habitual. Thus, the good social habit was formed in accordance with a social purpose. This, in turn, formed the action and, consequently, the circumstances of the individual. Helen Bosanquet summed up the point well when she stated:

a man's circumstances depend upon what he himself is; but this does not mean that there is always a conscious choice, that he always knows he is rejecting one circumstance in favour of another. More often he is simply attracted to what interests him, and that depends upon what he already has in his mind. If he has no interests in the higher sense, then his appetites and habits will make his circumstances.[74]

The aim, she maintained, was to establish new interest 'which will be a clue to guide his life.'

The defective quality of the COS casework method has often been cited. Certainly their contemporaries in the 1890s and 1900s singled it out, with great relish, for criticism.[75] Beatrice Webb objected to the exclusive sect of 'well-to-do' rigorously questioning and imposing themselves on the poor. Henrietta Barnett disliked their rigid system of classification and their clothing themselves, in Canon Barnett's words, 'In the dirty rags of their own righteousness'.[76] J. A. Hobson raised even more serious claims against the casework method.[77] He argued again that the COS classification system was too rigid, only presenting the mere husks of fact. The subtleties of a case escaped them, from the simple fact that it was treated as a case! He continued that the values of the investigator were not taken into account. The sound even of the COS worker's voices, their mode of speech, expressed the outward signs of patronizing superiority and class. The nature of casework seemed to be anathema to Hobson, especially for its critical, objectifying status.

Bernard Bosanquet stated in a paper in 1898 that 'Charity Organization work has always seemed to me an almost ideal training in the higher logic – the logic of Idealism.'[78] His wife· Helen Bosanquet reported of her husband in his biography that 'the application of knowledge in the sphere of practical charity could not fail to appeal to him, and he delighted in showing how here, again, wisdom and depth of thought justified itself in practice.'[79] The question was, though, What precisely was that relation that Bosanquet and his wife saw between the philosophy and the casework practice? It seems that a number of relations are implied. These can be brought out under the ideas of an 'Idealistic logic', the 'nature of Ideals' and 'respect for individuals'.

IDEALISTIC LOGIC

The idea of an Idealistic logic has not been introduced to investigate it in its totality, but to consider certain aspects relevant to social work. One of these implications is the construction of reality in terms of a whole. To look at a problem, especially a social problem is to see a many-sided phenomenon. The real problem is not grasped by trying to understand one characteristic. Concentration on one element will mean automatically the exclusion of a range of other characteristics which may be pertinent to the real situation. To try to determine the reality of an object from one viewpoint effectively debars one from a range of other considerations (*omnes determinatio est negatio*). The Idealistic view aims at a total comprehension.

Logic, Bosanquet described, not exactly in a contemporary sense, as an 'attribute of mind which makes us unable to rest in the face of contradiction.'[80] Facts were for him expressions of a partial view of reality. Investigation would show them full of contradictions. Idealism in social work brought with it the faith in reality as a whole. Thus the logic of social work was not be tolerant of one-sidedness and partial facts, but to investigate the structure of the whole situation. As Bernard Bosanquet argued: 'Social workers are surely more than anyone familiar with the transformation which experience undergoes as more light is thrown upon it and fresh points of view emerge . . . the logic of Idealism – the demand to realize unity – is the most disquieting of all ferments.'[81] Social facts when compared, he wrote 'criticize each other', since they are all partial aspects of one reality.[82]

Casework, like philosophy, must look for the order in the myriad of social details. Bosanquet described the process of philosophizing as beginning with the appearance of the world, the *prima facie* facts. The facts themselves tell the philosopher little; he must look below this apparent face to the social and economic causation underlying it. Eventually, in the third stage, the underlying patterns can be discerned. The comprehensive view can be gained through the consideration of the many-sidedness of a problem. This third stage Bosanquet called philosophical knowledge. He cited the COS conception of casework as being equivalent to this third stage.[83]

In this third stage, in Bosanquet's view, walls became transparent (a somewhat disquieting notion).[84] This transparency could only come about through the individualization of cases. The individual nature of casework entailed the recognition of the 'infinity of mind', as in philosophy. Thus each case was to be taken as a unique problem to be thoroughly investigated. Each unique combination of elements had to be grasped in every case. The infinite variety and possibility was simply an everyday hazard for the social worker.

One of the distinctions that Bosanquet continually utilized was that of the concrete and abstract. Abstraction, in Hegelianism, was a process of isolating components from a total reality. The concrete was necessarily the comprehensive. There is some sense in this view if it is translated into a more secular language. Each individual is a meeting-point of a nexus of family, neighbourhood, economic and general social forces. To investigate a problem in relation to that individual without taking into consideration all the possible reasons for that problem, that is to say the nexus in which he is involved, would be to create a totally wrong picture.

The imperfection and problematic nature of the individual case was something that should spur the social worker to resolve contradiction, and not just to tide the individual over a difficult period. 'Our work', Bosanquet argued, 'is nothing but examples of this process, from completing the enquiries on a case, to introducing some order into the medical charities of London; and to feel and master the way in which imperfect realities demand to be completed is that very innermost mainspring of life and faith which we call Idealism.'[85] The social worker and the philosopher were thus spurred by the passion and logic of reality, which was completeness and wholeness.

It is at this point that we can see a connection with the previous section on mind and action. Bosanquet stated explicitly that the social worker values mind above body and intelligence above comfort. The mind judges, feel and values. As we have seen, it is also the determining factor, through will, of the types of values and consequent actions. Thus the true object of casework is the mind. To modify the mind, that is to change it structure of values, to implant new values, is radically to alter the man and his activity.[86] In so doing the social worker, for Bosanquet and Loch, was well on the way to a solution to problems. Bosanquet claimed that this view of the COS casework method presented a far more profound vision than any mere collectivist or individualist proposal.

These ideas lay behind Loch's and Helen Bosanquet's conceptions of 'thorough charity', that is, detailed investigation, case histories, checking out details from all possible sources, assessing the character, social conditions, family and working habits, etc. Thus Idealistic logic was seen to be at the core of social casework.

THE NATURE OF IDEALS

The false view of ideals was seen by Bosanquet to be that of utopian fancy or sentiment. This idea derived from the false separation of ideals and reality. Ideals were not to be separated from facts. Idealism as Bosanquet put it, was the doctrine that went 'deeper and deeper into the heart of facts', and tried to correct their imperfections.[87] The Idealism of philosophy and social work was '(a) having faith that the world of facts has an idea, principle, order, organisation working in it, and (b) having the passion and wisdom to make ourselves the instruments through which this idea or principle or organisation asserts itself in the light of day.'[88] True Idealism in philosophy and social work demanded a capacity 'to dive into the core of appearance'. The worker needed considerable imagination. The ideals he sought were not for Bosanquet exalted phenomena; on the contrary, he described them as including all the perfections and imperfections of reality.

The Idealism which Bosanquet advocated for social work was that which aimed at finding the best in people. It was a somewhat optimistic faith in an ideal order within the appearance of the world. It aimed at a comprehension of the ideal within the whole in its concrete form. It aimed also at a transformation of the appearance, in the direction of reality, through casework. This social work Bosanquet described as love embodied in reason. It took into account the subjective, unique circumstances of the individual case, and tried through a thorough investigation to find the root of the apparent problem and to direct the individual back towards the order implicit in life.

One of the central facets of the COS pursuit of proper training facilities for social workers was to develop, through a school of social science, a form of training to allow students to develop the capacity to see from many sides on a practical and theoretical level was the fundamental aim.[89] The student must in one sense see what is good before he tries to do it. It was, to the Bosanquets, an artistic process. Helen Bosanquet stated that 'there is always something of the artist about the true philanthropist, and the harmony of life which he aims at creating is hardly less important than that of the painter, the poet, etc.'[90] She also argued, in another of her papers, that social workers took upon themselves a heavy responsibility of intentionally influencing men's lives, and consequently, they must consider deeply what kind of influence they will assert.[91] The same demand was echoed in other papers by society workers and writers, especially for a training in the concrete mind.[92] The training was thus essentially a training in ideals, which Bosanquet saw as knowledge of the logic of reality.

RESPECT OF INDIVIDUALS

This principle was probably the most widely utilized idea in social work. It stands centrally in the COS view of casework and in much of their social work philosophy. Octavia Hill's biography reports that her view of the relation between the individual and the state was based on her belief in the dignity of man, also that her idea of true help in social work was a caring for the individual.[93] Much of Loch's discussion on the question of charity was based on his conceptions of love and duty. Thus he often spoke of a 'church of charity'.[94] Bosanquet had spoken in similar terms of charity and casework being the unity of reason and love and devotion to the individual. As Eileen Younghusband wrote, the cos view of casework 'so far as its principles are concerned, is rooted in the Judaeo–Christian and democratic tradition of respect for the value of each individual person.'[95] In fact, in a later essay she includes all social workers in this bracket.

Una Cormack argues in a similar vein in one of her essays, although she picks out stages in the growth of casework. Ultimately, she says, casework begins with an act of friendship, of sitting down with someone to understand their problems. She goes on to say that in dealing with casework overall, one must take into account the early reformers' concern for their neighbours 'their respect for every man's individuality, their belief in every man's obligation to do his duty'.[96] In a more recent essay she develops this form of argument, although still circumspectly. She states carefully at the end of her paper that 'it is tempting to conclude that it was largely Oxford Idealism that characterized social work and its principles when they were first launched into the world, in the sixties and seventies of the last century . . . based upon respect for the individual as an end in himself and an autonomous member of the ideal kingdom of ends.'[97]

The foregoing argument that leads to this conclusion is very interesting. She claims that the message of the early social workers was bound up with the idea of respect for and the intrinsic value of the individual. The concern was not with monetary distribution or moral persuasion but new resources in life, intellect and feeling. The concern was expressed through friendship, which in its cos context derived much from the work of Octavia Hill. This friendship was tempered by a severe notion of responsibility and influence. Cormack noticed in her research that the common foundations of social work lay in Oxford. J. S. Mill was not the prevalent influence in this case. The dominant group who conducted the most passionate defence of the individual were the Idealists. For Cormack, the peculiar character of the work of the Idealists was their attempt to show the unity of theory and practice, and also the relevance they tried to bring to philosophy.[98] Their thought, as was argued in the section on

Idealistic logic, worked in terms of 'wholes', that is to say, the family, personality, and district. Mõre pertinently, their aim in charity and society was the development of the moral character of the individual. She continues that although the influence was at a fairly low level of appreciation 'the interaction between Oxford philosophy and social casework and reform also developed well into this century.'[99]

Cormack sees Kant as possibly the seminal influence behind this movement. She argues that his moral philosophy is of capital importance for understanding the course of social work principles, especially in terms of trying to influence the individual to think for himself, to will the structure of his own life as a practical, moral and charitable principle. The present account concurs with Cormack's arguments, especially in relation to the cos. It seems true to say that the casework, especially at the end of the last century, was based on a devotion to the individual and a respect for his personality. This personality was characterized by the categories of independence, self-restraint and a capacity to structure one's own circumstances through the wide social purpose of the will. The subjective dilemma of the individual found subjective aid in the reason and sympathy of casework.

In the book *Methods of Social Advance,* C. S. Loch contributed a paper entitled 'If Citizens Be Friends'. The theme of his, and all the papers in the book, he stated, was that ultimately 'society is based on charity – on love working through the individual and the social life.'[100] The process of social advancement he believed was dependent on this principle. He went on to argue that treating the individual with reverence, also the family and community, was achieved by thorough understanding. Part of this understanding is seen through the role that each individual played in the common good. Part of the function of charity Loch saw as the prevention of the destruction of the social organism by ensuring that each part fulfils its social purpose.

All parts of the state, the individuals, families and communities, Loch saw as 'parts and expressions of one social life' having one common interest. The individual accepted the customs and structures of the state since it was his real interest. He argued that at each point charity helped the individual to understand his or her responsibilities to the common interest of the social organism. It was guided, he stated, 'by the ideal, the pattern of the good that will be'.[101] As he argued in another work, the common good was really only individual good harmonized to a common end.[102] Charity, in this process, he understood as *agape,* a unity of reason and love. It helped individuals to realize their true interest and will, and thus, in classical Idealist terms, their freedom. The fruit of individuality and freedom was seen in the fulfilment of rights, obligations and duties. The charity worker, in helping others, was fulfilling his social obligations and developing himself, through his devotion to the common interest.

The love of our neighbour, Loch argued, 'means love according to the intelligence, energy and morality of our better self'.[103] This love recognized the importance and value of the social institution of the family. Its social purpose was directed at helping men and women to rally to the demands of their better selves. Charity did not deal with a class of poverty-stricken individuals, but it individualized each case, as failing to realize its true will and the ideal order of society and life. Loch's vision was one of a scientific religious charity – a friendly army, as he put it, of well-trained workers, helping people to fulfil their social obligations. The ultimate aim of this work was to achieve the common good, this being a society based upon mutual service, a service which expressed the real will, thus the general will. It is no wonder that there was an antipathy to the ideas of rich and poor and class conflict. It is maintained here that charity, as understood by Loch and the Bosanquets, was essentially T. H. Green's idea of the common good and mutual service. The idea of the general will or common good was admittedly a very ambiguous term. To try to define or locate its precise meaning is virtually impossible. Analytically, it is arguable that the concept is more or less bankrupt. However, it can still be said to have influenced the thought and actions of the cos members like Loch. To them it was meaningful.

Bernard Bosanquet's actual conception of it was analogous to his idea of the individual will, that is to say, the dominant idea which rules society. Many would say this was a wholly unrealistic notion. How are such statements about it to be verified? Surely it takes no account of the automatic clash of interests and divisions in societies, and the consequent impossibility of general agreement. Also, how can several wills be conceived of as one will, unless each explicitly willed the same proposition? Where precisely is it to be located? Is it present in the voting system, public opinion or in some other institution? Bosanquet seems to deny these latter possibilities.[104] If it was contained in peoples' ordinary work and job (station and duties), how did this relate to the competitive struggle of the market system?[105]

The basic problem in defining the general will was that of taking it out of context. It was a constituent part of a social vision. To grasp its meaning, it must be placed within the context and criteria of that vision. In this sense, the vision will determine, to an extent, its reality. Verification will take place within this context. To appeal to clashes of interest, divisions and a multiplicity of wills, is to appeal to *prima facie* theorizing, in Bosanquet's terms. The competitive struggle is a difficult idea, yet Bosanquet's answer seems relatively clear. Conflict and contradiction are intrinsically part of life. Competition is a determinate component of human development. This does not mean that a real interest or will might not lie in values of harmony, or in art or religion, which transcend competition. This admittedly does not get over notions of unlimited accumulation, which remain unresolved within the nexus of Green's and Bosanquet's arguments on property. However, mutual service and the general will were, within the context of the COS vision, important descriptions of, and criteria by which to justify, COS actions.

Certainly the key idea of citizenship followed from the conception of the general will and service. The good citizen was one who fulfilled his social obligations to his fellow men, in terms of the common interest. The idea appears unrealistic, but it is undeniable that many held to it. Lewis Nettleship, for example, asked his readers to imagine that 'all human beings felt permanently and universally to each other as they now do occasionally to those whom they love best'; he continued that in so far as we can imagine such a state 'it would be one in which there would be no individuals at all, in which individuality means mutual exclusion ... there will be a universal being in and for another ... a common consciousness.'[106] This is the kind of idea implied in citizenship. This is the citizen that Loch called for, at times almost in an Hellenic vein, in his work on charity organization. Citizenship was the crowning capacity of character, independence and recognition of the common good; in other words, Green's ideal self.

'The world of reality', Bosanquet stated, 'is the world of value.'[107] These values, as we have attempted to show, were seen on ascending scale. The higher value was seen as being able to dominate the mind and will, and also to bring wide social purpose. These values were conceived of as allowing the individual to structure his own life in terms of his interests. The object of COS work was to try to guide individuals to these values as part of the mutual service implicit in the ideas of citizenship and the common good. However, the COS vision was not limited to their own organization. Certainly Loch and the Bosanquets saw their work as an embryo of a total social movement aiming at a nationwide acceptance of the theories of solidarity and social obligation.[108] As Loch argued in 1904: 'I hoped that some day there would be formed a large association of persons drawn from all churches and all classes . . . who would find in charity a common purpose.'[109] Charity was thus symbolic of what all men should be doing, that is, trying to be good citizens and serving one's fellow men. This kind of argument has some interesting implications. Bosanquet claimed that 'the essential foundation of all sane political thinking is the supremacy of absolute values in the self-moulded life of community.'[110] The question remains, what type of values were being promoted?

Bosanquet became involved with and supported associations like the Home Arts and Industries Association, the Cottage Arts Association, and other such craft groups. He knew and had met William Morris in Oxford and deeply admired the man and his work. He described the work done by such associations as missionary. Essentially, the work was guided by small groups of volunteers giving evening classes to the wage-earning artisans. The crafts were seen as a unity of manual and artistic precision, designed, as Bosanquet put it: 'to be to these rough lads and men what our music and picture galleries . . . are to us.'[111] Bosanquet imagined that through craftwork a certain change could be produced in the workman's mind; 'a new perception is awakened, a new interest is acquired; he sees things to which he was blind before, and enjoys things to which he was insensible before.'[112] In other words, for Bosanquet art training intensified the values of life and encouraged self-help and self-maintenance. This he saw as therapeutic training, in that men gained self-respect, pride and value in their work.

Bosanquet wished to argue that the true conception of social equality was an identity of enjoyment, of art and artistic creation.[113] The 'vulgar exclusiveness' of the rich and the 'enforced narrowness' of the poor might be broken down in a common life of citizenship and appreciation of the higher values.[114] This social pride he thought would have a consequent revitalizing effect on the whole community, from local to national level.

Bosanquet's optimism on this topic became unbridled. The values of art represented the higher values, as in citizenship. These values, when dominating the minds of individuals within the community, had no ethical limit. As Bosanquet stated, 'there is nothing, I repeat, that cannot be done by change of interest; there is very little that can be done without it.'[115] This devotion to the higher values Bosanquet contrasted with luxury and sensuous pleasure. Art was bound up with life and work, not with exclusive luxury or pleasure. If, he argued, it could be rightly understood, it could change our whole economic system and social stratification. It could he thought, wipe out the drink bill, and London could become a 'paradise', if only citizens' minds could adopt these values. Art was thus intimately related to the fulfilled human personality and the earthly perfection of society. William Morris's influence is very noticeable here.

Another interesting implication of the value argument is bound up with the issue of democracy. Many theorists have taken Bosanquet to be a harsh individualist or conversely an absolutist. Both ideas imply an anti-democratic tendency.[116] Admittedly these are very vague notions, yet none the less they are widely held. However, a number of peculiarities arise in relation to Bosanquet's and Loch's vision of society.

First, in discussing various forms of society Bosanquet expressed admiration for the idea of guild socialism. Secondly, he supported the idea of workmen's ownership of the means of production and also profit-sharing. Thirdly, he believed that the working class should develop their own ethos and culture.[117]

His admiration for guild socialism was based on its strong emphasis on self-government, as implied by the idea of workers' co-operatives. These forms of social organization expressed the self-help and self-development of the working people; consequently they were developing their own ethos. They were not reliant upon other classes or the state. These ideas were interestingly summarized in one of Bosanquet's papers in terms of a 'practical society'.[118] This society was to be based on convenient districts, with members pursuing their vocations, and caring for one another through local committees, councils and legal institutions. These groups would be pursuing the public interest, yet would have to be aware of the extreme flexibility and complication of modern life. Pride and value would run through all the institutions, dwellings, streets and museums. The picture is virtually that of an ideal Jeffersonian society, based on self-help, where all forces in the state are approximately equal, and, as many would be tempted to point out, blind to the nature of emerging industrial civilization and large-scale enterprise. However, in affirming the value of the working-class ethos, the value of the self-conscious creativity of the individual, the opposition of art and luxury, etc., Bosanquet was not exactly expressing anti-democratic tendencies. Possibly the pluralist implications and the 'individualist' quality to many of his conclusions give even more relevance to Bosanquet's favourite expression relating to the unity of the ideal and the practical – 'here or nowhere is your America!'

To coin a rather extended phrase, the vision of society for the cos, was, in the eyes of these authors, an 'ethical-pluralist-democracy'.

IDEALISM AND THE POOR LAW

Beatrice Webb and Helen Bosanquet were both members of the Royal Commission on the Poor Law which reported in 1909.

Mrs Webb wrote in her second autobiographical work *Our Partnership*, that the contending sides of the Poor Law dispute were those who stood up for the Minority Report: the Liberal press, organized labour, officials of the preventive services, and a section of the public; and those who were against; the *British Medical Journal*, the British Medical Association, private philanthropists and their voluntary aid committees, and the Hegelians, led by Bernard Bosanquet.[119] As the Minority Report encapsulated the social theories of the Webbs, so likewise did the Majority Report embody the view of the cos. Bosanquet had claimed in an article in 1910, that the Majority Report represented part of the cos 'social vision'.[120] Since the Webbs has placed some of their central theories into the Minority Report, which Beatrice Webb claimed as having 'a philosophic basis in the whole theory of the enforced minimum' [121] the reports, in principle, can be said to represent two different social theories of poverty.

Without entering into the minutiae of the reports, the main proposals of both will be briefly summarized. The Majority Report stood for a national system of labour exchanges, Public Assistance Committees and Voluntary Aid Committees. The latter two committees were envisaged as working co-operatively. The ideas put forward by the Goschen Minute of 1869, which advised co-operation between Poor Law Guardians and voluntary societies, were to be generalized. Charities would register with the Voluntary Aid Committees, and persons not relieved by this group would be referred to the Public Assistance Authority. It was thus a dualistic arrangement, which many took for the old Poor Law, and a reinforced cos, merely with different names.

The Minority Report proposals, apart from the agreement with the Majority Report that the old Poor Law ought to be radically changed, were for a Registrar of Public Assistance, the break up of the 1834 Poor Law and its division into a range of committees dealing separately with children, the sick, mentally defective, the aged, etc. The able-bodied ought to be treated by the Ministry of

Labour, again as a separate unit from the sick or old. Both reports agreed on a penal system for the intractable residuum of paupers. The Minority Report was a radical break with the past, it wished to establish a pluralistic framework of committees dealing with all the various aspects which had in their minds been previously associated with the stigma of desitution and poverty.

The general criticisms that were voiced, from the Majority view, were that the Minority ignored the faculty of independence. In other words, the failure of independence was not always related to educational deficiency, bad health or market fluctuations. Some cases needed specialized casework from the voluntary bodies. The range of committees proposed by the Minority was also taken to task as producing a multiplicity of overlapping committees. The argument continued that the Minority ignored the family and its essential social role. Further criticisms were involved with the expansion of free treatment and public expenditure.

The Minority answered these criticisms by stating that the idea of independence, or the moral factor of destitution, was only obscuring the old deterrence idea, and that under this cloak the sick, aged, children and mentally defective were to be lumped under the stigma of pauperism. The 'multiplicity of officers' argument was denied by stating that each officer would know his sphere, questions and purpose, and therefore there would be less overlapping. The family, the Minority argued, was disintegrating because preventive help was not forthcoming. Specialized committees, they felt, should take the importance of an intact family seriously. The expansion would eventually lessen expenditure by attaining more effective cures. Further criticisms were made by the Minority of the overlapping in the Majority situation, that is between the existing publicly-organized hospitals, etc., and the new proposals regarding health. The voluntary system was also attacked as licensing irresponsible amateurs, a point which must have particularly irritated the COS.

The intention here is not to enter into a detailed examination of the reports, but rather to investigate the ideals of character and intervention by the state, which characterized one of the central dichotomies between the two reports. What did Bosanquet mean in his discussion of the citizen character, and what were the Webbs' objections?

Bosanquet's central article in the *Sociological Review* was taken by his opponents as summing up the Majority's case.[122] Bosanquet regarded the two reports as having read the events differently. Whereas the Majority regarded the evils as arising from the failure of earlier reforms to adjust to new demands and conditions, the Minority, he wrote, felt the evils were present in the system itself. The Majority wanted to remove hindrances, the Minority to break up the system. The aims of the Majority were to provide help that was preventive, curative and restorative. These aims were to be carried through by the dual organs of the Public Assistance Committees and the Voluntary Aid Committees. Helen Bosanquet made a similar point, distinguishing between the unwilled incapacity and wilful incapacity, or as she later argued, that in drawing a distinction between those who are driven to seek public assistance by temporary misfortune, and those who habitually rely upon it, the commission had made a new departure. New departures or not, the distinction was central. Charity, to the Bosanquets, was an essential aspect of civilized group life. It forged a path between the caprice of private independence and organization by the state. It can be conceived of basically as organized voluntary action. Bernard Bosanquet argued that it was a principal social laboratory. Institutions would grow from this inventive work. He maintained that charity in its semi-independent voluntary form was an aspect of the general will.

The principal notion to which Bosanquet was led was the respect for the self-maintaining character. The failure of character was moral since it was bound to the failure of the will of the individual to look to the social common good. Many could become destitute due to trade cycles and changes in the forces of production due to invention, etc. These could be dealt with by the Public Assistance Committees, presumably after a screening by the voluntary aid committees. The cos before this report had, in fact, pioneered the separate treatment of mental defectives, and the blind and sick, as distinct from the Poor Law. Some, however, in the cos estimation, needed more than health care or the three Rs. 'Social therapeutics' was to be concerned with the whole person, the individual who needed individualized treatment from trained social workers. The point as to whether all individual cases were curable remained ambiguous. The role of the so-called residuum remained more problematic. Were they to be referred to a refurbished Poor Law, in the form of the Public Assistance Board, or were they to be regarded as curables? The subjects of pure misfortune did not really need social therapeutics, yet neither did the residuum in the older usage of the term by the cos. In this case who qualified for the social laboratories?

It remains true, however, that the cure of the whole person, whoever that person may be, remained central to the Majority. As one critic of the Minority put it: 'offering the administrators segments of *homo sapiens* rather than entire human beings, made it difficult for them to remember the humanity and dignity of the people they were regulating . . . Mrs Webb knew that study of human relations was necessary for the survival of modern society: but for all her faith in scientific method and in specialists, she was a prisoner of her categories and failed to see that casework was a specialism.'[123] The COS in the Majority were concerned, where poverty arose, with the whole man and not segments of the problem. In fact, there is a peculiar fallacy here relating to the idea of overlapping, which was one of the principle criticisms by the Minority of the Majority.

The Webbs' method was to relate the problem to specific services, i.e. those dealing with lunacy, medical care, unemployment, etc. This was proposed as against the older methods of relating the problem to charity and the public assistance or Poor Law institutions. With the growth of municipal hospitals and asylums the Webbs felt that considerable overlap would take place between the municipal and voluntary bodies. But what of the man whose problem with his family related to his unemployment, and who was consequently suffering mental distress and illness? Did the Webbs mean that the specialized bureaucrats would not overlap in dealing with his unemployment, medical care and family problems? Did they believe that the palliatives offered would solve the problem? Surely there was a fallacy here of knowing the exact boundaries of one's work. Where does medical, psychological help and assistance begin or end? The Majority view – that purely economic help could be adequately covered by the Public Assistance Committee, while complex social problems ought to be dealt with by voluntary, inventive, yet organized casework, dealing with the whole man – would mean far less overlap than the plurality of bureaucratic administrators advocated by the Minority Report.

Bosanquet wanted an army of social healers, trained and united by a common purpose. For the failed will, a thorough trained investigation was needed. The change posed by this idea was, to Bosanquet, built upon the principles of 1834, which he thought negatively recognized the virtue of the restored individual. In this sense change is probably a misnomer, and evolution would be more appropriate. The actual treatment, he argued, should have no stigma attached to it. It aimed at restoring the capacity for citizenship in all individuals.[124]

This concept of citizenship was, as we have seen, central to Bosanquet. As he wrote in one of his articles: 'We start from the idea of democratic citizenship.'[125] This notion of citizenship entailed the theory of mind. Independence was described as 'a certain completeness of will and ideas, and outwardly a certain degree of success in the control of circumstances'. Pauperism was a failure in this citizenmind – a 'defective participation in the social mind'. This pauper spirit was wholly in the mind of the individual and was only disguised in the outwardly wealthy. Mind referred to powers and capacities and these were strengthened or weakened by social conditions. The COS, throughout their later work and especially in the Majority Report, aimed at strengthening the mind by adequate help in social arrangements, and the 'formation and execution of a plan which enlists on its side the mind of the distressed person, and gradually evokes and restores in him that capacity for control of circumstances.' It was this emphasis on the dual aspects of public assistance and casework charity, that prompted Bosanquet to remark that the difference between the reports was 'that the preventive system of the Majority, while covering all the details which the other can suggest, is also so adjusted and adapted as to appeal to a preventive force which the Minority have never contemplated at all.'[126]

The essential plea that Bosanquet made was that if the Minority wished to speak of the causes of poverty, it ought not to restrict itself to general preconditions for poverty, as in old age or sickness They were not strictly causes of poverty, unless related to specific individuals and having passed through the mediation of mind. The individual case and the mind involved were seen as the area of causation relating to poverty, the background to this being the preconditions, for instance, unemployment, etc.

The Webbs, of course, had a very different view of the matter. They felt that both reports had destroyed totally the 1834 Poor Law principles, which they believed had been at the centre of the COS. Sidney Webb saw the 1834 principles as resting on an atomic view of society, which he envisaged as being superseded by the more responsible and interventionary view.[127] This point of course ignored the fact that the Poor Law itself was harshly interventionary. Disregarding this, Sidney Webb continued his argument with the accusation of overlapping, implicit in the Majority view, which was an ambiguous point. Webbs' own argument in the *Sociological Review* revolved around two main propositions. First, that the COS and the Majority wanted to restructure the Poor Law and to change it. Webb took this proposition, as a rod to beat the COS for ever having supported the Poor Law, to show that their timid proposals contradicted the evidence, and to castigate them for holding on to old ideas. The second proposition maintained that the COS and the Majority wanted to humanize, widen and strengthen the Poor Law; in other words, to make it function more efficiently. Webb took this proposition to show their ignorance of the decline of the Poor Law and the growth of intervention by the standard overlapping of institutions. It is obvious that both propositions are contradictory, but the question is, did the COS and the Majority hold both? As the Webbs remarked in another work: 'The whole wording of the lengthy document points in one direction [that is, the Majority], and nearly all its definite proposals in another.'[128] One of the older facets, which the Webbs felt the Majority and the COS clung to, was the idea of the moral defect of the citizen character, which Beatrice Webb described as one of those 'abstract controversies, which delighted the early Victorian'.[129]

In fact, this controversy was taken more seriously by the Minority Report on Scotland, a section of which the Webbs appended to their *English Poor Law Policy*. The notion of the moral defective was associated by the report with the stigma of pauperism and deterrence. The report also regarded this position as 'the only philosophical argument that we have encountered.'[130] The report went on to refute this argument by asking, Do the child, disabled, aged, and feeble-minded suffer from defects in the citizen character? The same question was asked about the unemployed. The conclusion, apart from the familiar criticism on overlapping, argued that although 'individuals in all sections of the destitute may be morally defective, and this in all sorts of different ways, the great mass of destitution is the direct and . . . almost inevitable result of the environment.'[131]

Although Beatrice Webb had commented on the Royal Commission that 'What . . . is clear, is that the COS party are desperately anxious to slur over everything which distinguishes one destitute person from another',[132] she and her husband could write that character and the moral factor of destitution were the supreme issue.[133] The COS believed in individualizing cases, but relating this to character; was it not obvious that this view of destitution would be advanced, especially since she partially agreed with it herself? It is not, however, such an obvious point if it is looked at in a different light. The moral factor and character can be and were very ambiguously interpreted. As J. H. Muirhead remarked in his account of the two reports, *By What Authority?*, it was no part of a true collectivism to neglect the role of character.[134] Collectivism is by no means opposed to character. Yet the question remained: What was character? Both reports recognized, with varying emphases, the role of character. Were the Webbs, in holding on to the moral character, harping back to the old Poor Law? Were the COS, in seeking an alternative to the Poor Law, in recognizing the key influence of the environment, in creating poverty, and in suggesting a flexible Public Assistance Authority, looking to the spirit of the times of 1900?

The ambiguity of the role of character can be illustrated by examining the COS argument. On the idea of the 'standard of life', the COS were progressively pushed by the logic of their arguments to an acceptance of certain state-maintained levels. Total independence or dependence were equally illusions. Man begins as socially dependent. Through childhood and youth he is reliant upon the guidance of institutions. Allowance for this guidance was accepted by Loch, Bosanquet and the COS generally. The conscious concern with individual independence was an emphasis on the individual's role, his character, will, interest, and fundamentally, mind. The characteristic Idealistic principle, that the good of the state lies ultimately in the good will of the individuals comprising it, is the key element here. This good will needs maintenance, to some degree, in order to function. It needs guidance until maturity, and then continued training and education. In other words, although the COS admitted the need for individual responsibility, forethought, thrift, etc., they also saw particular worthwhile elements of will to develop. This carries the implication of a far more strict form of guidance than has usually been associated with the COS.

Responsibility for one's own actions and character, in the COS view, required that welfare should be constructed on the joint basis of Poor Law and charity. The structure of equality of opportunity was added to this, in the sense that individuals might have the possibility of improving their actions. Yet, as the more direct usage of the equality of opportunity doctrine implies, this idea of responsibility could only be partial. The responsibility is demonstrable in the distinction between the deserving and undeserving poor, helpable or worthwhile and unhelpable and worthless. The COS admitted, within their arguments, the partial responsibility of some, since deserving meant that the poverty was not solely causally related to will or character. The pursuit of adequate pensions, hospitals, asylums, convalescent homes and adequate sanitation admitted the role of environmental responsibility for certain categories of destitution.

Throughout the 1900s an increasing self-consciousness about principles, arguments and social change took place in the COS, which was reflected in the Majority Report. This report encapsulated many of the tensions within the theories of the society. In one sense it brought them to a head. Certainly, the extremely critical attitude to the Poor Law, the intrinsic flexibility of the Public Assistance Committees and the greater readiness to accept state activity on problems like unemployment, caused some heart-searching and surprise within the COS camp. Probably the society did not come to an equilibrium of sorts till it changed its name to the Family Welfare Association.

One of the main reasons for this tension was not due to the fact of some isolated, anachronistic Victorian social theory, but more to the actual COS conception of casework. Casework encapsulated the COS view of social work. It included within its framework a range of concepts which found their logical unity in the social theory. This social theory contained an oscillating principle on the partial nature of individual responsibility. Casework, as advanced by Bosanquet and Loch, led to the inference that economic matters were not the sole problem of social work. Economics and environment were but facets of one total problem. It was the individuals, the family, and specifically the minds and consciousness, which formed the complex relation to economic, environmental, domestic and medical problems. The mind, in this context, was viewed as centrally important. It needed a central stimulus, an idea, to guide and organize the complex process of action. Mind, in this situation, was seen as dominating the environment and circumstances. Yet, within the premises of this argument it had already admitted that mind *per se* was created and structured within the environment, that is to say in conditions of housing, sanitation, familial relations, training and general education.

The state, through the Public Assistance Board or voluntary charity, could investigate cases and assess needs. Yet, in admitting this the COS added a partial aspect, a qualification to the idea of mind dominating the environment. Some intervention was needed, but the amount varied. Yet increasingly, on practical grounds of state activity, and also on the grounds of what precisely were individual needs, the COS was pushed back into admitting more environmental foundations to the individual, especially through the partial notion of responsibility. Yet in so doing they could not abandon the principles of mind and character, since this would have meant throwing overboard their *summum bonum,* including casework.

The COS were thus caught in a dilemma. The dilemma was essentially that of recognizing what the Webbs saw as the old idea of character and moral factor of poverty; yet this was coupled with the recognition of what the Webbs saw as a modern idea, namely that of the environmental and economic root to poverty. The COS had, in fact, been circling the problem throughout the 1890s. Yet the questions remained as to how far individuals were allowed to fall before the state intervened, and how far was state intervention compatible with the individual's self-development and character? In this sense Sidney Webb was probably correct in his estimation of the Majority Report. The COS were either consciously or unconsciously affirming two propositions which were apparently contradictory. In fact, it would seem arguable that the COS were aiming at some kind of synthesis, which was more in tune with the actual spirit of the time than were the Webbs' ideas. The tone of the Majority Report was basically confusing and certainly not homogeneous. Thus, again it reflected the attitude of its contemporaries. This point may also account for its greater popularity – a paradox which seemed to have piqued the Webbs.

The Webbs, although in appearance presenting a far more homogeneous picture, also saw to a degree the importance of individual choice, character and morality. Yet the impression is gained that they never really grasped it. The beautiful passage from Beatrice Webb's diary hints at their real conception, where she stated: 'We staked our hopes on the organised working-class, served and guided, it is true, by an elite of unassuming experts who would make no claim to superior status but would content themselves with exercising the power inherent in superior knowledge.'[135] The Webbs' superior knowledge, however unassuming, strode out firmly on moral issues. 'If families which prefer dirt, disorder, and disease', remarked the Webbs' laconically, 'are to be forced by persistent pressure, to mend their ways, what a terrible restriction on the liberty of the individual.'[136] In the same tone they wrote: 'We recommend ... the systematic enforcement of parental responsibility.'[137] The Webbs had no sympathy for the work-shy and lazy. Detention colonies were suggested for this group. Great emphasis was also placed upon the enforced minimum, in order to clean up the base of society. The individual's work, the disorder and cleanliness of the home, the parental responsibility, wages, and presumably the birth-rate and type of infant, would all be part of the enforced minimum. This would be part of the job for the unassuming elite of superiors. As one critic has remarked: 'the Webbs, who after all were the Minority Report, preferred to emphasize the duties of citizenship and had no confidence in actual citizens.'[138] This remark finds ample evidence in the Webbs' work.

The cos and the Majority, aware of the problems of environment, wanted to have confidence in the rights and duties of citizenship. In so doing they became trapped in a classical dilemma, which was easily exploitable and never really resolved. This is not to argue for any crude conclusions regarding the certitude of either report. However, it seems necessary to qualify severely any attitude regarding the predominance of the Minority in historical writings. In fact, the two represent, at times, mere emphases of the same point. On other questions, the Majority, although less settled and clear-cut, demonstrates far more adequately the intrinsic difficulties that many felt regarding the nature of reform and poverty. Some of these difficulties can be seen in the logic of the cos and Bosanquet's arguments. The Majority Report was a key example of these difficulties.

Finally, the foregoing arguments demonstrate unequivocally that Idealist social theory lay at the heart of social practice. This current of theory runs through all the thoughts of Bernard Bosanquet, his wife Helen Bosanquet, and C. S. Loch. In this case the central problem of the Idealist position is that of the relation of the individual and his development to the state. In the cos case it comes out forcefully yet paradoxically. At the same time, the Idealists in the cos were quite right to see the point that any well-developed theory of citizenship is going to be forced to take some account of the practical obstacles to the development of a sense of citizenship, and in particular poverty, which as Hegel pointed out destroys the links between individuals and the mediating institutions of society, creating a penurious rabble of paupers.

7 Toynbee Hall: The Settlement and Civic Idealism

Every locality, often, is however imperfectly and unconsciously, a body which has a mind. It is, an idea which enters into us, the spiritual reflection of our adjacent surroundings, both human and rational. ... The neighbourhood is for the mind its immediate picture of the World into which its future of society on a whole must be fitted.

B. Bosanquet

If the COS embodied the idea of seeking to enable disadvantaged individuals to become to become more effective citizens, Toynbee Hall and the settlement movement generally was an attempt to try to improve the situation of neighbourhoods and communities so that they could become transformed into environments within which individual citizenship could become more effective, and in which a sense of civic idealism could flourish. In *The Philosophical Theory of the State* Bernard Bosanquet provided an eloquent defence of the Idealist view that the neighbourhood was an 'ethical institution'. For this to be realized the neighbourhood had to be transformed from a mere aggregation of individuals in physical proximity into a community of individuals who shared a common purpose in their locality. This, in Bosanquet's view, can often be observed in modern society[1] and in some aspects at least the university settlement movement of which Toynbee Hall, named after Green's friend and disciple Arnold Toynbee, was the first institutional embodiment of this ideal of community.[2]

Initially the movement began in Oxford and its immediate inspiration came from Canon Barnett. As Pimlott wrote: 'Young Oxford was becoming more and more conscious of the deficiencies of the economic system.'[3] It was Canon Barnett who tapped the consciences of the young students. At the time Barnett was nicknamed the unpaid professor of social philosophy. He put forward the relatively simple idea that by residence among the poor, students would be able to serve their generation more effectively. Scott Holland, a Balliol graduate and pupil of Green, wrote in the *Commonwealth* (July 1913): 'Barnett came down and preached in our college hall, and the whole university laid hold of his idea and understood. He came as a prophet just when it was wanted, and men saw in his settlement proposal exactly the opportunity which their gathering interest in the problems of poverty demanded for its exercise and fulfilment. He surprised us by his quiet common-sense.'[4] Barnett, as many have noticed, seemed at the right moment to give concrete form to a strong undercurrent of feeling in Oxford. He acted as a catalyst for the latent feelings of civic duty.

These feelings of duty and responsibility touched upon a raw nerve. Many undergraduates seemed sublimely ignorant of the social conditions of urban poverty.[5] To Barnett and others this only testified to the deplorable divisions between classes in the community. Barnett essentially was part of the broader movement in the late nineteenth century which began to place a greater emphasis on the environmental conditions of poverty. He still expressed himself very much in the moral and religious context of his age; for instance, he defined social reform as 'a removal of certain conditions in and around society which stand in the way of man's progress towards perfection.'[6] In essence, his 'empirical socialism', as Beatrice Webb called it, was synonymous with a practical Christianity.

The call to duty and responsibility was essentially part of this context. 'Which of us', Barnett asked with moral conviction, 'having once seen a Whitechapel alley at five o'clock on an August afternoon and realising what it means . . . could go and enjoy our afternoon tea, daintily spread on a shady lawn, and not ask himself questions about his own responsibility?'[7] Many including the young Arnold Toynbee, seemed to have asked themselves this same question. Several of the early manifestations of this sense of duty had what now seems to be a patronizing quality. Werner Picht, the first historian of the settlement movement, had like Toynbee himself defined the settlement as 'a colony of members of the upper classes, forming in a poor neighbourhood'.[8] Another early settlement enthusiast the MP Sir John Gorst, pointed to them as a fulfilment of 'the obligation which the classes which possess culture and leisure have towards those who are less highly endowed.'[9] Admittedly, in many cases this kind of practice was overtly patronizing. Yet on the other hand, Toynbee Hall and other settlements were a protest by the more privileged members of society in universities against the sin, as Beveridge put it, 'of taking things for granted, in particular, taking one's own social position or conditions for granted.'[10]

This manifestation of social conscience and duty found an apt theoretical basis in the idea of citizenship. Elizabeth Macadam stated in her work in the 1930s on what she called the new philanthropy, that 'Toynbee Hall and its successors were visible symbols of the new spirit of fellowship and equal citizenship.'[11] The democratic impulse to establish equal citizenship was fundamental to Arnold Toynbee, T. H. Green, and Canon Barnett, and the settlement movement. It was through active participation in the civic life, with intelligent concern for the public interest that the individual was able to realize his true self. As Alfred Milner remarked of Arnold Toynbee: 'he was in the thick of every movement to improve the external conditions of life of the people – better houses, open spaces, free libraries ... stirred to the depths of his soul by the ideal of a bolder civic life.'[12] It was the mark of most who came under his influence that they were deeply impressed with the idea of their individual duty as citizens and filled with an enthusiasm for social equality.[13]

Arnold Toynbee, like many of the Idealists, spent much of his time developing the idea of active citizenship. He was a keen advocate of training schemes for citizenship, which in fact Toynbee Hall attempted to introduce within their general educational pro- gramme.[14] The cult of citizenship formed virtually a secular religion. It was, as some Idealists put it, part of the *best* we know, this being the essence of religion.[15] Yet this idealism, as Milner put it, could only justify its existence by energetic devotion to the good of mankind.[16] It was in this sense that Toynbee Hall was attempting to spiritualize the forces of the future, or as Barnett maintained, was attempting to 'raise the buried life' or the 'Christed self' of each man and woman. The religion of Toynbee Hall was basically a practical Christianity, probably more closely attached to a liberal theology. For many like Mrs Humphry Ward, this practical religion was expressed in the vision of a humanized Christ incarnated in an active life of citizenship and social reform, in Mrs Ward's case in University Hall and later the Passmore Edwards settlement.[17]

However, it was misleading to argue, as did D. O. Wagner in the 1930s, that 'Toynbee Hall is in a very real sense a monument to the social power of the Church of England as well as Arnold Toynbee.'[18] Many churchmen like Bishop Gore, Canon Scott Holland and Stewart Headlam were active social reformers, but they were a minority. Also, the Toynbee settlement was criticized by the official Anglican Church as being indifferent to religion. It was not concerned to preach a particular dogmatic faith.[19] It took pains, especially in Barnett's case, to dissociate itself from the concept of a mission. The settler was not there to proselytize, but to learn and to teach vocational and cultural subjects. He was there to deepen his own understanding as well as to help and pass on his skills.

The Toynbee idea was to encourage the young student to come and perform his citizen's duty in a local neighbourhood. The original impetus of the student may have been an intellectual craving, a missionary zeal, a desire for equality or a disgust at intolerable social conditions, yet once in the settlement he was encouraged to simply make friends and be hospitable in the local community. The idea that Barnett put forward was that 'the foundations of a real thorough improvement of the social evils is a friendly mutual approach of those who give and those who need help, and that human sympathy is more valuable than material assistance.'[20] Thus, the original aim and ultimate end of the settlement was fellowship. This desire for friendship and fellowship, which lay at the foundation of Toynbee Hall, was symptomatic of a communitarian spirit latent in many social movements at the close of the nineteenth century. Ruskin, Morris, Carlyle, and the Idealists, and later R. H. Tawney, Belloc, and Orage, all in their different ways, looked to man as a socially harmonized being. This communitarian desire for a human social fellowship was partly an intellectual reaction to what they took to be the individualism of the mid-nineteenth century. It was also partly due to a sense of breakdown in older social norms in relation to the continuing expansion of industry and market values. In this sense, Elizabeth Macadam was correct when she stated that Toynbee 'brought a new community spirit into the philanthropy of the late nineteenth century.'[21] Toynbee Hall was a directly practical expression of a wider desire for fellowship, a unity of classes in the community. It is significant that Toynbee Hall's communitarianism derived from the Idealists. The practical attempt by men like Barnett and others to develop certain latent assumptions, had its theoretical embodiment in the work of such men as T. H. Green.

Toynbee Hall was offered essentially as a solution to the social problem. Its origins lay in the nineteenth-century desire, especially among intellectuals, for this total solution. To Barnett, settlement stood as an acknowledgement of the claims of all citizens to share in the good things of social life. These good things were culture, knowledge, beauty and cleanliness. In helping to lead and provide people with these good things, the settlements like Toynbee Hall hoped to mitigate class suspicion, to achieve greater social justice and to realize a more cohesive community. As we have seen, this aim related very profoundly to the ideas of the Idealist school. As many commentators have noted, Toynbee Hall was basically an Oxonian response to the social problem.[22] A recent scholar has pointed out that it expressed the spirit of Balliol College, Oxford, even though it came about through a lecture at St John's College.[23] Other settlements expressed different sentiments: Oxford House, for example, articulated the Tractarian high churchmanship of Keble College.

Although Oxford common rooms had widely different opinions, undoubtedly that of Balliol in the 1880s and 1890s, in political, social and philosophical matters, was dominated by the spirit and thought of T. H. Green. Arnold Toynbee or 'apostle Arnold' as his friends nicknamed him, according to Alfred Milner, occupied 'an almost identical position in religion, philosophy and social questions to T. H. Green.'[24] He looked to Green as a guide. He reported to his sister in a letter in March 1882, on Green's death, that 'I am sick and miserable today, for Green . . . whose lay sermons you have read and who, I loved deeply (more than I knew), died suddenly this morning.'[25] Toynbee's affinity with Green led to a fundamental agreement of aspirations. The role of civic conscience, the sense of duty, and the ideal of goodness in the practical civic life, were some of these. In the same way as Green had worked on the Oxford Council, Toynbee went to London to do his civic service for the people. Some of the more notable aspects of Green's teaching were the aim to develop the capacity and powers of each individual citizen, the emphasis on the power of organizing society to further conditions for this development, and the function of government to maintain the conditions in which morality, as the disinterested pursuit of self-imposed duties, could flourish.

It was in this context that Green had emphasized the role of citizenship. Those who realized the common purposes and moral aims of social life ought to work actively for their fellow men. This kind of impetus worked in political life for politicians like Asquith, Samuel and Haldane, in social work for men like C. S. Loch and Bernard Bosanquet, and in educative matters in the university settlements. Green's views were often interpreted as espousing a radical form of Liberalism in politics and theology. His civic theories provided a positive philosophical and practical call to duty. This call was intellectually satisfying and emotionally exciting and uplifting. It was no wonder that it turned the heads of so many young students, although many would say it had addled their heads. The settlements, especially Toynbee Hall, in this context, gained a great stimulus from Green's thought. As J. H. Muirhead wrote in his autobiography: 'it was chiefly in consequence of Green's teaching that the idea of duty to spread opportunity took hold of the young Oxford men who came into intimate contact with it in the 1870s and 1880s.' Muirhead linked this with the phenomenon of Toynbee Hall, the enthusiasm for Charles Booth's work, the interest in the Fabians, and other social movements.[26]

In fact, since many of the voluntary efforts and social reforms of the 1890s have become so familiar this century, and security for the poor and sick has become normal, it is often forgotten that the institutions which performed welfare functions were created through ideas originally shot through with idealistic fervour and humanitarian conscience.

The discussion of the social question and the duties of the young citizen were not limited to the heretical minority. Respectable college preachers at Oxford in the 1880s spoke out as strongly as others. K. S. Inglis reported in his work *Churches and the Working Classes in Victorian England* that J. F. Bright, the Master of University College, while deploring what William Morris had said in a visiting paper, nevertheless himself expressed similar sentiments to those of Morris on the contrast between the squalid conditions of the poor and the flourishing property owners.[27] Between 1883 and 1884, half the sermons in Oxford referred in some way to the social problem. As these sermons were consequently reported in the *Oxford Magazine,* which was not noted as a radical organ, this was worthy of attention.[28]

It was the attempt to throw light on the duties of citizenship that led to the idea of service, a concept discussed in Green's work. This service included the students, the universities as a whole, the teachers, politicians and churchmen. All alike, as citizens, were encouraged earnestly to serve their fellow men in the community. This point was well expressed by Arnold Toynbee in a lecture in London, when he more or less confessed to his working-class audience that the apathy of the middle classes in the nineteenth century was a sin. He asked his audience if he and his fellow students could serve the working class. 'It is not', he stated, 'that we care about public life, for what is public life but the miserable arid waste of barren controversies . . . we are willing to give up something much dearer.'[29] This 'something' that was to be given up was time, loved ones, and a life of study and leisure, in order to serve the masses.

He only pleaded with them not to see material civilization as an end in itself but as a means to a nobler life.

Other Idealists, like Edward Caird in Glasgow, were also involved in settlements. As Caird's biographers noted, the founding of the University Settlement Association in Glasgow in 1886, which was sited eventually in Cathedral Street under the name Toynbee Hall, owed its existence and early enthusiasm to Caird and his wife. 'Caird's sympathy', they reported, 'was strong with the poor, and with everyone held down and deprived of healthy citizenship.'[30]

It could thus be argued that although the work of Carlyle, Ruskin, Morris and many others had some effect on the origins of Toynbee Hall, the most immediate influence, as reported by Clement Attlee (an early Toynbee settler himself) was the teaching and practice of T. H. Green at Oxford.[31] To Attlee, Green's philosophy, 'with its emphasis on the right of every human being to a full opportunity of developing his faculties, and the need for ensuring the conditions under which those faculties could be exercised together with his lofty conception of the duty of the citizen in the modern state, were allied to personal service in the routine of municipal life and in voluntary social effort. The young men of the University, such as Toynbee, learnt their social philosophy from him.'[32]

Green's influence can be seen in two ways. First, as Canon Barnett noted, the first and most active settlers were those who had come under Green's influence directly through his teaching, or indirectly through his writings.[33] The general atmosphere of Balliol, through Green's civic practice and teaching in the 1880s, was wholly conducive and receptive to the proposals of men like Canon Barnett. Second, Green's influence can be seen as absolutely direct. Mrs Humphrey Ward, for example, reported in her recollections that she had founded her university settlement 'to show that the faith of Green and Martineau and Stopford Brooke was a faith that would wear and work'.[34] Green's message, as Mrs Ward put it, was concerned with 'life itself, the ordinary human life and experience of everyday as it slowly evolved through history.'[35] The Professor Grey of her novel *Robert Elsmere,* and the Professor Green of real life, became the impetus for her settlement activity.

In fact Green seemed at this time almost to have become a legend. the library at the Passmore Edwards settlement, now named the Mrs Mary Ward House, was devoted to the memory of Green, and the letters of his name were engraved into the fireplace. Mansfield House, a denominational university settlement, got into trouble with the *British Weekly* for laying a stone to the memory of T. H. Green in 1896. This memorial seemed to be connected to a studious ignoring of orthodox religion, which the paper felt might indicate that Mansfield House was turning into a second-rate Toynbee Hall.[36]

In sum, as Werner Picht noted, the origins of Toynbee Hall lay in a romantic social idealism.[37] In fact, a more apt term for this would be a civic idealism. The most coherent form of this idealism lay in the social and moral philosophy of idealism, especially that of T. H. Green. The call to practice the duties of citizenship, to fulfil obligations, to see the connections between the universities and the affairs of the world, were all forcefully present in Green's work and eventually in social movements like Toynbee Hall.

The origins of Toynbee Hall lay very much in currents of civic idealism. However, there were earlier forms of settler, who had a more directly missionary aim to their work. These religious groups and individuals went back as long as the concept 'charity' itself. The more explicit aim of settling among the poor to share their destitution was relatively novel, if still connected to the missionary zeal.

Examples of this early pioneering work were men like J. R. Green, Edward Denison and Moore Ede. J. R. Green came to the slums of Stepney in 1860. Ill-health stopped his activities as it was to check those of Arnold Toynbee, yet not before he had come into contact with other settlers like the Revd E. C. Hawkins of Hackney and the Revd Brooke Lambert. Lambert, in fact, had addressed undergraduates at Merton College, Oxford, in 1881, encouraging them to go to London. This early zeal was also expressed by John Ruskin who had meetings with Denison and another Oxford graduate, Holland, in 1886 in London, to discuss various possibilities for helping the poor. It was Holland who encouraged Canon Barnett to go to St Jude's parish in Whitechapel in 1873. Barnett kept in contact with Oxford, after taking up the St Jude's parish, and many students like Arnold Toynbee, Lewis Nettleship, Scott Holland, Sidney Ball, Alfred Milner and Arthur Hoare spent their vacations in the Whitechapel slums.

In 1883, the year of Mearn's *The Bitter Cry of Outcast London*, Barnett gave a paper in St John's College Oxford, entitled 'University Settlements'.[38] The substance of the paper was that the poor needed more than food. They needed *knowledge* and the *means* to develop themselves, means which had fallen to the rich. Barnett was not content with scientific charity. He described the age he lived in as that of the higher life, where the best things ought to be shared by all. 'It is', Barnett claimed, 'to members of the universities anxious to unite in a common purpose of improving the lives of the people that I make the suggestion that university settlements will better express their idea.'[39] The settlement was envisaged as being the common ground for all classes. Knowledge would be freely given. All men would be able to partake in what Barnett called the 'associated life'.[40] A warden was seen as directing the activities, not arbitrarily but imaginatively. The result was an assault on poverty – poverty being due partly, in Barnett's paper, to the division between classes. He felt that the university settlement provided 'a remedy which goes deeper than that provided by popular philanthropy'.[41] It was an ideal worthy of sacrifice since it looked to a community where the best was most common and where hunger and ignorance were eradicated.[42]

Barnett's paper which attracted so much attention, had been preceded by action. Picht reported in his study that in 1875 five undergraduates requested to stay at St Jude's.[43] Barnett agreed and the students worked with the cos, joined local clubs and generally entered into the community life. One of these students was Arnold Toynbee. He took a room at Whitechapel and joined the Tower Hamlets Radical Club, became a cos worker and also worked as a Poor Law Guardian. Although only staying approximately two weeks in Whitechapel, due to ill-health, it was in Oxford, as Mrs Barnett reported, that the 'subtle force of Toynbee's personality' had most effect.[44]

In June 1883 two Cambridge students wrote to Barnett wishing to do social work in East London. Barnett replied with a suggestion of hiring a house in the area. In November Barnett brought his ideas together in the St John's College lecture. A committee of students was formed to study Barnett's proposals in his November lecture. Their report was laid before the interested parties on 23 February 1884 and consequently adopted. Another committee was appointed, including A. J. Balfour, to buy a site in Whitechapel, and to try to interest other colleges in Oxford. The premises were purchased by a subscription, and after architectural work and building, the first residents slept in the hall on 25 December 1884.

The settlement movement developed from this time onwards. Caius was formed in 1887, St Hilda's in 1889, Mansfield House in 1890, Bermondsey in 1891, Canning Town in 1892, Browning Hall in 1895, and the Passmore Edwards in 1896. Werner Picht reckoned that by 1911 there were 45 such settlements. However, it was the example of Toynbee which provided a general theory and typical pattern to the settlement structure, and it was thus that Toynbee Hall was often called the 'mother of settlements'. The idea spread fairly quickly to America, as the COS movement had done, although it took on a slightly different complexion there in the neighbourhood idea, which will be discussed later. The Hull House Settlement was formed in Chicago by Jane Addams and Ellen Gates Starr, and the Henry Street Settlement was founded in New York.

Part of the difficulty of accounting for the work of Toynbee Hall lay in the method that Barnett adopted. He valued spontaneity and the ability to adapt to changing needs and circumstances. The 'one-by-one' formula, he valued highly enough to have embroidered on a picture above the main fireplace of Toynbee Hall. It was probably a method that Barnett had retained from his COS days. The basis of COS casework, as argued in the previous chapter, was a one-by-one method, judging each situation on its own merits as unique and comprehensive. As many noted of Toynbee Hall, its only programme was the lack of programme. The Hall was a place of perpetual change in activities defying adequate description. Beveridge probably put the point most succinctly when he stated that the essence of Toynbee Hall: 'lies in the individual lives of the residents. . . . Any full account of the settlement and any estimate of its significance would have to bring in the biographies of the residents and note all the movements which directly or indirectly emanated from their stay.'[45]

Although this seems to point to the conclusion that Toynbee Hall had no social philosophy, there are certain common threads which run through its work. Picht himself notes that the importance of the settlement lies largely in the educational influence on the actual members and on the neighbourhood.[46] Barnett also, as one scholar puts it: 'always viewed the settlement as an instrument of education. He thought that the social problem was at its root an educational one.'[47] This in fact seems to be a fairly common assessment of the work of Toynbee. Elizabeth Macadam, in the 1930s, praised the neighbourhood and educational work of the settlements, and argued that they were never more important than in her own decade, partly because of the work they did in establishing community centres on the newer housing estates.[48]

The question remained, however, What type of education was so centrally important? There was a formal unity in the various educational activities which was present in the origins of the movement. All these strands of education that were present in Toynbee Hall were essentially aiming at a corporate civic education. That is to say, all the various activities of discussion, clubs, local government work, primary and secondary level teaching, and social investigation, found a formal unity and stimulus in the theory of civic Idealism. The aim was some form of civic service. It was viewed in the context of the duties and responsibilities of citizenship. The aim was to demonstrate a high level of rationality. Citizenship recognized certain common aims of corporate life, and the 'one-by-one' idea was of key importance here, for the end of the social work and education was to help the individual to help himself. The principle that the state could only provide the conditions for the self-development of individuals was observed even more in practice in Toynbee Hall. Voluntary help could admittedly go one step further than the state and could guide the man or woman individually to self-realization. Yet the settlement could not achieve that self-realization for the individual. It was notable that Barnett, who was so enthusiastic for the developments of local government activity in East London early on in his career, should have been disturbed by the number of residents at the end of his time at Toynbee Hall who saw manipulation by local government as an end in itself.[49]

The aim of the settlement was thus, in Walter Besant's words, 'personal service; not money'. Besant saw the inspiration for this service in fictional characters like Robert Elsmere, especially in its appeal to broader views of humanity and religion.[50] Mrs Ward had written that the essence of lives like that of T. H. Green which inspired her work, was 'usefulness, social reform, the bettering of daily life for the many'.[51] Clement Attlee also noted that the settlements had opened a new era of social service, characterized by active sympathy and co-operation between classes.[52] The philosophy behind this and Barnett's work was based on the belief in the solidarity of the human race. This sense of solidarity and service was expressed by Canon Barnett in the Wadham House residents' book, when he wrote that 'communion represents the highest state of human development and for perfect communion there must be perfect individuals. It is hoped by the founders that Wadham House may offer an example of the common life satisfying to its members and helpful to its neighbours.'[53]

The settlement was thus to become a central and organic part of a neighbourhood. Its role was to educate the settlers and the residents of East London. The education was a civic one, in the widest sense of the term. To be a good citizen in Green's and Barnett's terms was to be self-supporting, knowledgeable, serving others, realizing common moral ends and aiming at some kind of self-perfection. It was thus that E. J. Urwick, as sub-warden of Toynbee Hall, wrote in the *Charity Organization Review* of 1902 that 'the ideal settler will make the fullest performance of a citizen's duties a first claim on his time, taking his share in the local administration and in the work of voluntary agencies ... making good management a part of his own personal responsibility, just as he makes the welfare of his individual neighbours a part of his personal interest.'[54]

The fundamental basis to the civic or corporate education was friendship, neighbourliness or hospitality. This to Barnett was a process of mutual learning. In a paper in the 1890s he expressed himself forcefully, and in distinctly Kantian terms: 'Hospitality', he wrote, 'is a duty enforced by experience as well as by command. It is the best expression of good will, the outward and manifest sign of the inward feeling of respect and sympathy.'[55] Urwick, in the article of 1902 cited above, expressed himself in similar terms, arguing that it was good-will that was wanted in the settlement and not good works.

According to Barnett, the process of hospitality was one where the giver and receiver became one in sharing. He argued that the idea had an ancient heritage, based on the personal nexus of human relationships. This he felt had been undermined by the cash nexus and had led to divisions between classes. Mere entertainment, teaching, or proselytizing could not overcome this division. What was needed was to develop personal relationships. Residents of settlements should live in a local neighbourhood and partake in its life and government without being religiously or politically affiliated. The object was to establish human friendship and community, based on mutual respect and goodwill.[56] Thinkers and workers could in this way come together and share their experience. In the process the thinker could put his expertise at the service of clubs, associations unions and co-operatives of working people. Barnett felt that the settler could learn as much as he could teach, and that culture would spread by contact on a friendly level. It was in this light that the noted 'smoking debates' developed on a friendly, informal, discursive level.

Another area of education was that of direct primary, secondary, vocational and cultural teaching. Settlements developed differently on this path. Oxford House was noted for its boys' work. The Manchester settlement at Ancoats was noted for its work with the blind. Mrs Ward's settlement developed the first non-residential physical defective school for crippled children. In 1893 the first children's play centres were formed. In the same vein in 1902 children's vacation schools were brought into being. Other women's settlements pioneered children's welfare clinics and nursery schools. Various classes for primary and secondary level teaching in literacy, mathematics and basic science were regularly given at Toynbee Hall, as well as craft subjects like woodwork. On a more cultural level, reading classes, drama, music and social science were taught.

Perhaps one of the most important areas of Toynbee teaching was at a higher level. University extension work in East London was based at Toynbee Hall. This kind of work developed into the founding of the Workers' Education Association, which was again based at Toynbee Hall. The short-lived London Ethical Society also began life there, as did evening classes and adult education.

Barnett's vision was ultimately an East End university. A writer in the *Toynbee Journal* in 1886 idealized this picture into a Utopian scheme.[57] The student body of the university was to consist of workmen and clerks from local co-operative factories. Their study was to be six hours per day for six years. Money being equally distributed in society, fees would present no problem. The tutors at this university were also to be employed in the factories, although professors would be engaged full-time on their studies. Courses in citizenship and political science would be compulsory for all. Barnett's conception, which was less Utopian, was eventually partially realized in Wadham and Balliol House, where teaching reached a very high level.[58] In Barnett's view settlers found 'that without more knowledge, power might be a causeless weapon and money only a means of degradation, and that without more education, local government could hardly be for the local good.'[59]

In his enthusiasm for education Barnett encouraged local pupil-teaching associations to base themselves at Toynbee Hall. He also campaigned for improved teacher-training facilities. R. B. Morant, an ex-Toynbee settler himself, was the main impetus behind the 1902 Conservative Education Act, which in its attempt to establish a ladder of learning principle, on a more formal basis, undermined some of the basic educative functions at Toynbee Hall, especially the idea of the working-class university. Alternatively, Barnett was never happy with a purely formal educational arrangement. The principle he desired was one where there is neither teacher nor taught. He wanted groups to come together to exchange and obtain information, and to create friendly relationships and feelings of inter-dependence.

This inter-dependence was of supreme value in Barnett's estimation. The club work was especially pertinent here. As Picht pointed out, 'Clubs are the ground on which human contact with the working-class is most completely achieved.'[60] Kathleen Woodroofe, in her work *From Charity to Social Work*, praised Barnett's ideas on club and group work as being the germinal conception from which group work theory has developed this century.[61]

Barnett, Woodroofe argues, realized that the aim to strengthen a person's own strength could better be achieved in a group with a common goal and sense of purpose. The individual in the atmosphere of fellowship and disciplined co-operation would be able to develop a feeling of self-respect. His or her capabilities would be able to come out in a group and consequently be valued by others. According to Woodroofe, Barnett more or less intuitively realized that groups organized round selected interests could compensate for the disabilities and harshness of urban poverty. They could, as Woodroofe put it: 'recreate that sense of intimate purpose which has once belonged to the village of an earlier age.'[62] In so doing, they could develop more emotionally sound personalities and more satisfying social relationships. This, Woodroofe argued, was an anticipation of modern group work or group dynamics.

This form of personal group work was matched by the more direct political activity of the Toynbee settlers. Some settlements became noted for specific types of political action, for example, Browning Hall for its campaigns on pensions. The work of Toynbee Hall in this area can be seen approximately in four different activities: first in local government, secondly in direct political activism outside the institutions: thirdly in its role as a social laboratory and centre of information: and finally in its training of workers and leaders.

Barnett confidently wrote in the early 1900s that 'a new spirit is moving our local government. It is obviously impossible to put its presence to the credit of Toynbee Hall; but it is fair to say that its residents have contributed by the share they have taken as members of various boards, as well as by the influences they have exerted.'[63] Barnett argued in this paper for the need for some active settlement members to enter local government in order to achieve things for the good of all citizens. It was in this light that the Whitechapel public library was founded.

Toynbee settlers were actively engaged in various political activities through local government, for example Poor Law Guardians and school managers. Through debates and canvassing they helped to educate electors to identify and participate in local issues. Percy Alden, the Warden of Mansfield Hall, contributed a paper on this topic in a volume of essays in 1895.[64] He argued that the settlements had been criticized for being partisan, yet he claimed that they existed to educate the public conscience and to crystallize public opinion. 'It is impossible', he stated, 'to value too highly the presence in any working-class district, of men with some amount of leisure time and education who are willing to take part in the public life of the locality.'[65] He believed that settlers needed to show the capacity for disinterested service. The ideas, imagination and broader perspectives of the students were always invaluable.

Interestingly, the figure that he asked the settlers to emulate was T. H. Green. In Alden's words, 'what Green did in Oxford, owing to his public spirit, disinterested motives, and untiring industry, university men, in a lesser degree perhaps, could do in every poor district.'[66] Toynbee Hall in the 1890s had two members on the London school board; other settlements were equally involved. These, Alden argued, could help in housing inspection, the creation of libraries, and social work. In so doing they would act as 'citizen students' helping to better the lives of the poor.[67]

A slightly less orthodox form of political work was the direct political activism and involvement in industrial disputes. D. O. Wagner recorded that in one year Canon Barnett was involved in 14 industrial disputes.[68] The line between certain types of philanthropic action and political action was not easily defined. In 1889, as Tom Mann recorded in his memoirs, the residents of Toynbee Hall were of considerable help to the dock strikers. In fact, the strike leaders were invited to dinner at Toynbee Hall, an action which Barnett had to explain carefully to many Oxford associates. In 1891 A. P. Laurie and Llewellyn Smith, in their capacity as Toynbee residents, organized a London busmen's strike with great success. Mrs Barnett was also deeply involved in the famous matchgirls' strike where she acted as a mediator.

It was in this light that Toynbee Hall was conceived of as a 'sociological laboratory', doing the patient work of research. The 1892 Toynbee Commission was organized under the auspices of the Toynbee Trust, for social research to look into the causes and effects of trade depression in East London. It was from this kind of practical study, in conjunction with a cos Committee, that W. H. Beveridge drew most of the material for his famous study of unemployment.

Beveridge viewed the settlement as a place of postgraduate education in humanity, and not just a place to pass through. Settlements produced, he states in his autobiography, a general culture in political and social views which broke down the watertight compartments of men's class and values.[69] He also suggested that settlements were clinics for social scientists, places where students of social science could gain practical experience. In the *Evidence for Voluntary Action*, Beveridge discussed the role of settlements in the

1940s which was one of giving advice and developing friendly relations in a neighbourhood, providing opportunities for training candidates for the social services, and finally for the study of local conditions and the initiation of experimental research.[70] Apart from the stronger emphasis on social work training this programme illustrated how little it had changed from Barnett's own day.

The final area of political action was more of an indirect result of settlement activity. It was also the subject for criticism. Toynbee Hall was often accused of being an elitist group, having little actual contact with the poor. As B. B. Gilbert remarked: 'In all its varying patterns, settlement work became fashionable. It commanded the time of young men with assured careers before them, and the money and patronage of the leaders of the nation.'[71] Asquith in fact coined the phrase of Toynbee Hall being a 'social laboratory'. However, of the actual figures who attended Toynbee Hall, a remarkable number became civil servants or active social reformers in the Liberal administrations of the first decade of the nineteenth century.

Those who worked on the Liberal reforms between 1906 and 1914 were men like W. H. Beveridge, R. B. Morant, Llewellyn Smith, Ernest Aves and W. J. Braithwaite. Other figures of note were J. A. Spender, E. J. Urwick, Clement Attlee, Max Beer and R. H. Tawney. All did their stint at Toynbee Hall and were duly affected or motivated by its civic idealism and stress on social conscience and duty. Although these men were in one sense an elite, they took their elitism seriously. This seriousness and earnestness was reflected in their social action, especially in the period of the Liberal administrations. As B. B. Gilbert noted: 'the researcher finds that nearly without exemption these men – junior members of parliament, private secretaries to Prime Ministers, permanent secretaries of ministers, junior civil servants – had settlement experience and continuous settlement contact in their background.'[72] Many of the ethical and political principles of these men were encapsulated in Barnett's *Practicable Socialism*. Their civic idealism and enthusiasm surrounded the National Insurance Act, the Trade Boards Act and other such reforms, which were virtually entirely constructed and piloted by men like Braithwaite, Morant, Llewellyn Smith and Beveridge.

The kind of reform that was aimed at here was to provide conditions for individual development. In decent wages, sanitary, health and insurance reforms, Barnett and many settlers saw a basis to civilized life. This practicable socialism was not revolutionary or directly redistributive. Economic equality was not the aim for

Barnett, but rather a social equality and harmony, a harmony of fellowship and citizenship. The settlement represented reform without institutions. It was the pursuit of providing conditions, means and guidance to the self-cultivation of the citizen, and a self-realization within the common purposes of the local community structure.

The idea of poverty that Barnett espoused was a relative one. As he argued in his *Practicable Socialism*: 'Poverty is a relative term. The citizen whose cottage home with its bright housewife and happy children, is a light in our land, is poor in comparison with some stately mansion. But his poverty is not an evil to be cured ... The poverty which has to be cured is the poverty which degrades human nature.'[73] Thus, although he was keen to go on with local government campaigns to support pensions and strikes for higher wages, he felt that a conception of morality needed to be conjoined to these activities. In principle, there was no limit to defining the extent of government interference.

Therefore, needs had an essentially arbitrary quality to them. Governmental interference on a national or local level could not achieve everything for the individual's needs. 'People', he argued, 'must raise themselves ... People therefore must have the education which will reveal to them the powers within themselves and within other men.'[74] Thus he did not want men to be instruments of a productive process or a cash nexus, but conversely to be equal citizens, enjoying equally the gifts of civilization. The process of achieving this could only be done by spontaneous friendship and education, a mutual learning about the associated life of fellowship. Barnett considered that, 'It is the poverty of their own lives which makes the poor content to inhabit uninhabitable houses.'[75] This poverty could, he thought, be removed by contact with those who have had the privilege of contact with the 'higher life'. He thus argued that friendship was the channel by which the knowledge which belongs to one class may pass to all classes. Poverty was thus seen as an inner condition. This was essentially a cos doctrine. Yet Barnett, going beyond this, gave a much larger play to environmental forces in helping to create this inner condition. He also felt that scientific charity was too cold and dogmatic to provide an adequate solution. It was only in friendship and education that the question of poverty could be resolved. Barnett's ideas here were close to those of the New Liberals like Herbert Samuel, H. H. Asquith and L. T. Hobhouse, although Barnett's particular emphasis was on voluntaristic guidance, rather than providing the statutory conditions for equal citizenship.

It is a supremely difficult task with any social movement to pin down with precision a firm theoretical influence. However, if one takes into account the aims, practices and major figures in the founding and work of Toynbee Hall, it is undeniable that Green's civic idealism played a crucial role, both as an emotive backcloth and as a direct theoretical stimulus. For Samuel Barnett, for Arnold Toynbee, settlement was a manifestation of social duty. To strive for self-perfection necessarily entailed striving for the self-perfection of others. One's own good and full satisfaction, as in Green's thought, entailed the common good. Toynbee Hall was a manifestation of mutual service, embodied in the pursuit of the common good. On a directly practical level, what Barnett would have called 'practical Christianity', it was an attempt to create the conditions for each person to realize his 'best self' or 'Christed self', echoing Green's theological sentiments. Citizenship was here viewed as a mode of divine service, incarnating the life of Christ in duties to others. Through responsible friendship and diverse forms of education, a community of mutual service could be built up. Toynbee Hall was thus viewed as a forcing-house for an ethical community, based upon the character development of both settlers and working people. The fundamental theme which underpinned the work of Toynbee was therefore the self-development and self-realization of all citizens in the neighbourhood. Toynbee Hall, as the mother of settlements, was seen to be the catalyst for a countrywide movement forming the basis for a more complete conception of the common good, and a deeper sense of community.

8 *Education and Citizenship*

Rights are to be regarded not as rewards but as opportunities. But opportunities could only be taken by the educated. With T. H. Green as their chief inspiration, philosophers such as Sir Henry Jones, MacCunn, Hetherington, Muirhead and Haldane flung themselves into the theoretical and practical questions of education.

G. B. Parry

I was then looking forward, in common with many of those with whom I associated in Oxford, to a reconstitution at no very distant time, of the middle and higher education of England, and, as I need not be ashamed to add, if not to a reconstitution of society through that of education, yet at least to a considerable change in the tone and to the removal of many of its barriers.

T. H. Green

It is clear that any theory of constructive citizenship is going to have something to say about education. Indeed this point was prefigured in the previous chapter. Citizenship requires that individuals should be able to act for themselves as effectively as possible, to define their own needs and to seek to make institutions more responsive. Character could not be developed without some development of the capacity of self-help and this capacity depends of course upon education, of understanding one's environment and the political context within which life is lived.

In order to examine more fully the relationships between Idealism and the theory and practice of education we shall look at the work of Richard Burdon Haldane, who was committed both to educational reform and Idealist philosophy. His own views on education were developed within a self-consciously Liberal perspective, although in the end it was the issue of education which profoundly influenced his decision to leave the Liberal party and become the first Labour Lord Chancellor.

Haldane's work on education, which has only recently been thoroughly recorded, extended into many areas. Apart from his 1889 speech on the Universities of Scotland Bill, his earliest concerns were with the University of London Bill. It was during his work on the latter Bill that Haldane, while propitiating Irish MPs, helped to lay down the basis of the Irish higher educational reforms. The 1897 University of London Bill was followed by further help to Sidney Webb in the founding of the London School of Economics (LSE). It was also during this period, up into the early 1900s, that Haldane called for an English version of the German Technische Hochschule, or the London Charlottenburg for South Kensington – a scheme which did not come to fruition for many years.

In England in 1900 there were five universities: Oxford, Cambridge, London, Durham, and Victoria. These were fundamentally federations of colleges. It was certain disputed federations, for instance of the college of Liverpool under Victoria, that led eventually to the campaign for independent universities in major civic centres. Haldane played a considerable role, although its extent has been disputed, in negotiating for independent university charters for Liverpool, Sheffield, Leeds and Birmingham. This role he later repeated in campaigns, public speeches, and behind the scenes manoeuvring, for the creation of the universities of Southampton, Reading, and Bristol, the last-named of which he became chancellor.

Apart from this work, Haldane took part in two Royal Commissions on university and higher education concerned with London and Wales, both of which he chaired, again with disputed success. Nor did he rest here. He had always been a firm supporter and lecturer for the Workers' Educational Association, and was also closely associated with the founding of the British Institute of Adult Education which in fact came into being in 1921 in his home at Queen Anne's Gate.

Haldane although an enigmatic man was a unique politician. The quality of this uniqueness is contained in his conception of theory and practice. He had certain guidelines to his work. These guidelines make his work comprehensible, in the sense that we can grasp his aims and methods. Probably the key element of this was self-consciousness. He interpreted and understood, as far as it is possible, himself and his work in terms of these principles. He acted in terms of the criteria embodied in these principles, conscious to a large extent of what he was doing and what he sought to achieve.

The main area of Haldane's activity in education was the universities. As a recent account has stated:

[Haldane's] prime educational interest was in the promotion of universities. But he wanted universities to be an integral part of a coherent system of education such as is only now, in the 1970s, beginning to develop in Britain. His vision was of a national education system with universities at the pinnacle, permeating (as he used to say) the whole education beneath them and, through adult education, beyond them.[1]

This work was coupled to his strong concern for extra-mural and university extension activity, which in point was a similar preoccupation of T. H. Green who had argued in 1877 that 'we are beginning to be made aware that if the people are to be made scholars, the scholar must go to the people, not wait for them to come to him.'[2] Green and Jowett had contributed to the pioneer work of university extension in Oxford, with an extension college attached to Balliol and at first run by Green.[3]

In 1918 Haldane had unselfishly given considerable support and advice to Fisher concerning the Education Bill. He had also argued for the creation of a University Grants Committee. Ashby and Anderson in their book maintained that Haldane's success lay 'in the foundations of our whole system of education'. Undoubtedly, the authors add, the university of London would have been reformed, civic universities would have been created, higher education would have acquired a University Grants Committee, and adult education would have flourished – 'but the style and tenor of these would . . . have been the poorer; and – equally important – all of them would have been delayed. It was Haldane who, patiently over decades, created in the public mind and among politicians a consciousness of the need for quality and balance in education.'[4]

Overall, his commitment to education was dominated by three preoccupations: firstly, a network of regional universities; secondly, educational provinces, permeated by provincial universities, from primary up to continuation classes; and thirdly, adult education. This work, considering his other activities and the opposition he encountered, met with considerable practical success. His governmental work in the Liberal party was most notably concerned with the reforms of the army, his Lord Chancellorship, and his seminal work on the machinery of government. His career, if one also takes into account his philosophical work and lifelong correspondence and friendship with men like Pringle Pattison, Bernard Bosanquet, F. H. Bradley, A. N. Whitehead and A. Einstein, stands as a phenomenal example of energy and enterprise, which not many have rivalled this century. For someone with his background it is perhaps obvious that he always tried to link educational vigour with matters of basic moral and political principle. Perhaps the most basic of these was the relationship between education and democracy.

In an interchange of letters with Asquith in January 1922, Haldane had argued that his public life had long been bound up with education. He claimed that he was still, although already in tow with the Labour party, in deep sympathy with the Liberal tradition. Yet, he added that the reforms in electoral fields could not be successful 'unless a systematic and far reaching policy of enlightening the people and developing their minds has a prominent place'.[5] He went on to argue that meetings over the country had shown a public demand for this policy. He believed that nothing short of this enlightened democracy could save any party before the electorate. This was his reason for leaving the Liberals and joining Labour, and was also part of his explanation for the Liberal decline. In his *Autobiography* he was less gentle with Liberalism; 'a new spirit' he argued 'was disclosing itself, a spirit that was moving the democracy to go beyond the old-fashioned Liberal tradition.'[6]

Asquith, somewhat irritated, replied the next day. He stated that he shared Haldane's view on the urgency of educational matters, and yet, as he put it: 'in the most friendly spirit', he took 'strong exception' to other points in the letter, for instance, that he, Asquith, did not seem to mention education in his speeches, and that Sir Donald MacClean was the only member of the Liberals who seemed to care about education.[7]

Haldane, not to be perturbed, replied with an insistent suavity: 'it is something further that I have searched for . . . something which many are now united in looking to . . . Much more is involved than a mere attempt to carry out efficiently the familiar programme for existing schools.'[8] This 'much more' Haldane relates to 'great principles' and the 'public mind', and thus we are left in the dark, as probably Asquith was.

In Haldane's mind, part of the spirit of permeation of the country by the universities was connected to this idea of the enlightened democracy. From the bottom of the society upward, he envisaged a ladder of learning. As Ashby and Anderson remark: 'he returned repeatedly in his speeches to the concept of a unified, articulated state system of education, a ladder from primary school to university, and beyond, adult education.[9]

Haldane saw education as the means by which an enlightened democracy might be produced. This particular concern was not everything to him. He admitted a range of other mental activities, for instance, religion and love of the beautiful. 'But we thought' he added, in relation to the adult education movement, 'that people whose minds were freed from the fetters of ignorance would develop these other phases more readily.'[10] This faith he wished to transmit to the Labour party; as he argued in a speech in 1921: 'I know what I would do if I were leader of the Labour movement. I would put every ordinary item of the programme in the second place . . . whatever the merits of these items, the first way to accomplish them is to educate your people.'[11] The inspired democracy was, Haldane claimed, the enlightened one.

The question remained though, of what was enlightened democracy. One of Haldane's answers was to overcome ignorance so that the masses might grasp the higher cultural interests. Another more covert reason was what Ashby and Anderson call 'his deepening conviction that democracy would not survive without an educated citizenship.'[12] The idea of democracy was becoming a positive and politically effective reality in his mind. Yet, in true style, he felt that its nascent powers needed to be guided. 'As their education and knowledge increase', Haldane stated with reference to the working people, 'they are pressing more and more each year for better social conditions and for a larger share in the fruits of industry.'[13] However democracy could not be driven. It could only be supplied with the knowledge and training which would guide it to seek its own salvation.

One of his fears was the 'collective mediocrity' which had so appalled J. S. Mill. Democracy he felt to be unduly jealous. In its early stages it tries to drag things down to a level which will not accommodate higher talents. He seemed to find a symptom of this jealously in the Labour party. Yet, connecting this problem with the idea of the civic university, he argued that 'the true remedy is to break down the class barriers by making provision for enabling the youth of eighteen to go on.'[14]

Writing the above in 1914, he had modified his views by 1928, when he stated that, education was not there 'to create class consciousness, or even merely to get rid of class consciousness'.[15] The function of education was to teach people that they had a right to get such instruction from the state as would 'free them from the depressing effect of circumstances for which they were not responsible'.[16]

His ambivalent attitude in these passages to class consciousness may be explained by his dalliance with the Labour party, which probably would not have taken kindly to the aim of education as undermining class divisions. As we have seen, Sir Henry Jones took the view that it was in its appeal to class, rather than community or the common good, that the Labour party corrupted the citizenship of the working man.

Another more explicit aim was equality of opportunity. He argued in relation to the adult education and university movement that 'the student would feel that he had been assisted towards equality with his fellow citizens, not absolute equality ... but in the sense of having something more like even chances with his fellow citizens.' This Haldane called the equal chance of self-development.[17] In a speech to the House of Lords, which his first biographer Maurice quotes at length, Haldane argued for some prophetic developments in education to enable children to have the necessary opportunities. He advocated the extension of elementary school age, the improvement and extension of secondary schools, inducement to pass to higher schools and colleges, the development of technical colleges, and the expansion of infant welfare and pre-natal care. The growth in education, Haldane envisaged as freeing the working population from the fetters of ignorance and capital.[18]

In putting his case for equality of opportunity, Haldane tended to oscillate, arguing in another speech that 'you cannot in practice give educational opportunity to all classes.'[19] Few of the children, he admitted, from the working classes, could climb the narrow ladder of learning.[20] He suggested the pragmatic solution of giving as many as possible the chance to ascend. 'Nevertheless', Haldane added, 'education must be diffused among the working class.'[21] The methods he suggested for this were vocational training, evening classes and continuation schools. His ideas seemed to be connected to those of the German theoriest Kerschensteiner.[22] Kerschensteiner's theories were directed at young workers wanting a general education with practical training. He aimed to enlist employers' and employees' sympathies to enhance industrial capacities by making more use of industrial training.

Haldane argued the point in another address, that in the quantitative extension of universities there would be a qualitative decrease in standards of work. The education of the working people, he stated 'is the new problem of the twentieth century'.[23] The solutions he put forward were extra-mural work, WEA lectures, which he acclaimed as a 'priceless experiment', and extension work. Haldane considered that if a man worked eight hours, slept eight hours, and took four hours for meals, he *still* had time for leisure activity.

This leisure, Haldane argued, 'is to furnish in the way I am suggesting to you, by that contact with the inspired teacher which introduces him to new regions, thus that man will utilise his leisure time for communing with the greatest souls the world has ever seen.'[24] In Haldane's perception these great souls were men like Hegel, Kant and Plato. This kind of idea relates back to Haldane's idealization of Scottish life, with poor, but neat homes, full of strong, healthy men and shelves of books. In one address he advocated the idea that most teachers' horizons would be extended by teaching the rugged miner, and that a more comprehensive mind may be thereby attained.[25]

There is a paradox, however, in this argument, which Ashby and Anderson noted, but perhaps not strongly enough.[26] It is encapsulated in an introductory work of 1906, where Haldane argued for the 'penetration of the mass of our people by the spirit of higher education'.[27] The question is, what kind of penetration? One important suggestion was that the people of England needed to be well led. Therefore he advocated a thorough training of our higher leaders.[28] In other words, the idea of university education was to train an intellectual elite of leaders who would benefit the whole community in some way. The working people were to be penetrated with the second best, namely, adult education and the WEA. The question was though, what was this penetration for? Haldane seemed here to play with a number of ideas: firstly, vocational training, implying that cultural higher interests cannot be of any primary use; secondly, that cultural interests, for instance the miner reading Plato, would occupy leisure time very fruitfully; and finally that one or both of these would break the fetters of ignorance. The reader is never quite clear here whether education is to be mass-based or elitist. It would seem that Haldane was aiming at something between the two but could never quite resolve it in his own mind.

The elitist implications were certainly developed in some addresses. For instance, in 1910, when addressing the university College of Wales, he stated: 'it is in the universities with their power over mind, greater in the end than the power of any government or church, that we see how the soul of the people at its highest mirrors itself.'[29] The university is envisaged as the brain of the state and the soul of the people. It was the measure for Haldane of civilization and the health of the organic state. If the selection is limited qualitatively and quantitatively this implies a strong elitist notion relying on intellect, which is a strange bedfellow for democratic mass education.

There are two arguments that Haldane utilized, at different points, to justify the unity of these elements. The first is of explicit Idealist origin, which in F. H. Bradley's phrase, is bound up with accepting one's station and duties. The second is more ambiguous and relates to economics and industry.

In the first, the background lies with the assumption that each individual has some capacities and powers. It is the duty of the state to enable the man to fulfil his latent abilities and powers, and this constitutes his self-development. Yet this process can involve hardship and difficulty. Haldane utilized Bosanquet's idea of 'soul-moulding' to explain this. It is constituted by an acceptance and struggle with contingency in one's particular station.[30] This process of accepting one's station and duties and making the best of it, he described in another speech, as finding the infinite in the finite. It is a characteristic Hegelian idea, which Haldane saw as being aware 'of the immanence of the divine in the humblest and saddest consciousness', that is to say, that every particle of life is saturated with spirit, the idea, or *Geist,* and to gain a wider view, is to grasp this universal in the particular job, role or station.[31]

Thus, Haldane's conclusion was that those who do not qualify for the elite or universities ought to be satisfied if they are in work which matches their abilities, as long as they have had the chance for some educational advance. Haldane thought that whatever level one reached in society 'the mind that is really free is the mind that chooses to submit itself to toil and discipline'.[32] For Haldane, this was the substance of self-development. It was also the source of chaffing letters from G. B. Shaw, and charges of hypocrisy from Mrs Webb.[33]

Haldane's second argument, like the first, can be said to be a mystificatory appeal for the status quo, with the qualification of a more open and intellectually-based elite. The basis of the argument was Haldane's assumption that the old days of the capitalist versus wage earner were over. 'Today', Haldane confidently asserted in an Eighty Club dinner of 1913, 'anyone can get as much capital as he likes if only he is a great organiser.'[34] Yet the basis of this development is first, to develop the scientific potential in industry, and second, to raise the general educational standard of the workforce. The more academic scientific knowledge enters the industrial field, and the more intelligent the work-force, the more competitive the industry will be. As he stated in another lecture: 'An enlightened policy in education is the order of the day . . . and if we are to hold our own, even in the making of money, we dare not fall behind or lag.'[35]

The focus of the argument has changed in this economic idea. The purpose of education was to create an elite of scientific advisers, and an intelligent work-force capable of more complex tasks, who might also strive, if they should have the wherewithal, after capital themselves. The linking concept here is effective competition and industrial potential. The purpose of education thus appealed to the national emolument.

Haldane's strongest statement of this position is in his *Education and Empire*, where he described the commercial position of the nation and empire as a 'sacred trust'.[36] Yet he coupled this defence of 'the application of science to the training of our captains of industry' with the idea of culture pursued as an end in itself.[37] Thus he envisaged a 'double function' for education in the enlightened democracy.[38] The German Technische Hochschule, or in Haldane's terms the London Charlottenberg for scientific research in relation to industry, was to be matched by the continued study of the humanities for their own sake. The problem with Haldane's double function is again a paradox concerning the ends of education. The principle tries to unite a utility-based view of education with an 'education for its own sake' view. This may well be possible, but apart from commending it, he did not adequately explain how it would come about. He clearly admired the German system of Gymnasium to university, and Realschule to technical institution, yet in another paper in 1916 he complained of the division between the humanities and the sciences.[39] His main point was to argue that all knowledge is eventually one. If you study literature of history, it should give a sufficiently wide outlook and intellectual curiosity to investigate the sciences as part of the spirit of knowledge and humanity. All ideas if pursued deeply enough, again in the Hegelian dialectical mode, take the enquirer beyond them. This is a very important point. The Idealists tended to stress the importance of general education rather than narrow technical learning and this of course has had important, indeed some would argue disastrous effects on the British administrative system. The aim should not just be to train experts, but to enable the personality 'to make the best of itself.'

However this does not solve the problem. Are scientists and industrialists likely to see consistently beyond their own subject? The sciences are divided into various disciplines. Are scientists or industrialists likely to study the other parts of their own profession or subject, let alone its wider humanistic implication? The same holds true for those working in the humanities.

Haldane does unfortunately throw hostages to fortune. At one point he speaks of the British workman as the industrial unit who needs to be kept healthy and efficient for the sake of the industrial organism. This was part and parcel of the wider campaign for national efficiency. In this sense, the elementary school aimed to produce the minimally efficient workman. The secondary school produced a class of well-educated citizens. The university, as the handmaid of the state and the pool of talent, produced the intellectual elite. Yet this elite would have divided ideals of education, for example between the scientific and humanistic. Also how would the lower echelons of this educational order be supposed to acquire the broader, more reflective outlook, which is presumably the province of universities, if all they are trained for is to be efficient industrial units?

Part of Haldane's optimism for education stretched to the solution of certain basic divisions in society. In this he followed Green who in his lecture on 'The Work to be Done by the New Oxford High School for Boys' (in the third volume of his collected works) argued that education was the great social healer, that those who experienced a common education would, despite their different social circumstances, have a sense of fraternity with one another. They would be free from social jealousies and animosities however different their circumstances in life might be. Green saw that a common education could be a great vehicle for the growth of equality in citizenship, an equality which was at that time absent because the school system itself encouraged social exclusiveness and created 'new divisions'.

The aim of a common basic education was, as Green argued (p. 476), in his lecture: 'As it was the inspiration of Moses that all the Lord's people should be prophets, so with all seriousness and reverence we may hope and pray for a condition of English society in which all honest citizens will recognise themselves and be recognised by each other as gentleman.' Haldane felt that following this lead education would solve, for example, the divisions between labour and capital. Haldane called in one address for the 'national mind' – a mind which would unite knowledge, science and productive co-operation.[40] This he thought required a reflective habit of mind. Yet again, who had this habit? The reflective habit, Haldane described at one point, as a process of mental development and moral discipline, a harmony of character and intellect. What school or even WEA lecture gave this kind of training?

These questions remain unresolved in Haldane's arguments. He was conscious of the difficulties of an enlightened democracy, yet it was possible, as his sister stated in her autobiography, that 'despite all we said on platforms, we were not "of the people", nor did we truly understand their needs. We were in great measure Whigs still and we enjoyed the pleasant atmosphere of Whig society.'[41] This kind of implication seems to pervade many of Haldane's writings and correspondence. It was this kind of optimism which allowed him to say of social problems that 'these things solve themselves if only you get the right spirit into your people.'[42]

Beatrice Webb in *Our Partnership* described ironically Haldane's conversion to collectivism as 'vaguely metaphysical'. She stated that one could spend hours dinning the right side of the question into him, yet he held her off with retorts of how narrow she was, and 'that it was impossible for the cultivated representative to do more than grasp certain large principles.'[43]

Oddly enough, Haldane complained of a similar point with the Webbs in a *Contemporary Review* article in 1890. 'Mr Webb' he stated 'and his colleagues in the Fabian society are philosophers . . . They illustrate the advantages and disadvantages of that much abused article – the abstract mind in politics.'[44] The theory which he claimed they adhered to, and which to Haldane constituted their 'ideal', was collectivism. He continued in the article to argue that this theory or ideal could not be imposed at one stroke. A great many changes in institutions, opinions and motives must precede it. The method he wished to advocate was that of inclining the people towards collectivism.[45]

The actual sources of Haldane's mild collectivism do not lie in Karl Marx or Sidney Webb. The underpinning for his theory he discussed in a *Progressive Review* article in 1896. The argument, in sum, was that the older Liberal questions of franchise and disestablishment were no longer viable as policies. The new situation was the 'social question'. Liberals were moving into fields of progressive thought, for example the relations of capital and labour and municipalization. This he described as a changed attitude of the 'time spirit'. The key architect of this change who 'expressed the necessities of our generation in the matter of social progress better than any one else' was to Haldane, T. H. Green. Haldane made particular reference to Green's 'Freedom of Contract' lecture.[46]

After quoting a long passage from Green's lecture, Haldane argued that Green's language 'may be taken as defining generally the aim and tendency of the party which looks as much to distribution as to production, and which claims that only so can the Liberalism of today be true to its mission.'[47] The impact of this language, he felt, had not been fully grasped by the Liberal party.

The same point was made by his sister in a wider context. To her, the mid-1880s signified a time of great hope. The intellectual side of this was dominated, she argued, by T. H. Green and Arnold Toynbee, who provided an outlook not only satisfying to reason but also encouraging to those who wished to give practical help. She added that 'this movement which was founded on the Idealist philosophy dominated by Hegel, influenced us greatly.'[48]

Thus the basis of Haldane's collectivism was Idealistic philosophy, fundamentally in the style of T. H. Green. Haldane's concern was to change or incline the people towards this collectivism, but not to impose it. In a speech to the Eighty Club in 1892 he argued that collectivism was gradually taking root.[49] The desire to vindicate the claims of labour to a larger share in the produce of industry he saw as developing a sense of the public interest. Municipalization ought to be encouraged and Liberals should identify themselves far more with the labour movement.

It was during the 1890s that Haldane seriously took up his championship of education. It is possible to say that his increasing emphasis on educational matters, as opposed to his dalliance with Fabian collectivism was a result of his realization that his form of mild collectivism could be far more effectively brought about by education. The 'educative state' was a means to the self-development and active citizenship of its members.

J. H. Muirhead, a contemporary of Haldane, wrote of him:

once having mastered the principles of Hegel's philosophy in a way that few of the younger men had done, he devoted himself to the consistent application of what he conceived to be true in them to the main problems of life . . . From his own multifarious experience he was, thus, able to return to philosophy, as he was constantly doing in lectures and books, to illuminate his text from departments of activity for the most part unfamiliar to his audience or his readers.

Muirhead added that he had not known 'any philosopher belonging to . . . the second generation of British Idealists who used with greater effect, what he found in the teaching of Hegel and Goethe.'[50]

9 Citizenship, Human Nature and the State

It is false to maintain that the foundation of the state is something at the option of all its members. It is nearer the truth to say that it is absolutely necessary for every individual to be a citizen.

Hegel

Anyone who has the idea of transforming society by political action must in consistency have in mind an order of priority among human activities and therefore a specific norm or standard of human excellence.

S. N. Hampshire

In this book we have tried to depict the Idealist political vision of citizenship and we have looked at it at a number of levels: its source in T. H. Green's securalized Pauline moral thinking, its philosophical underpinning, and the practical forms in which it manifested itself. However, we began the study with the question of whether we need a theory of citizenship and the state, in the sense of a theory which would connect political institutions with some account of human capacities and powers. We noted that modern political science has to a great extent displaced the ideas of both citizenship and the state. Having looked at the Idealist arguments in some detail we are now in a position to look more clearly at these questions and to seek some appraisal from our own standpoint of the Idealist position.

As we have seen, a theory of citizenship of the sort that Green, or for that matter Plato, Aristotle, Kant and Hegel advanced, would seek to connect an understanding of political life, action and experience with a conception of man, his needs, capacities and powers, in an attempt to throw mutual light on each and to provide some concrete detail for the worn platitude that man is a political animal.

In what sense is this true? Are political institutions purely instrumental, mechanical devices for settling conflicts of interest, for making sure that as many people as possible get as much as possible of whatever it is they want, and removing discontent. Or does politics have more of an expressive and moral character – that in political life and activity certain important capacities and moral relations between persons are realized, capacities and relations which atrophy and die in the absence of certain sorts of political institutions. Theories of this latter sort have been under considerable attack for the past 40 or 50 years. As *normative* theories, seeking to advance a view of human capacities and relations, and of the institutions which would embody them, trying in effect to specify the nature of the good life, they have suffered from the growth and pervasive influence of empiricism in intellectual life; as *idealistic* theories they have suffered from what is thought to be a more 'realistic' view of politics as exemplified in the quotation from Buchanan at the opening of chapter 1.

Views of citizenship, the individual and the state which connect political life with moral notions like human capacities, self-respect, interdependence and mutual obligation, and which see will and voluntary commitment at the basis of the state, are going to be classified as metaphysical. We have no obvious way of giving an operational definition to the concepts involved, and we have no way of verifying, or more appropriately, falsifying, theories which involve these concepts. Such theories could not be part of a political science which seeks to be empirical and behavioural. Not only are such theories unfalsifiable, and therefore metaphysical, it is not clear even on what basis they could be advanced. While metaphysical argument has made something of a comeback in philosophy generally, it has not yet been made clear how recent developments in metaphysics are going to help in the formulation of a foundation for theories of human nature and conceptions of political life. We may have moved some way from the 1930s, and some of the crudities of the positivist analyses of both metaphysical and moral argument have died away, but nevertheless fully developed metaphysical theories of politics are still rare. Those which do exist, for example, Rawls' *A Theory of Justice*, and Nozick's *Anarchy State and Utopia*, leave the individual's relation to the state obscure, as in Rawls, or neglect the metaphysical basis of the theory, as in Nozick.

The problem has not just been that of positivism in philosophy, but of more general and deep-rooted issues, both in society and within social and political science. We need to explore some of these issues before it becomes profitable to consider whether the political theory of Idealists such as Green, Bosanquet, Caird, and others, can offer anything complementary and enhancing to contemporary political understanding.

Any conception of citizenship is going to be developed against a background of other notions such as community, common good, common interest, and welfare. However, it is precisely these notions which have become increasingly problematic over the last century or so. Clearly concepts of this sort, in order to be operative, have to assume some value consensus. They draw upon and express assumptions about what is common to citizens, in terms of their values, interests, needs, and in the case of community, attitudes towards one another. However, it is just these assumptions that have become increasingly problematic. The growth of secularization, decline in religion, urbanization and ethnic diversity, have all led to an increasing moral diversity – a diversity which must and has affected the ways in which people think about their own nature, their needs, wants and interests. Thus ideas such as the common good have become much more difficult to define, in contrast to a situation in which there would be much more moral and cultural homogeneity. Indeed, the point is driven home very clearly in Idealist attempts to advance a philosophical theory of the common good as a basis for citizenship. If the establishment of the common good requires elaborate metaphysical argument, the critic might say, does this not show that the idea is at best practically problematic, at the worst totally irrelevant?[1] Where the concept is useful and operative, citizens see their needs and interests in the same way, they do not need the direction of metaphysical argument to come to an understanding of the basis of their common life.

So too with community. The concept of community has been a central intellectual and practical problem within the liberal tradition. The liberal tradition has its origin in the critique of traditional communities, and has not known really what to do with the concept since.[2] A tradition of voluntaristic individualism can certainly make sense of partial communities which individuals with similar interests may join voluntarily, but such partial communities may well be incompatible with one another, and there is no guarantee that a society composed of voluntaristic partial communities is going to have the basis of a common life. On the other hand, the idea of an overall political community seems equally problematic given the diversity of goals and interests in modern society. A sense of overall community would seem to require an overall agreement on goals and interests which seems absent in liberal society; alternatively, it would seem to require the imposition of a set of goals, which is incompatible with the central voluntaristic presuppositions of liberal society. We lack a rich conception of political community, and with it a sense of membership and citizenship, and therefore of the way in which the state could embody the moral purpose of the community. An appeal to community is beguiling, but seems to be wholly indefinite.

The problem in trying to understand and provide an account of concepts which seek to capture the sense of sharing a common political life and identity have also been exacerbated by the growth of mass society and with it mass democracy. Obviously a notion of citizenship is going to be much easier to handle in a small homogeneous society than in a large mass society in which all citizens have political rights and aspirations, but may equally represent radically divergent needs and interests. The Idealists thought that the sense of common life could only be made clear and articulate by metaphysical argument; not, as the critic would have it, a remote and abstract argument, but rather one which would develop and render explicit conceptions and values which in fact were to be seen *as part of ordinary everyday consciousness*. This was a consciousness however, which, as Green argues without equivocation in the *Prolegomena to Ethics,* was not fully explicit:

It may thus fall to the moral philosopher, under certain conditions of society and intellectual movement, to render an important practical service. But he will render it simply by fulfilling with utmost completeness his proper work of analysis. As a *moral* philosopher he analyses human conduct; the motives which it exposes, the spiritual endowments implied in it, the history of thought, habits and institutions through which it has come to be what it is. He does not understand his business as a philosopher if he claims to do more than this.[3]

Philosophy makes explicit and rational what is implicit and unconceptualized in actual moral endeavour.

At the same time, normative theories of citizenship have to face another range of objections, those posed by various 'realist' theories of politics which would deny both the need for and possibility of such a theory. In this context we can perhaps distinguish several different stands of argument and analysis. Elite theorists such as Pareto and Mosca, and those who have followed them, argue that a view of politics which gives a central role to citizenship is in fact illusory.[4] Political power in any society will always be exercised by an elite, and at the very best the involvement of the citizen is limited to choosing between competing elites, on political agendas drawn up by the elites and on goals determined by them. Notions such as common good, social justice, welfare and community are a tissue of consoling illusions through which the real exercise of political power is disguised. The idea that in the final analysis the relationship between the state and the citizen is a moral one, to be justified by an appeal to moral principles and constrained by those principles is hopelessly idealistic. The power of the state is the central and unavoidable fact of politics, and the idea that will and not force is the basis of political relationships, that it is will which gives the exercise of state authority its legitimacy, is an idealistic illusion which an empirical treatment of politics will reveal is out of place. It is part of the success of the neo-Machiavellian view of politics that we no longer find such a view offensive or shocking and this illustrates the depth of the problem facing idealist theory in gaining a foothold in contemporary political thinking.

A similar argument is deployed by Marxists. The idea that a sense of legitimacy can be given to the modern state by an appeal to moral argument is just a form of bourgeois moralism. In a capitalist society the state ultimately represents class interests: the interests of those who own the means of production. Of course, in the Marxist view of the state, those who exercise power will seek to foster the view that the state is a moral entity acting in accordance with a range of moral principles such as justice, welfare, democratic legitimation and so forth, to disguise its fundamental class character. This argument was most elegantly advanced by Richard Crossman in his essay 'The Theory and Practice of British Freedom', in *Planning for Freedom: Essays in Socialism*: 'Their concept of the state as an instrument of positive good is the concept of a new ruling class, whose sense of moral responsibility, unlike that of the aristocracy demands a philosophic justification of their new power.'[5]

A Marxist will see the ideological importance of the appeal to moral principles in a class society: only by the permeation of society by such a consciousness of its legitimacy will such a state be able to secure its power to act without provoking dissent and crisis, but such conceptions embedded in the consciousness of citizens are forms of *false* consciousness. Such forms of false consciousness inhibit the development of *class* consciousness, and thus the appearance of a socialist society in which for the first time in human history human beings will be able to be fully self-determining, although not technically as *citizens* because the state, the necessary correlate of citizenship will wither away. Again we find the awareness of the importance of the state having the appearance of a moral entity, and citizens of having a sense that they stand in a principled relationship with political authority, but at the same time the view that such a sense is fundamentally illusory and that a necessary condition of human liberation consists in breaking through the bonds of this illusion. This again is a central form of political 'realism' in the modern world which would see an Idealist conception of politics as not merely false but as ideological, as fostering a view of the nature of politics which renders the future advancement of human freedom more difficult.

A more modern view, but one which nevertheless has a central role in modern political understanding, tends to neglect the state and its direct relationship with the citizen, concentrating rather on intermediate groups and their role in the political processes of deliberation and decision. Pluralism in the hands of writers such as Dahl and Polsby has developed no real theory of citizenship and the state. Studies of the individual's relationship to interest groups abound, and there are many sophisticated studies of the ways in which groups gain access to decision-making and affect decisions, but there is no clearly articulated theory of the state, and in consequence no developed account of citizenship. Of course, Idealists were very interested in group activity and can lay some claim to being a major historical influence upon the development of pluralist political theory, but they were convinced that any theory of group activity in politics should relate to the important parameters of the individual citizen, his capacities and powers on the one hand and the state and the principles on which its relationship with individuals and groups should be conducted on the other. It is just this comprehensive framework in modern pluralism which is lacking and, of course, part of the reason for this is obvious: pluralism is one of the straight outgrowths of an empirical, behavioural approach to politics. Any comprehensive theory of the type sought by Idealists would have to make metaphysical and moral assumptions which are incompatible with the behaviourist methodology which has given pluralism such a central place in modern political science. In addition, such a methodology has to be concerned with the articulated interests of individuals and groups, and it must study how the decision-making system is influenced or fails to be influenced by them. This in turn yields a wholly interest-based view of political activity. Interests are advanced and defended, decisions are made and conflicts of interest are adjudicated, but there is no conception at all that politics may have a less instrumental role in human life, that the world of politics may constitute a world within which certain distinctively human capacities and moral powers might be realized and expressed.

Such wholly instrumentalist views of politics go hand in hand with behaviourism just because such a view rules out of court any appeal to moral or metaphysical arguments. Nevertheless, it is extremely important to realize how this effectively closes off a whole tradition of looking at politics, going back to Aristotle and Plato, coming through Rousseau, Hegel and the Idealists, to Hannah Arendt and Charles Taylor.

A further illustration of this is the tendency to utilize economic theory in the understanding of politics. The temptation to use economic techniques is obvious, or at least is thought to be. Economics is by far the most developed social science and the one which appears to conform most clearly to a recognizably scientific paradigm. However, here again it is important to see how far the introduction of such models into political science forecloses certain kinds of ways of both studying politics and characterizing the world of politics; ways of understanding politics which include the Idealist tradition. In *An Economic Theory of Democracy*[6] by A. Downs, or *The Calculus of Consent*[7] by Buchanan and Tullock, we find a theory which claims to be a form of scientific realism, and of course it yields a wholly instrumental view of politics. It assumes that the only possible basis for men to form a political community is rational self-interest. But we need to make a central point, namely that this is a pseudo-realism, as notions of the individual, of rational economic man, of preferences, are not derived in some uninterpreted manner from palpable observation. These notions involve considerable metaphysical constructions and indeed constructions which, when applied to politics, rule out alternative conceptions in the light of this misplaced scientific realism.

The other major challenge to a constructive theory of citizenship such as the Idealists wished to advocate is posed in the growing disillusion over the past few years with interventionist government and a desire, given theoretical articulation in the work of thinkers such as Hayek and Nozick to restrict the function of government. These last two thinkers, see the state as having a general umpiring role, rather than being an institutional structure serving certain central moral values. This neo-liberal position leaves very little room for a rich notion of citizenship. The duty of the citizen is to observe the general rules of the game – the game being the pursuit of their own particular purposes and interests, and to observe the rights of others to pursue their own good in their own way. Citizenship is defined in terms of forbearance – in not interfering with the rights of others, rather than in actively participating in the realizing of certain communal values through political activity and political institutions.

The Idealists' theory of politics thus faces intellectual and social obstacles which go very deep into our culture and colour our view of the nature of science and politics. At the least an understanding of such a theory and its subsequent elaboration in detail would provide us with an alternative view with which to compare more modern views which, as we have seen, place the emphasis upon 'realism' and a much more modest view about the nature of man and the purposes of politics.

The Idealist theory of human nature on which their concept of citizenship rests is normative in at least two respects. In the first place the conception of human nature in question is used as a moral standard to criticize or to endorse the nature of actual states and the quality of citizenship to be found within them; secondly the conception of human nature is itself normative in the sense that it involves some grading or ordering of human powers and capacities. This point of course is clear from Green's talk about the best of oneself and Bosanquet's idea of 'the real will'. The theory is also thought to be problematic in the sense that views of human nature, as normative are thought to be 'essentially contestable' and therefore not really capable of bearing the moral weight which is being placed upon them. Normative theories of human nature cannot be verified and are not amenable to scientific treatment; therefore they have lost their place in liberal–democratic theory which must be relevant to a culture so marked by scientific success and scientific procedure.

This kind of criticism is likely to lead in the direction of what we have called 'negative' citizenship; that is to say that, since we are no longer confident in the rational basis of conceptions of human nature and accounts of central human purposes and needs, we should reject the view that the state has any specific purposes to fulfil, in favour of the view that its job is to secure a framework of law and rules of order within which individuals with their own and widely different purposes may pursue their own ends in their own way. As Dworkin argues, one central strand in liberal political theory

supposes that political decisions must be so far as possible, independent of any particular conception of the good life, of what gives gives value to life. Since the citizens of a society differ in their conceptions the government does not treat them as equals if it prefers one conception to another.[8]

Such a state, if in fact we wish to use the term,[9] will be nomocratic rather than telocratic, and the duty of citizens will not be the attempt to make the best of themselves through the pursuit of a common good, but rather to be attentive to the need to maintain the legal framework which secures the space for them to realize their private, non-civic selves. Such accounts of the nature of liberal democratic citizenship are now popular and influential, and are to be found in many recent works of political theory, explicitly in Hayek's *Law, Legislation and Liberty* (Vols I–III); in Nozick's, *Anarchy, State and Utopia*; in Oakshott's *On Human Conduct*; and in De Jouvenal's *On Power*. It also finds expression, although in a complex form in Rawls' *A Theory of Justice*. Such works endorse a negative view of citizenship and a limited or minimal role for the state.

However, it would be quite wrong to draw a clear line between these works and those of the Idealists in terms of the overall metaphysical assumptions which they make. It is clearly the case that Hayek, Nozick, Rawls, and other thinkers, in the same kind of tradition as, for example, Buchanan and Tullock develop their accounts of negative citizenship and the state utilizing various assumptions about human nature and capacities. These may be, as in Hayek, assumptions about human cognitive capacities; in Nozick, assumptions about human beings as right holders; in Buchanan and Tullock, assumptions about maximizing; and in Rawls, limitations on altruism and a propensity for rational maximizing and, more controversely, an aversion to risk.[10] All of those thinkers are able to develop very rich, detailed and plausible political theories from their accounts of human nature – but the fact is that they are utilizing assumptions about human nature, and these assumptions are either normative in themselves or have very strong normative implications. As such they are on all fours with Idealist theories. So if we are willing within modern political theory to take the work of say, Rawls, Nozick, and Hayek seriously, then it cannot be the case that their claim to serious consideration lies in their refusal to tie the nature of the state to central human capacities and powers, as the Idealists clearly and explicitly did. On the contrary, modern analytical philosophers do exactly the same thing but because their assumptions about human nature and human cognitive capacities are more limited, their conceptions of citizenship and the state are also limited.

Consequently it is far too bland to think that because we seem to lack any clear way of resolving arguments about human nature we are compelled into a nomocratic rather than telocratic theory of the state, and a negative rather than an active view of citizenship. Those theories which underpin negative theories of citizenship also make assumptions about human nature and the limits of human capacities.

If this is so, then it is natural to turn attention to the kinds of arguments which might be thought to be able to underpin accounts of human nature. Here we face the problem that in Anglo-Saxon philosophy, at least since the decline of Idealism after the First World War, the general tendency in moral philosophy has been towards one or another version of non-cognitivism. Despite their intentions, intuitionist theories *in effect,* are very little different from emotivism and decisionism, in the sense that intuitionists were not able to provide a rational procedure for arbitrating clashes of intuition, and emotivists such as A. J. Ayer and C. Stevenson, and decisionists such as R. M. Hare are explicit in acknowledging that there are, at the end of the day, no rational ways of settling moral disputes. Granted that disputes about human nature, involving as they do questions about grading and ordering human capacities, are normative disputes, then it would seem that we lack a procedure for deciding rationally about the nature of man and his capacities, and thus the character of citizenship and the nature of the state.

However, there is an interesting reflexivity at work here. It has been pointed out, particularly by Iris Murdoch and Alasdair MacIntyre,[11] that moral theories of the non-cognitivist sort themselves embody assumptions about the nature of man, and more obliquely about the sort of society in which we live. The view of man which, as it were, 'lurks behind' emotivism and prescriptivism is one which sees human nature more in terms of action rather than contemplation, of choice rather than deliberation, and commitment rather than adherence to commonly accepted standards. Iris Murdoch, for example, argues that this conception of human nature is to be found in *Thought and Action*[12] by Stuart Hampshire. Hampshire takes the view that theories of human nature are essentially contestable as part of an argument which, if Murdoch is correct, rests upon a particular view of human nature. In the same way as political philosophers such as Hayek and Nozick need 'a theory of the state to overcome the theory of the state', so non-cognitivist moral philosophers presuppose a theory of human nature as part of an argument designed to show that conceptions of human nature have no ultimate cognitive defence. In MacIntyre's view the concept of man presupposed by non-cognitivist moral philosophy has a wider importance in that it is itself a reflection of the collapse of generally agreed communal moral standards. As we shall see, this argument is important and will re-emerge.

If modern moral philosophy is enmeshed in reflexivity in its thinking about human nature, it is tempting to try to put arguments into a wider perspective and to take the view that it is not to moral philosophy as such that we should look for arguments about human nature, but to metaphysics. It is in metaphysical theories that we shall find the basis for both an understanding of morality and an account of human nature. Certainly, those who have taken the view that theories of human nature are essentially contestable have usually argued that conceptions of human capacities are part of a general metaphysical perspective, and draw what support and plausibility they may have from that overall perspective. Certainly, in the case of the Idealists this is true. Green's account of human powers is part of a general metaphysical theory deployed in the *Prolegomena to Ethics* and most of the Idealists followed Green in writing metaphysical works, against the background of which their theories about human nature and politics are developed. Indeed some of the disputes between the Idealists about the fundamental nature of man are disputes at a very high metaphysical level – as for example between Bosanquet and Andrew Seth over the nature of human individuality. It is therefore plausible to suggest that in seeking to appraise Idealist political philosophy we have ultimately to take into account the validity of their metaphysical writings.

If Idealist politics are a deduction from their metaphysics then clearly the plausibility of their political views are going to depend upon the validity and truth of metaphysical writings of this sort. However there is a difficulty here which parallels the difficulty which appeared in the discussion of moral theory. It is certainly true that even those who in the heyday of positivism regarded metaphysics as nonsense would now retract this view. Ayer, for example, in *Metaphysics and Commonsense*[13] argues that metaphysical theories are rather like policies, rather than attempts at an objective depiction of the nature of what there is from some kind of Archimedian stand-point. The difficulty with such a seemingly tolerant view is that we have no independent criteria for assessing policies. We cannot appeal to the nature of reality to 'see' whether a particular metaphysical 'policy' depicts that reality correctly, because what counts as part of reality is determined by the 'policy'. To assume that we can appeal independently to the nature of the world itself assumes that the policy account is false. On the other hand we could take the view popularized by Strawson and say that metaphysics should attempt to describe the conceptual framework which we actually have. This presumably gives us an objective basis on which to arbitrate between moral metaphysical theories. However, such a view has difficulties of its own – is there any *one* metaphysical theory which can account for the concepts which we actually employ? And what of the status of revisionary metaphysics – the attempt to suggest a different conceptual framework – which equally fits the case of Idealism? Strawson[14] acknowledges the importance of revisionary metaphysics, but we are left unclear why it is important, other than as an exercise in human imaginative and constructive powers, and in terms of what criteria we could rank rival revisionary metaphysical frameworks. So again there seems to be very little chance of appealing to metaphysical argument as some kind of independent 'bed rock' for assessing the validity of rival conceptions of human nature and thus of politics.

This protracted excursion into metaphilosophy has been an attempt to show that there is nothing in the nature of modern philosophical thinking to allow us to rule out the Idealist political thought as mistaken in principle. We may lack adequate philosophical resources to render a final reckoning of its validity, but there is nothing to preclude the legitimacy of this kind of enterprise. If we liken metaphysical argument less to mathematics or science and more to literature and poetry,[15] then we may cease to regret the fact that we lack the resources to give the philosophical vision a *final* appraisal. It is part of the human situation and predicament that we should be unable finally to arbitrate between different conceptions of human nature and politics. This does not mean, however, that we should abandon such theories because, as we hope to have shown, even those who seek to do so become entangled in assumptions which the limitations of their theories make illegitimate. Nor does it mean that we are wholly devoid of canons of criticism any more than we are in the case of poetry and literature. If we accept Hampshire's view that: 'The nature of the human mind has to be investigated in the history of the successive forms of its social expression; the greater the historical sense of variety, the more adequate the philosophy will be.'[16] This may give us some clue to the way in which Idealist political theory may be criticized. Are there large features of our social and political experience which we regard as central and important which Idealism ignores?

This may seem on the face of it to be an overly sociological and historical way of appraising philosophical argument. However, there are two replies which can be made to such a criticism. In the first place, if there is more in common between metaphysical arguments about the nature of man and poetry and literature than there is between such arguments and science and mathematics, then we can hardly avoid judging them finally in terms such as, 'Does such a conception of human nature and politics speak to our condition?', while realizing of course that there would be some disagreement about what our condition is. Secondly, such a mode of sociological and historical appraisal seems particularly appropriate for the Idealists. Hegel, in his great works on the relationship between the human mind and its social and political embodiments, argued that: 'The Ego is by itself only a formal identity. Consciousness appears differently modified according to the difference of the given object and the gradual specification of consciousness appears as a variation in the characteristics of its objects.'[17]

While Green in a similar vein argued a similar case: 'The divine mind touches, modifies, becomes the mind of man, through a process which mere intellectual conception is the beginning but of which the gradual complement is an unexhausted series of spiritual disciplines through all the agencies of social life.'[18] Because Green specifies the human good and the realization of definitive human powers in terms of forms of social life – because the good cannot just be a good for individuals it follows that the relevance of Green's thought for our own social life is of crucial importance to the overall coherence of his theory.

In pursuing this line of appraisal we shall be concerned with a number of closely connected issues – citizenship and social class, citizenship and the market, morality and the community. Although they are interrelated we shall attempt to disentangle these various threads in criticism.

As we have seen, it has often been argued that the Idealist view of citizenship neglects the reality of class relationships. Moreover, it is sometimes seen as part of the ideology of Liberal capitalist thought which seeks to disguise class relations by means of securing a sense of legitimacy to the Government through the dissemination of a notion of citizenship based upon a common good which in fact is illusory in a class society. The civic idealism of Green and others becomes therefore a form of false consciousness, but one which fulfils an important ideological function. Perhaps the basis of this argument has been developed most trenchantly by C. B. Macpherson in *Democratic Theory*:

T. H. Green rejected possessive individualism but, unwilling or unable to see what it was that made it untenable (i.e. the appearance of the possibility of a class based social democracy), went to the concept of the Greek city state for a pattern. The tendency of Idealism as a whole was to disguise from itself, and so divert attention from the class basis of political problems. The Idealists' concept of the state as a moral idea rather than a Benthamite mechanism appears as the crowning concept of a chain of thought starting from a moral rejection of class conflict and class political action arguing that the frustration of humanity was due to faulty political concepts, and finding the remedy in instilling into the political structure a more rounded concept of the state which would recognise and embrace the claims of society as well as the individual.[19]

It is certainly difficult to disagree with the central point here. The Idealists did reject class conflict and class politics. This can be seen in their theoretical writings and, as we have seen, in the assumptions behind their approach to the settlement movement and the development of education, both of which were seen as solvents of class antagonism. The whole argument can be seen very clearly in Sir Henry Jones's critique of the Labour party's class appeal in his article 'The Corruption of the Citizenship of the Working Man'. It is then not surprising that Marxists should make this claim about the British Idealists when in essence the same point had been made by Marx against Hegel, among others, in his essay 'On The Jewish Question'. The problem is, as we have seen, that the Idealists wished to stress a conception of human nature and citizenship which made a great deal of man as a developer of his capacities and powers, as against the Benthamite form of utilitarianism which stressed man's role as a consumer of utilities, a rational maximizer. At the same time they endorsed the operation of the market, with the inequalities to which that would lead and the ownership of private property and the right of accumulation. At the most, their welfare proposals were attempts to ensure that those who were disadvantaged would be able to act more effectively in the market.

The Idealist reply to a criticism such as that of Macpherson would be on several grounds. In the first place they would in fact reject the view that the economic market should be seen wholly in terms of competition and the destruction of a sense of community and fellowship. While Macpherson, and Marxists generally see the market as being characterized by possessive individualism, which is incompatible with the realization of the human powers and capacities that Idealists wished to see flourishing, those Idealists who wrote about the market tended to try to revise the understanding of it. They tried to show that, despite the motives which go into the operation of the market, nevertheless the market does lay down forms of mutual interdependence, and its differentiation of function does lead to differential but complementary and harmonious realization of a range of human capacities. In this the Idealists followed Hegel's lead in *The Philosophy of Right*. Hegel, as he sees it, seeks to do full justice to the individualism of the market, while at the same time arguing that the market and the social classes involved in economic production involve mutual interdependence, and lead to the harmonious development of human powers and social solidarity between classes.[20] On this view the market, far from being incompatible with the realization of those 'higher' powers of human kind which Idealists wished to see realized, is in fact a necessary, irreversible form of progress towards both the realization of human powers and of the common good between individuals. The market is not wholly 'lost to particularity' and lost to morality: as Hegel argues in *The Phenomenology of Spirit*:

The labour of the individual for his own wants is just as much a satisfaction of those of others as of himself, and the satisfaction of his own he attains only by the labour of others. . . . As the individual in his individual work already unconsciously performs a universal task, so again he also performs the universal work as his conscious object; the whole becomes, as a whole his own work, for which he sacrifices himself and precisely in so doing he receives back from it his own self.[21]

and in *The Philosophy of Right* the point is made more generally:

. . . by a dialectical advance self-seeking turns into the mediation of the particular through the Universal, with the result that each man is earning, providing and enjoying on his own account in *eo ipso* producing and earning for the enjoyment of everyone else.[22]

Drawing upon this kind of perspective, as Sir Henry Jones argued, the system of economic life was misconceived as 'a realm of otherness'. The market does have an ethical spirit realizing individual powers and also a form of solidarity. This second part is taken up by MacCunn in his essay on 'Fraternity' in *Ethics and Citizenship*. As he says in a revealing passage:

Be our sentiments what they may, even if there be no sentiment at all, the relation of man to man is not hostility but mutual serviceability . . . The true influence lies in the words of George Eliot 'I have more need of him because his treasure differs from mine.'[23]

However, this passage shows the difficulty in this attempt to show that the market is not necessarily pervaded by possessive individualist values. It makes a sense of community or fraternity depend upon the upshot of activity undertaken for another purpose and not on sentiments of fraternity. I seek to maximize my utilities and in so doing I became implicated in a scheme of co-operation and mutual interdependence; when I realize this I understand that the market realizes communal values. However, there are two closely connected difficulties with this. It means that fraternity need not be an intentional relationship – as MacCunn so clearly says in his essay.[24] Secondly it is assumed that when economic actors come to understand the patterns of mutual interdependence and differentiation of which they are a part, this will then enter into their motivations as economic actors – as Hegel clearly says: 'this becomes the conscious object of my labour', and as Henry Jones says: 'we must moralise our social relations as they stand.' This is all very well, and as a critique of individualist *laissez-faire* as an abstract and one-sided way of looking at markets it may have its point, but as it stands it is much too bland. We are told nothing about the effects on economic activity which these changed perspectives and changed motivations will produce. Can a market still be sustained when this consciousness is internalized and becomes part of our economic perspective? So the Idealist response to a radical critique, questioning the compatibility of the market with values such as self-development, character and the common good, may well make an appeal to the idea of a moralized market, but unfortunately this conception is just not worked out. The perspective in which all within a system of market inequalities all respect differential forms of human excellence, and in which these inequalities still connect together a form of unintended solidarity, is very suggestive and is to be found in Rawls' *A Theory of Justice.* However, it is not developed in any detail by even the Idealists or Rawls.

The other strategy which is clearly adopted by Green was to argue that the common good must primarily be sought in objects which cannot be competed for, and therefore are not subject to market competition. Obviously Green recognized that some measure of economic security was necessary to the enjoyment of such non-economic commodities and other types of goods which will develop character and self-realization. However, one clear pattern of argument would be that such a conception neglects the way in which largely unfettered market activity is likely consistently to make inroads into the range of goods which is able to be bought and sold. Both Richard Titmuss and K. E. Boulding[25] have drawn attention to the way in which these attitudes and goods, which make for social integration, can become matters of economic exchange. This tendency in markets was not noticed by Green, and if it is correct (and it seems to be an attested feature of markets – knowledge and education would be examples of such goods), would undermine Green's confident assertion that the common good can be found in objects which do not lend themselves to competition. The other aspect of this is that even non-economic commodities can still yield positional advantages and lead to inequalities in a market society. Here again education would be a good example. If there are a range of positional foods of this sort, as Fred Hirsch argues,[26] then again Green's easy distinction vanishes.

It seems therefore that the Idealists had rather facile answers to questions about how character, self-development and a common good could be developed within a society whose economic life was characterized by market activities. A moralized capitalism is all very well but we are not really told anything about the detail of this, and yet it is crucial to meeting the Marxist objection.

The other major difficulty is with the notion of community itself. This may seem somewhat paradoxical in that the sensitivity of Idealism to the value of a sense of community has often been taken as one of the movement's strengths.[27] In contrast to the individualism of a liberal, democratic perspective based upon some form of Benthamite utilitarianism, Idealist thought seemed to promise a way of reconciling individualism with the claims of collectivity. Indeed this idea is central to the Idealists' notion of common good. Green argues in the *Prolegomena to Ethics,* as we have seen, that the idea of a common good does not admit of the distinction between good for self and good for others. However, there are a number of problems with this conception and to explore them sheds light on Idealism in a number of different ways.

In the first place, for the Idealist, this common good, the basis of community life, is finally given form in the role of the state seeking to provide the conditions within which this common good may be realized. As we have seen, Idealism provided one of the major steps towards the development of the interventionist state through which the various interests which divide citizens, for example, in the economic field will be able to be reconciled, as they were for Hegel, in the state. However, there is a growing disenchantment with the view that the state can be the vehicle of community, and this seems to be so for two reasons. In the first place, the state seems too impersonal an institution to secure a sense of community, moreover at the level of lived experience at least, the attempt to tie the state to the realization of certain capacities and powers seems to fail. Secondly, the interventionists' state is seeking to secure welfare, far from becoming a source of community identity, becomes in fact the source and the aspect of social discontent. Once the state has some responsibility for welfare it becomes the object of competing and irreconcilable claims. These two ideas might seem to come together in the work of a theorist like Robert Nisbet who explicitly counterpoises the value of state to that of community.[28] Full community is not to be found in the state but rather in specific, partial voluntary groups, and he goes on to argue that 'liberation of the social from the political may yet prove to be the greatest contribution to stability and freedom alike in this century.' Of course Idealists from Hegel onwards have wanted to claim that the state will be able to grant a certain amount of autonomy both to the individual and to partial communities, but nevertheless only state structures will be able to secure a sense of overall community within a nation, as opposed to the partial and restricted communities of civil life. However, after the growth of the interventionist state over the past 100 years or so, the most marked feature of the contemporary world seems to be the attempt to appeal to the values of community in order to decentralize and weaken the power of the state – a state which for the Idealists was to be the most general and universal form of community. In the view of critics, despite the good intentions of supporters of state intervention to secure a sense of constructive citizenship and community, there is no clear dividing line to be drawn between the enabling state and the controlling state. G. A. Kelly has aptly summarized this view: 'Whatever the state is in our mental image it is not the instrument by which what is best in the community is raised to the surface, it is not the locus of the common good.'[29]

However, the alternative version, which in our day is perhaps to be found best in Hayek and Nozick, would remove the state from the distributive arena altogether, with the effect that the rationalistic outcomes of the market and their all too evident inequalities would be legitmized. Disadvantage is a matter of hard luck to be relieved by philanthropy, and community is to be found in partial voluntary groups having a common interest; any sense of overall community is abandoned. This is a central political question of our day and one to which Idealist theory gives one sort of answer. As Kelly has pointed out, the issue lies at the heart of the Western tradition in political theory: 'Over centuries, political philosophy expended vast intellectual resources in quest of the rationale by which men could live well in a community and how they could suffer a superior and in some ways sovereign power that would enhance these arrangements.'[30]

This certainly encapsulates the central impetus of Idealist thought and in a sense this tradition, although under attack from the radical liberalism of Hayek. There is another sense too in which the Idealists' moralistic approach to community, citizenship and the common good is vitally important to the liberal social democratic, welfare tradition. In the first chapter we looked at the distinction drawn by Peter Clarke in *Liberals and Social Democrats*[31] between 'moral' and 'mechanical' reformers. It seems clear that during the middle years of this century, social democratic reformism has been dominated by the mechanical model. A more just and more equal society could be achieved by using the dividends of economic growth to improve the position of the worse-off members of society, while maintaining the living standards of the majority. Because growth would allow levelling up to take place, there would be no great need for a strong sense of altruism between citizens, sense of the common good, or public spirit as civic virtue, in order to secure a more just society. Few people would be made worse-off in the pursuit of social justice and fairness. This mechanical reformism is most clearly associated with the writings of Anthony Crosland.[32] However, the decline in the capacity to maintain economic growth has made it important again to consider the moral basis of a just society and how the sense of justice could be developed within society so that citizens would in fact be prepared to make sacrifices to improve the chances of the worse-off. The dilemma presented here has been most cogently stated by Fred Hirsch in *The Social Limits to Growth*. He postulates a return to an agreed morality, common good, or *sittlichkeit*, as the only possible way to underpin a reformist morality.

The Idealists in some respects did face this problem, of how a sense of common good and community-based action could be developed within a society marked by individualism. It is surely no accident that the last great restatement of the intrinsically moral dimension of social democracy was developed by R. H. Tawney, who sat at the feet of Edward Caird, and whose thought was permeated with Christian attitudes. This point has been made very well by David Harris in a recent contribution to *Democratic Theory and Practice*:

In coming to a judgement about the possibilities of returning the social to democracy, it is important to decide whether the account of the social upon which one is relying is closer to Tawney's than Crosland's. . . . In some important respects Tawney is more nearly right than Crosland. . . . Tawney may well have been right that public-spiritedness, a commitment to public purposes rooted in a sense of community membership, is a precondition of achieving a wider range of socially acceptable outcomes than Crosland admits. Perhaps a wide range of social outcomes needs to be actively, intentionally and collectively pursued.[33]

To recognize that one is a member of a community, and to respond to the moral demands which this involves, is crucial to the moralistic as opposed to the more mechanistic, invisible hand procedures of mid-century social reformism. The Idealists were at the very beginning of this way of thinking. Some of their specific ideas in this area are worth holding on to, perhaps particularly in relation to poverty and social work. It is a frequent criticism of the social democratic response to poverty in the past 30 years that it has led to the establishment of a centralized, professional, bureaucratic administration, with management on the one side and clientism on the other. This has the effect, as Titmuss notes, of further depleting the sense of community, citizen altruism and voluntary commitment. The great strength of Idealist thought in the sphere of social work, both individualized and communitarian, is that they were absolutely right in seeing it in the context of social and moral theory. Social work in the middle years of this century has been bedevilled by wholly inappropriate medical analogies and a misplaced pseudo-medical language. The growth of professionalism and expertise based upon this has driven voluntary activity to the margin. The situation of social work in the context of a moral theory of citizenship, an account of human capacities, and the nature of political community, is a much more appropriate way of conceiving the activity. It is humanistic and preserves much more the sense of the dignity of the person than does talk about social health, social pathology, adjustment and the like.[34] Indeed, the growth of managerialism and professionalism in these spheres may thus be seen as a lack of confidence in the possibility of achieving some kind of moral agreement within society.[35] When a sense of community and the common good have collapsed there is pressure to turn what are at root moral issues into problems of technique, expertise and management.

On the other hand, an over-emphasis upon a communitarian approach to welfare, based upon ideas of citizens responding to one another's needs out of a concern for the common good, does have very definite dangers. If welfare is seen on the basis of altruism, voluntary effort and charity, as opposed to being a right which has a positive legal form, it is not at all clear that effective citizenship could be encouraged.

Idealists such as Bosanquet and Green were worried about the maintenance of self-reliance and character in the provision of welfare benefits, but it is not at all clear that these qualities in individuals, important though they are, are necessarily developed through welfare seen as charity. It might be thought that effective citizenship – having the material means for self-develoment and self-reliance, might be much more likely to be developed if welfare was seen as a right and an entitlement. While it may be a duty to be benevolent, no specific individual has a right to another person's benevolence. This might well mean that the receipt of charity would be discriminating and stigmatizing, with unfortunate consequences for a sense of self-reliance and citizenship.[36] Whereas if there is a legal right to welfare, which is thought to represent a fundamental human right, this is perhaps more likely to involve a greater sense of dignity and self-reliance on the part of the disadvantaged. If, as the Idealists maintained, the possession of material means is a condition of citizenship, then it seems a small step to say that the provision of such means is a right which citizens must have. Otherwise, citizens would be dependent upon the charitable impulses of others but, because of the discriminating character of benevolence, a particular individual may not be a recipient, even if legally he is a citizen. The maxim 'from each as he chooses to each as he is chosen' is fair enough if a particular citizen happens to be among the chosen, but it seems an odd basis for self-reliance and a haphazard way of securing a common sense of citizenship. At the same time to see welfare as a right rather than a gift does not avoid the moral difficulties mentioned earlier. A theory of human rights has to be grounded in some commonly accepted morality.[37] This morality may not be of a communitarian sort, but it is nevertheless a morality, and the difficulty of grounding it is not avoided.

The problem of grounding any sort of morality is very acute for us, whereas for Green the problem did not appear so difficult. He took the view that he was bringing into a rational and exoteric form, a moral consciousness, a Christian consciousness which was already implicit and immanent in the minds of citizens. In his view, this rational secularized form of political and moral theory did not stand outside the consciousness of ordinary men and women in an abstract and disembodied way. It was implicit in their conception of themselves and their relations between one another. The further inroads of secularization and moral pluralism have made this assumption difficult to accept today and impossible to imitate. Its vocabulary and its presuppositions are now inappropriate and, to the secular conscience, alien. However, as we have seen, the vision of civic idealism, of constructive citizenship is, despite the vagaries of Idealism itself, an important one, and the attempt to tie together a theory of the state and some account of human capacities and powers, is still a central part of the vocation of the political philosophers. In this sense then, there is still a case for looking at the Idealists, not just as a group of philosophers who were historically important in the development of Liberalism and social democracy, but also as thinkers who posed central issues in this tradition – issues which are again emerging. In his assessment of the Idealists, Collini states in his magisterial work that their mode of thought 'was embedded in a set of assumptions which no longer demands our allegiance, and addressed to a range of problems which no longer commands our attention.'[38] The argument of this book is that while the first of these judgements is true, the second is not.

Notes and References

CHAPTER 1 *The State, Citizenship and Idealism*

1. T. H. Green (1836–82), educated at Rugby and Balliol College, Oxford. Green was subsequently Fellow of Balliol and Whyte's Professor of Moral Philosophy, University of Oxford 1878–82. His major works *Prolegomena to Ethics* and *Lectures on the Principles of Political Obligation* were published posthumously.
2. H. Jones (1852–1923), educated at Glasgow University where he was a pupil of Edward Caird. Subsequently Professor of Moral Philosophy, University of St Andrews, and Professor of Moral Philosophy at Glasgow University. Author of *Idealism as a Practical Creed, The Working Faith of a Social Reformer, Social Powers, Principles of Citizenship,* knighted 1912.
3. B. Bosanquet (1840–1923), entered Balliol College 1867. Fellow and Tutor, University College, Oxford, (1871–81). Professor of Moral Philosophy, St Andrew's University 1903–08. Prominent figure in The Charity Organization Society.
4. D. G. Ritchie (1856–1903), Fellow and Tutor at Jesus College, Oxford. Subsequently Professor of Logic and Metaphysics at St Andrews University. An early Fabian.
5. W. Wallace (1843–97), educated St Andrews University and Balliol College, Oxford. Fellow of Merton College from 1867. Succeeded T. H. Green as Whyte's Professor of Moral Philosophy in 1882.
6. E. Caird (1835–1908), educated at St Andrews University and Balliol College, Oxford. Fellow and Tutor Merton College, Oxford. Subsequently Professor of Moral Philosophy, Glasgow University 1866–93 and Master of Balliol 1893–1907.
7. R. B. Haldane (1850–1928), educated Edinburgh and Göttingen. QC 1890. MP for East Lothian 1885–1911. Secretary of State for War 1905–12. Lord Chancellor 1912–15 and from 1924–25 in the first Labour Government. Opposition leader in the House of Lords 1925–28.
8. P. Clarke, *Liberals and Social Democrats,* Cambridge, 1978.

9. See V. Bogdanor, *Multi-Party Politics and the Constitution*, Cambridge, 1983.
10. G. Lichtheim, *Marxism*, London, 1961, p. 220.
11. M. Pugh, *The Making of Modern British Politics*, Oxford, 1982, p. 112.
12. K. Dyson, *The State Tradition in Western Europe*, Oxford, 1980, p. 191.
13. F. Hayek, *Law, Legislation and Liberty*, Vol. II, *The Mirage of Social Justice*, London, 1976.
14. M. Friedman, *Capitalism and Freedom*, Chicago, 1962.
15. R. Nozick, *Anarchy, State and Utopia*, Oxford, 1974.
16. R. Terrill, *R. H. Tawney and His Times: Socialism as Fellowship*, London, 1974.
17. A. Warde, *Consensus and Beyond*, Manchester, 1981.
18. F. Inglis, *Radical Earnestness: English Social Theory 1880–1980*, Oxford, 1982.
19. A. Ulam, *Philosophical Foundations of English Socialism*, Harvard, 1951.
20. J. Rawls, *A Theory of Justice*, Oxford, 1972.
21. D. Marquand, Introduction to *John P. Mackintosh on Parliament and Social Democracy*, London, 1982.

CHAPTER 2 *'The Word is Nigh Thee': The Religious Concept of Idealism*

1. T. H. Green, *Collected Works*, ed. R. L. Nettleship, London, 1885–88, Vol. 3, p. 93.
2. H. P. Liddon, *The Divinity of Our Lord and Saviour Jesus Christ*, Oxford, 1875, p. 44.
3. A. Toynbee, Notes and jottings in *Industrial Revolution*, London, 1969, p. 246.
4. A. MacIntyre, *Secularisation and Moral Change*, Oxford, 1972, p. 29.
5. A. Toynbee, *Preface to Witness of God*, London 1884, p. 8.
6. T. H. Green, *Collected Works*, Vol. 3, p. 169. For a recent discussion of these themes see R. Sennett *The Fall of Public Man*, Cambridge, 1977, ch. 5. For Hegel's view see Wohl, *Theologische Jügendschriften*, Tübingen, 1908, p. 224.
7. R. Glockner (ed.) Hegel's *Samtliche Werke* Stuttgart, 1927, Vol. 9, pp. 1–30, para. 247.
8. F. C. Baur *Lehrbuch der Dogmengeschichte*, Tübingen, 1847, p. 56.
9. For a discussion of this aspect of Hegel's thought see L. Colletti, *Marxism and Hegel*, London, 1973.
10. These issues can only be touched on in the present context. For a full discussion see W. Pannenberg *Jesus: God and Man*, London, 1968.
11. T. H. Green, *Collected Works*, see Vol. 3, p. 146.

12. D. F. Strauss, *The Life of Jesus*, translated by George Eliot, edited with an introduction by P. C. Hodgson, London, 1973, p. 777.
13. H. P. Liddon, *The Divinity of Our Lord*, p. 146.
14. T. H. Green, *Collected Works*, Vol. 3, p. 239. Italics added.
15. See Green's essay 'The Conversion of Paul', *Collected Works*, Vol. 3, p. 186.
16. Ibid., p. 189.
17. Ibid., p. 121, 'philosophy on its part is seen to be the effort towards self-recognition of that spiritual life of the world, which fulfils itself in many ways but most completely in the Christian religion and to be thus related to religion as the flower to the leaf.'
18. Ibid., p. 221.
19. Ibid., p. 225.
20. Ibid., p. 227.
21. Ibid., p. 233.

CHAPTER 3 *A Metaphysical Theory of Politics*

1. T. H. Green, *Prolegomena to Ethics*, A. C. Bradley (ed.), Oxford, 1906, p. 12.
2. Ibid., p. 22.
3. Ibid., p. 31.
4. Ibid., p. 41.
5. Ibid., p. 208.
6. T. H. Green, *Collected Works*, Vol. 3, p. 233.
7. T. H. Green, *Prolegomena*, p. 103.
8. Ibid., p. 206.
9. Ibid., p. 189.
10. Ibid., p. 206.
11. Ibid., p. 210.
12. Ibid., p. 219.
13. Ibid., p. 219..
14. R. B. Haldane (ed.), *Essays in Philosophical Criticism*, London, 1884, p. 201.
15. T. H. Green, *Prolegomena*, p. 231.
16. Ibid., p. 251–2.
17. Ibid., p. 281.
18. Ibid., p. 289.
19. Ibid., p. 220.
20. Ibid., p. 220.
21. Ibid., p. 220.
22. Ibid., p. 283.
23. Ibid., p. 288.
24. See R. Plant, 'Hegel's Social Theory', *New Left Review*, 1977, 103–4.

25. Sir Henry Jones, *The Working Faith of a Social Reformer*, London, 1910, p. 114.
26. A. Toynbee, *Industrial Revolution*, p. 251. The view is also to be found in E. Caird's 'College Life' in *Lay Sermons*, Glasgow, 1907.
27. A. J. M. Milne, *The Social Philosophy of English Idealism*, London, 1962, p. 49.
28. Sir Henry Jones, *The Principles of Citizenship*, London, 1919, p. 89.
29. J. MacCunn, *The Ethics of Citizenship*, Glasgow, 1894.
30. J. H. Muirhead and H. J. W. Hetherington, *Social Purpose*, London, 1922, pp. 291–2.
31. E. Caird, *Lay Sermons*, p. 37.
32. J. H. Muirhead (ed.), *Birmingham Institution Lectures*, Birmingham, 1911, p. vii.
33. J. H. Muirhead and H. J. W. Hetherington, *Social Purpose*, p. 122.
34. J. S. MacKenzie, *An Introduction to Social Philosophy*, Glasgow, 1895, p. 175.
35. E. Caird, *Lay Sermons*, p. 70.
36. B. Bosanquet, 'The Kingdom of God on Earth' *Science and Philosophy*, London, 1927, p. 344.
37. T. H. Green, *Lectures on the Principles of Political Obligation*, London, 1966, p. 224.
38. Ibid., pp. 227–8.
39. Ibid., p. 225.
40. Ibid., p. 227.
41. Ibid., pp. 217–20.
42. Ibid., p. 45.
43. J. MacCunn, *Ethics of Citizenship*, p. 56.
44. W. Wallace, 'Natural Rights', *Lectures and Essays on Natural Theology and Ethics*, Oxford, 1898, p. 258, p. 289.
45. T. H. Green, *Lectures*, p. 220.
46. J. S. MacKenzie, *The Manual of Ethics*, London 1897, p. 298.
47. B. Bosanquet, *Aspects of the Social Problem*, London, 1895, p. 311.
48. H. J. W. Hetherington, *Life and Letters of Sir Henry Jones*, London, 1924, p. 137.
49. C. B. Macpherson, Oxford, 1973, p. 120.
50. Ibid., p. 175.
51. Ibid., p. 201.
52. R. Nozick, *Anarchy, State and Utopia*, Oxford, 1974.
53. Wallace, *Lectures and Essays*, p. 318.

CHAPTER 4 *'Freedom in a more Subtle Sense': The Political Context of Idealism*

1. A. Toynbee, 'Are Radicals Socialists?', *Industrial Revolution*, p. 203.

2. This is especially true of groups such as the Rainbow Circle and the editorial board of *The Progressive Review*. Various articles by Haldane in the *Contemporary Review* are also of great interest in this context; see particularly 'The Liberal Party and Its Prospects', Jan. 1888.
3. See A. Bullock and M. Shock, *The Liberal Tradition from Fox to Keynes*, Oxford, 1967, p. xxxi.
4. T. H. Green, *Lectures*, pp. 225–7.
5. See O. MacDonagh, *Early Victorian Government 1830–1870*, London, 1977, pp. 15–16.
6. R. B. McCallum, *The Liberal Party From Earl Grey to Asquith*, London, 1963, p. 52.
7. See M. Barker, *Gladstone and Radicalism*, Sussex, 1975, p. 11.
8. Ibid., p. 13.
9. A. Toynbee, *Industrial Revolution*, pp. 215–16.
10. Ibid.
11. T. H. Green, *Collected Works*, Vol. 3.
12. T. H. Green, *Lectures*, p. 41.
13. A. Toynbee, *Industrial Revolution*, p. 219.
14. M. Barker, *Gladstone and Radicalism*, pp. 14–15.
15. A. Toynbee, *Industrial Revolution*, p. 219.
16. T. H. Green, *Collected Works*, Vol. 3, p. 367.

CHAPTER 5 *The New Liberalism and Radical Philosophical Idealism*

1. H. H. Asquith, A. Acland, Edward Grey, H. Samuel, L. T. Hobhouse, J. A. Hobson, W. H. Beveridge, R. B. Morant and W. J. Braithwaite were educated in Oxford in this period. In addition R. B. Haldane, though not a pupil of Green's, was a disciple and made some contribution to Idealist philosophy.
2. Such as Tweedmouth, Bryce, Elgin and Rippon, for instance.
3. This area has expanded in the last few decades. See specifically S. Collini, *Liberalism and Sociology: L. T. Hobhouse and Political Argument in England 1880–1915*, Cambridge, 1979; Michael Freeden, *The New Liberalism: An Ideology of Social Reform*, Oxford, 1978; Peter Clarke, *Liberals and Social Democrats*, Cambridge, 1978; A. F. Havinghurst, *Radical Journalist: H. W. Massingham*, Cambridge, 1974; J. Allett, *New Liberalism: The Political Economy of J. A. Hobson*, Toronto, 1981. See also P. Weiler, *The New Liberalism: Liberal Social Theory in Great Britain*, New York, 1982.
4. J. R. Hay, *The Origins of the Liberal Welfare Reforms 1906–14*, London, 1975.
5. This is a common view in historical work of the period; see M. Bruce *The Coming of the Welfare State*, London, 1966; H. V. Emy, *Liberals, Radicals and Social Politics 1892–1914*, Cambridge, 1973, p. 296.
6. Emy, *Liberals, Radicals*, p. 165.

7. B. B. Gilbert, *The Evolution of National Insurance in Great Britain,* London, 1966, p. 448.

8. Compare Colin Cross, *The Liberals in Power 1905–14,* London, 1963; T. Wilson, *The Downfall of the Liberal Party,* London, 1968; A. Briggs, 'The Political Scene' in S. Nowell-Smith (ed.) *Edwardian England 1901–14,* Oxford, 1964; K. O. Morgan, *The Age of Lloyd George,* London, 1971.

9. Thomas Jones, *Lloyd George,* Oxford, 1951, p. 90. See also M. Freeden, *The New Liberalism,* p. 160.

10. See E. Halevy, *The Rule of Democracy 1905–1914,* London, 1961; L. Masterman, *C. F. G. Masterman, A Biography,* London, 1939, pp. 202, 246.

11. Hay, *The Origins of the Liberal Welfare Reforms,* p. 40.

12. See H. Pelling, *Popular Politics and Society in Late Victorian Britain,* London, 1968, especially the first essay.

13. A. Briggs, 'The History of Changing Approaches to Social Welfare', in E. W. Martin (ed.), *Comparative Developments in Social Welfare,* London, 1972, p. 17.

14. See H. Pelling, *Popular Politics,* p. 2.

15. See Halevy, *The Rule of Democracy,* p. 120.

16. See K. D. Brown, *Labour and Unemployment 1900–4,* London, 1971; P. Thompson, *Socialists, Liberals and Labour,* London, 1967, J. R. Hay, *The Origins of the Liberal Welfare Reforms,* p. 29; P. F. Clarke, *Lancashire and the New Liberalism,* Cambridge, 1971, p. vii.

17. See Emy, *Liberals, Radicals,* p. 124 'intervention and socialism had become interchangeable terms.' This is true to some extent and of course precipitated Toynbee's lecture 'Are Radicals Socialists?', *Industrial Revolution.*

18. A. M. McBriar, *Fabian Socialism and English Politics 1884–1914,* Cambridge, 1962, pp. 238–9 and p. 242. See also Freeden, *The New Liberalism,* p. 145.

19. See Thompson, *Socialists, Liberals and Labour,* p. 238; and McBriar, *Fabian Socialism.*

20. See M. Petter, 'The Progressive Alliance', *History,* Vol. 58, 1973, p. 49.

21. A. Briggs, *Social Thought and Social Action; A Study of the Work of Seebohm Rowntree,* London, 1961, p. 50.

22. General Sir J. Maurice, 'Where to Get Men', *Contemporary Review,* Vol. LXXXI, 1902.

23. E. Halevy, *Imperialism and the Rise of Labour, 1895–1905,* London, 1961, p. 316; Emy, *Liberals, Radicals,* p.vii–viii; A. Briggs, *Social Thought,* p. 55.

24. A. Toynbee, *Industrial Revolution,* pp. 216–19.

25. G. Lichtheim, *Marxism,* London, 1967, p. 292.

26. C. F. G. Masterman, 'The Social Abyss', *The Contemporary Review,* 1902.

27. C. F. G. Masterman, *The Condition of England,* London, 1902, p. 105.
28. C. F. G. Masterman, *The New Liberalism,* London, 1920, p. 131.
29. C. F. G. Masterman, *The Heart of the Empire,* London, 1901, reissue, Sussex, 1973, p. 50.
30. G. P. Gooch, 'Imperialism', in Masterman *Heart of Empire,* p. 397.
31. C. F. G. Masterman, *The New Liberalism,* p. 152.
32. *Towards a Social Policy,* London, p. 52.
33. H. N. Brailsford in H. J. Massingham (ed.) *HWM: A Selection from the Writings of H. W. Massingham,* London, 1925, pp. 96–7.
34. Ibid., p. 93.
35. H. W. Massingham, introduction to Winston S. Churchill, *Liberalism and the Social Problem,* London, 1909.
36. Ibid., pp. xxi–ii.
37. Ibid., p. xxii.
38. Lucy Masterman, *C. F. G. Masterman,* p. 78.
39. Winston Churchill, *The People's Rights,* London, 1909, p. 137.
40. Ibid., p. 116.
41. Ibid., p. 156.
42. T. Jones, *Lloyd George,* p. 41.
43. L. T. Hobhouse, *Liberalism,* London, 1911, p. 128.
44. Ibid., p. 130.
45. L. T. Hobhouse, *Democracy and Reaction,* London, 1904, p. 116.
46. M. Richter, *The Politics of Conscience: T. H. Green and his Age,* London, 1964, p. 374.
47. T. H. Green, *Lectures,* p. 29.
48. T. H. Green, *Prolegomena,* p. 237.
49. T. H. Green, *Lectures,* p. 34.
50. W. H. Fairbrother, *The Philosophy of T. H. Green,* London, 1896, p. 109.
51. 'The Church of England and Social Reform', *The Progressive Review,* Vol. 1, No. 4, 1897, p. 321.
52. S. Paget (ed.), *Henry Scott Holland Memoirs and Letters,* London, 1921, p. 212.
53. H. Jones, *The Principles of Citizenship,* London, 1919, p. 49.
54. L. T. Hobhouse, 'The Ethical Basis of Collectivism', *The International Journal of Ethics,* Vol. VIII, 1898, p. 140.
55. J. A. Hobson, *The Crisis of Liberalism,* London, 1909, p. 77.
56. H. Samuel, *Liberalism,* London, 1902, p. 6.
57. *Second Chambers in Practice,* London 1911, p. vi.
58. J. Bowle, *Viscount Samuel: a Biography,* London, 1957, pp. 17, 325.
59. H. Samuel, *Liberalism,* p. 387.
60. C. F. G. Masterman, *The Heart of Empire,* p. 30.
61. B. B. Gilbert, introduction to C. F. G. Masterman (ed.), *The Heart of Empire,* p. xiii.
62. L. T. Hobhouse, *Liberalism,* p. 137.

63. See G. Spillar, *The Ethical Movement in Great Britain*, London, 1934, p. 1.
64. B. Bosanquet, *The Civilisation of Christendom*, p. 2.
65. H. Jones, *Social Powers*, Glasgow, 1913, p. 98.
66. J. S. Mackenzie, *Introduction to Social Philosophy*, Glasgow, 1895, pp. 131–2.
67. Ibid., p. 140.
68. J. H. Muirhead and H. J. W. Hetherington, *Social Purpose*, pp. 291–2.
69. H. Jones, *The Idealism of Jesus*, London, 1919, p. 25.
70. *Nation*, 4 July 1908, p. 478.
71. T. H. Green, *Collected Works*, Vol. 3, p. 432.
72. Ibid., p. 375.
73. L. T. Hobhouse, *Liberalism*, p. 143.
74. L. T. Hobhouse, *International Journal of Ethics*, pp. 155–6.
75. H. H. Asquith, *Speeches 1892–1908*, London, 1908, p. 92.
76. Ibid.
77. Ibid., pp. 252–3.
78. R. B. Haldane, 'The New Liberalism', *Progressive Review*, Vol. 1, No. 2, 1896, pp. 141–2.
79. R. B. Haldane, *Autobiography*, London, 1929, p. 214.
80. H. Samuel, *The Good Citizen*, Liverpool, 1954, pp. 6–7.
81. T. H. Green, *Collected Works*, Vol. 3, p. 374.
82. H. H. Asquith, Introduction to Samuel, *Liberalism*, p. xi.
83. Ibid., p. 6.
84. *Towards a Social Policy*, p. 121.
85. H. W. Massingham, Introduction to Churchill, *Liberalism and the Social Problem*, p. xxii.
86. W. H. Beveridge, *Unemployment: A Problem of Industry*, London, 1912, p. 12.
87. Ibid., p. 136.
88. See J. A. Hobson, 'The Social Philosophy of Charity Organisation', *Contemporary Review*, LXX, 1896.
89. H. Samuel, *Liberalism*, p. 11.
90. See Bowle, *Viscount Samuel*, p. 17.
91. T. H. Green, *Prolegomena*, p. 219.
92. T. H. Green, *Collected Works*, Vol. 3, p. 376.
93. T. H. Green, *Prolegomena*, p. 286.
94. See T. H. Green 'Liberal Legislation and Freedom of Contract'.
95. C. F. G. Masterman, *The New Liberalism*, p. 135.
96. J. A. Hobson and M. Ginsberg, *L. T. Hobhouse*, London, 1931, p. 79.
97. See E. Barker, *Political Thought in England 1848–1914*, Oxford, 1951, p. 46.
98. See A. Toynbee, *Industrial Revolution*, pp. 217–19; H. Jones, *The Working Faith of a Social Reformer*, London, 1910, p. 56; J. MacCunn, *The Ethics of Citizenship*, Glasgow, 1894, p. 81; J. S. MacKenzie, *An Introduction to Social Philosophy*, especially the chapter on 'The Social Ideal'.

99. J. A. Hobson, *Confessions of an Economic Heretic*, London, 1938, reprint Sussex, 1976, p. 138. See also J. Allett, *New Liberalism: The Political Economy of J. A. Hobson*, ch. 2.
100. Ibid., p. 148.
101. See H. V. Emy 'The Land Campaign: Lloyd George as a Social Reformer', in A. J. P. Taylor (ed.) *Lloyd George: Twelve Essays*, London, 1971, p. 36.
102. J. A. Hobson, *The Evolution of Modern Capitalism*, London, 1926, p. 432.
103. Ibid., p. 434.
104. B. B. Gilbert, Introduction to C. F. G. Masterman, *The Heart of Empire*, p. xvi.
105. L. T. Hobhouse, *Liberalism*, p. 123.
106. Ibid., p. 128.
107. L. T. Hobhouse, *The Metaphysical Theory of the State*, London, 1918, p. 60.
108. L. T. Hobhouse, *Liberalism*, pp. 153–4.
109. J. A. Hobson and M. Ginsberg, *L. T. Hobhouse*, p. 178.
110. Ibid. See also S. Collini, *Liberalism and Sociology*, p. 121.
111. J. A. Hobson, *The Evolution of Modern Capitalism*, p. 407.
112. J. A. Hobson, *Confessions*, p. 143.
113. C. F. G. Masterman, *The New Liberalism*, p. 216.
114. P. Alden, *Democratic England*, London, 1912, p. 214.
115. Winston Churchill, *Liberalism and the Social Problem*, pp. 318–19.
116. J. H. Harley, 'Second Chamber in France and Switzerland – the Referendum', in *Second Chamber in Practice*, p. 14.
117. Ramsay Muir, *Liberalism and Industry*, London, 1920, p. 29.
118. T. H. Green, *Collected Works*, Vol. III, p. 369.
119. T. H. Green, *Lectures*, p. 133.
120. T. H. Green, *Collected Works*, Vol. II, p. 513.
121. T. H. Green, *Lectures*, p. 210.
122. See A. Toynbee, *Industrial Revolution*, p. 219; E. Caird, *Lay Sermons*, p. 42; J. S. MacKenzie, *Outlines of a Social Philosophy*, p. 57.
123. L. T. Hobhouse, *Democracy and Reaction*, p. 224.
124. L. T. Hobhouse, *Liberalism*, p. 210.
125. J. A. Hobson, *The Crisis of Liberalism*, p. xii.
126. Ibid., p. 80.
127. Ibid., p. 109.
128. *The Times*, 15 Oct. 1906.
129. H. Samuel, *Liberalism*, Introduction, p. x.
130. H. Samuel, *Liberalism*, p. 64.
131. W. Lyon Blease, *A Short History of English Liberalism*, London, 1913, p. 7.
132. Ibid., p. 8.
133. *Towards a Social Policy*, p. 120.

134. This was a consistent theme in both New Liberal and Idealist theorizing.
135. *Nation*, 2 May 1908.
136. T. H. Green, *Collected Works*, Vol. 3, p. 371.
137. Ibid.
138. See D. G. Ritchie, *The Principles of State Interference*, London, 1891.
139. T. H. Green, *Prolegomena*, p. 344.
140. Andrew Seth, *Hegelianism and Personality*, London, 1887.
141. H. Samuel, *Liberalism*, p. 6.
142. See J. R. Hay, *The Origins of the Liberal Welfare Reforms*, p. 35–6; Churchill, 'The Untrodden Field of Politics', *Nation*, 7 March 1908.
143. P. Alden, *Democratic England*, p. 24.
144. M. Freeden, Introduction to Hobson, *Confessions*, p. ix.
145. See M. Freeden, 'Biological and Evolutionary Roots of the New Liberalism in England', *Political Theory*, Vol. 4, No. 4, 1976, pp. 485–6; see also Freeden, *The New Liberalism*.
146. J. H. Muirhead, *Reflections of a Journeyman in Philosophy*, London, 1942, pp. 160–61.
147. H. Samuel, *Memoirs*, London, 1945, p. 25.
148. H. Samuel, *Liberalism*, Introduction, p. x.
149. *Nation*, 2 May 1908, p. 144.
150. *Nation*, 7 Nov. 1908, p. 211.
151. Ibid.
152. Ramsay Muir, *Liberalism and Industry*, p. 30.
153. D. G. Ritchie, *Principles of State Interference*, p. 138.
154. Ibid., p. 147.
155. Sir Henry Jones, *The Working Faith of a Social Reformer*, p. 10.
156. E. Caird, *Lay Sermons*, see 'Salvation and Hereafter'.
157. *Second Chambers in Practice*, with a Preface by A. Parsons, p. vi.
158. Ibid.
159. See H. V. Emy, *Liberals, Radicals and Social Politics*, pp. 287–9.
160. E. Barker, *Political Thought in England*, p. 65.
161. H. C. G. Matthew, *The Liberal Imperialists: the Ideas and Politics of a Post-Gladstonian Elite*, Oxford, 1973, p. 249.
162. L. T. Hobhouse, *International Journal of Ethics*, p. 143.
163. J. A. Hobson, *Confessions*, p. 126.
164. W. H. Beveridge, *Power and Influence*, London, 1953, p. 51.
165. C. F. G. Masterman, *The Condition of England*, p. 150.
166. Ibid., p. 150.
167. H. Jones, 'The Corruption of the Citizenship of the Working Man', *Hibbert Journal*, Vol. X, 1911–12, p. 176.
168. Ramsay MacDonald, *Hibbert Journal*, Vol. X, 1911–12. It is interesting to note that in the view of A. H. Birch 'the view of politics that is presented in MacDonald's book *Socialism and Government* is nearer to the Idealist view than any other', A. H. Birch, *Representative and Responsible Government*, London, 1969, p. 102.

169. C. F. G. Masterman, *How England is Governed*, London, 1921, p. viii.
170. Ibid., p. 262.
171. M. Richter, *The Politics of Conscience*, p. 77.
172. J. Muirhead and H. J. Hetherington, *Social Purpose*, p. 291.
173. Ibid., p. 97.
174. J. MacCunn, *Six Radical Thinkers*, London, 1907, p. 220.
175. H. Jones 'The Education of the Citizen', *The Round Table*, Vol. VII, 1916, p. 472.
176. A. Toynbee, 'The Education of Co-operators', *The Industrial Revolution*, p. 226.
177. W. Wallace, *Lectures and Essays on Natural Theology and Ethics*, p. 150.
178. Ross Terrill, *R. H. Tawney and His Times, Socialism as Fellowship*, London, 1974, p. 177.
179. Ibid., p. 211.
180. T. H. Marshall, *Citizenship and Social Class*, Cambridge, 1950, quoted on p. 5.
181. Ibid., p. 9.
182. Ibid., pp. 65–6.
183. C. F. G. Masterman, *New Liberalism*, pp. 45–6.
184. *Nation*, 22 May 1909, p. 266.
185. L. T. Hobhouse, *Liberalism*, p. 202.
186. C. Gore (ed.), *Property, Its Duties and Rights*, London, 1915.
187. Ibid., p. xiv.
188. Ibid., p. 57.
189. A. Toynbee, 'Wages and Natural Law', *Industrial Revolution*, p. 156.
190. A. Toynbee, 'Are Radicals Socialists?', in *Industrial Revolution*, p. 220.
191. G. Stedman Jones, *Outcast London*, London, 1976, p. 7.
192. H. Jones, *The Principles of Citizenship*, p. 148.
193. *Progressive Review*, Vol. I, No. 3, 1896, p. 258.
194. *Nation*, 2 May 1909.
195. J. A. Hobson, *Imperialism: A Study*, London, 1902.
196. H. Samuel, *Liberalism*, pp. 343–4.
197. Ibid., p. 345.
198. J. H. Muirhead, *The Service of the State*, London, 1908, p. 106.
199. Ibid., p. 110.
200. G. K. Chesterton, *Autobiography*, London, 1936, pp. 273–4.
201. H. Belloc, *The Servile State*, London, 1912, p. 6.
202. M. Freeden, *Political Theory*, p. 487; also Freeden, *The New Liberalism*.
203. Ibid., p. 476.
204. Ibid., p. 478.
205. Ibid., p. 480.
206. Ibid., p. 485.

207. See H. Jones, 'The Social Organism' in A. Seth and R. B. Haldane, *Essays in Philosophical Criticism*; J. H. Muirhead, *The Service of the State*; J. S. MacKenzie, *An Introduction to Social Philosophy*.
208. M. Freeden, *Political Theory*, p. 482.
209. D. G. Ritchie, *Darwin and Hegel*, London, 1893, p. 69.
210. E. Barker, *Political Thought in England*, p. 148. S. Collini also argues in his recent book that Hobhouse's use of evolution was in fact dressing up familiar philosophical notions in scientific clothes. Hobhouse, he says, 'owed more to Green than to Darwin', S. Collini, *Liberalism and Sociology*, p. 174. Freeden, in one sense, overemphasizes the evolutionary and biological side, especially in his book on the New Liberalism, see S. Collini, 'Political Theory and the "Science of Society" in Victorian Britain, *Historical Journal*, XXIII, 1980, pp. 203–31.

CHAPTER 6 *The Charity Organization Society: Poverty and Citizenship*

1. For discussions of Hegel's views on poverty see S. Avineri, *Hegel's Theory of the Modern State*, London, 1972; R. Plant, 'Hegel's Social Theory', in *New Left Review*, 1977, pp. 103–24, and 'Hegel on Economic and Social Integration' in *Hegel's Social and Political Thought*, D. P. Verene (ed.), Sussex, 1980.
2. C. L. Mowat, *The Charity Organisation Society 1869–1913: its ideas and work*, London, 1961; M. Rooff, *A Hundred Years of Family Welfare*, London, 1972, G. Stedman Jones, *Outcast London*, p. 301; see S. Collini, 'Hobhouse, Bosanquet and the State: Philosophical Idealism and Political Argument in England 1880–1918', *Past and Present*, No. 72, 1976.
3. A Briggs, *Social Thought and Social Action*, p. 21.
4. Anon., *Charity Organisation Reporter*, Vol. 1, No. 8, 1872, p. 42.
5. C. P. B. Bosanquet, *London, Some Account of its Growth*, London, 1868, p. 139.
6. C. S. Loch, 'The Programme of the Charity Organisation Society', *The Charity Organisation Review* No. 163, 1910, p. 48.
7. A. Briggs, *Social Thought and Social Action*, p. 20; B. B. Gilbert, *The Evolution of National Insurance*, p. 51.
8. A. Briggs, *Social Thought and Social Action*.
9. B. B. Gilbert, *The Evolution of National Insurance*, p. 52.
10. A. Briggs, *Social Thought and Social Action*, pp. 21–2.
11. D. Owen, *English Philanthropy*, Oxford, 1965, p. 222.
12. C. L. Mowat, *The Charity Organisation Society*, p. xi; D. Owen, p. 211; M. E. Rose, *The Relief of Poverty 1834–1914*, London, 1974, p. 25.
13. B. Bosanquet, *Social and International Ideals*, London, 1917, p. 112.
14. H. Bosanquet, 'Thorough Charity', *The Charity Organisation Review*, No. 101, June 1893, pp. 208–9.

15. C. S. Loch, *Charity Organisation and Social Life*, London, 1910, pp. 367–8.
16. B. Bosanquet, *The Civilisation of Christendom*, p. 362.
17. B. Bosanquet, *The Philosophical Theory of the State*, p. 152.
18. B. Bosanquet, *The Aspects of the Social Problem*, p. 290; H. Bosanquet, *Social Work in London*, London, 1914, p. 190.
19. C. S. Loch, *Charity Organization*, London, 1905, p. 105.
20. C. S. Loch, *Old Age Pensions and Pauperism*, London, 1882.
21. H. Bosanquet, 'The Poverty Line', *Charity Organisation Review*, 1903.
22. See B. Bosanquet, 'Character and Its Bearing upon Social Causation' in *Aspects of the Social Problem*, pp. 105–6.
23. B. Bosanquet, *Essays and Addresses*, London, 1889, p. 24.
24. C. S. Loch, *Charity and Social Life*, p. 367; also B. Bosanquet, *The Philosophical Theory of the State*, p. 181.
25. B. Bosanquet, *The Philosophical Theory of the State*, p. 191.
26. J. H. Buckley, *The Victorian Temper*, New York, 1951, p. 3.
27. W. E. Houghton, *The Victorian Frame of Mind 1830–1870*, New Haven, 1957, p. xiv.
28. T. H. Marshall, *Social Policy in the Twentieth Century*, London, 1967, p. 167.
29. C. L. Mowat, *The Charity Organisation Society*, p. 38.
30. S. Rowntree, *The Poverty Line: A Reply*, London, 1901, p. 28.
31. R. Pinker, *Social Theory and Social Policy*, London, 1970, pp. 29–30.
32. B. Webb, *My Apprenticeship*, London, 1926, p. 206.
33. G. V. Rimlinger, *Welfare Policy and Industrialisation in Europe, America and Russia*, London, 1971, p. 71.
34. M. Rooff, *A Hundred Years of Family Welfare*, p. 46.
35. R. L. Nettleship, *Philosophical Remains*, London, 1901, pp. 162–3.
36. B. Bosanquet, *The Philosophical Theory of the State*, p. 79.
37. B. Bosanquet, *The Civilisation of Christendom*, p. 382.
38. C. S. Loch, *Charity and Social Life*, p. 352.
39. H. Bosanquet, *The Family*, London, 1906, p. 259.
40. B. Bosanquet, *The Principle of Individuality and Value*, London, 1912.
41. C. S. Loch, 'The Development of Charity Organisation', *The Charity Organisation Review*, No. 86, 1904, pp. 64–5.
42. J. A. Hobson, *Contemporary Review*, 1896, p. 720.
43. H. and B. Bosanquet, 'Charity Organisation: A Reply', p. 115.
44. B. Bosanquet, all quotations from *Aspects of the Social Problem*, pp. 103–6.
45. Ibid., p. 105.
46. C. S. Loch, 'The programme of the Charity Organisation Society', *The Charity Organisation Review*, p. 50.
47. H. Bosanquet, 'Meaning and Methods of True Charity', *Aspects of the Social Problem*, p. 171.
48. Ibid., p. 97.
49. B. Bosanquet, *The Civilisation of Christendom*, p. 202.

50. B. Bosanquet, *Social and International Ideals*, p. 267.
51. B. Bosanquet, *The Philosophical Theory of the State*, pp. 158–61.
52. B. Bosanquet, *Social and International Ideals*, p. 229.
53. B. Bosanquet, 'The Antithesis Between Individualism and Socialism Philosophically Considered', *Charity Organisation Review*, No. 69, 1890, p. 363.
54. See U. Cormack, 'Developments in Casework', A. F. C. Bourdillon (ed.), *Voluntary Social Services: Their Place in the Modern State*, London, 1945, pp. 86–117, for historical development of idea of casework specifically in relation to the concept of character.
55. C. S. Loch, *Charity and Social Life*, pp. 367–8.
56. B. Bosanquet, *Science and Philosophy and Other Essays*, London, 1927, pp. 334–5.
57. B. Bosanquet, *Some Suggestions to Ethics*, London, 1918, p. 56.
58. B. Bosanquet, 'Life and Philosophy', in J. H. Muirhead (ed.) *Contemporary British Philosophy*, London, 1953, p. 52.
59. M. Richter, *The Politics of Conscience*, pp. 203, 267.
60. B. Bosanquet, *Philosophical Theory of the State*, p. 198.
61. J. H. Muirhead, *Reflections by a Journeyman in Philosophy*, p. 95.
62. B. Bosanquet, 'The Reality of the General Will', in *Aspects of the Social Problem*, p. 322.
63. Ibid.
64. Ibid., p. 323.
65. T. H. Green, *Prolegomena*, pp. 108, 117.
66. See H. Bosanquet, *The Standard of Life and Other Essays*, London, 1898, pp. 115–16.
67. Ibid., p. 125.
68. Ibid., p. 129.
69. H. Bosanquet, *The Strength of the People: A Study in Economics*, London, 1902, p. 30.
70. Anon, 'The State and Parental Control', *The Charity Organisation Review*, No. 68, 1902, p. 79.
71. Ibid.
72. C. S. Loch, 'The Problem of the Unemployed', *The Charity Organisation Review*, No. 119, 1906, p. 248.
73. C. S. Loch, *The Charity Organisation Review*, 1904, p. 64.
74. H. Bosanquet, *The Strength of the People*, pp. 51–2.
75. See B. Webb, *My Apprenticeship*, pp. 202–3.
76. Mrs H. Barnett, *Canon Barnett: His Life and Work*, London, 1910, pp. 263–5.
77. J. A. Hobson, *Contemporary Review*, 1896, p. 724.
78. B. Bosanquet, 'Idealism in Social Work', *Charity Organisation Review*, No. 15, 1898, p. 123.
79. H. Bosanquet, *Bernard Bosanquet: A Short Account of His Life*, London, 1924, p. 52.
80. B. Bosanquet, *The Charity Organisation Review*, 1898, p. 127.

81. Ibid., p. 129.
82. B. Bosanquet, *Social and International Ideals*, p. 77.
83. Ibid., p. 171.
84. Ibid., p. 169.
85. B. Bosanquet, *The Charity Organisation Review*, 1898, p. 124.
86. B. Bosanquet, *Social and International Ideals*, pp. 181–2.
87. B. Bosanquet, *The Charity Organisation Review*, 1898, p. 124.
88. Ibid., pp. 122–3.
89. B. Bosanquet, *Social and International Ideals*, pp. 77–8.
90. H. Bosanquet, 'Methods of Training', *Charity Organisation Review*, No. 44, 1900, p. 109.
91. H. Bosanquet, *The Charity Organisation Review*, 1893, pp. 206–7.
92. See J. H. Muirhead, 'Foundations of Social Interest', *The Charity Organisation Review*, No. 98, 1904; also E. J. Urwick, 'A School of Sociology', in C. S. Loch (ed.) *Methods of Social Advance: Short Studies in Social Practice*, London, 1904.
93. See E. Moberly Bell, *Octavia Hill*, London, 1942, p. 113.
94. C. S. Loch, *Methods of Social Advance*, p. 190.
95. Younghusband, *Social Work and Social Change*, London, 1964, p. 17.
96. U. Cormack, 'Developments in Casework', in A. F. C. Bourdillon (ed.) *Voluntary Social Services*, p. 112.
97. U. Cormack, 'Oxford and Early Social Work' in A. H. Halsey (ed.) *Traditions of Social Policy*, Oxford, 1976, p. 120.
98. Ibid., p. 112.
99. Ibid., p. 119.
100. C. S. Loch, *Methods of Social Advance*, p. 189.
101. Ibid., p. 190.
102. C. S. Loch, *Charity and Social Life*, p. 367.
103. See C. S. Loch, 'Christianity and Social Questions', *The Charity Organisation Review*, No. 71, 1902, p. 236.
104. B. Bosanquet, *Aspects of the Social Problem*, pp. 324–8.
105. For Bosanquet on my station and duties, see B. Bosanquet, *Essays and Addresses*, London, 1889, p. 15.
106. Nettleship, *Philosophical Remains*, p. 42.
107. B. Bosanquet, *Suggestions in Ethics*, p. 65.
108. See C. S. Loch, 'Solidarity Considered as a Test of Social Condition in England', *The Charity Organisation Review*, No. 154, 1909.
109. C. S. Loch, *The Charity Organisation Review*, 1904, p. 68.
110. B. Bosanquet, *Social and International Ideals*, p. 319.
111. B. Bosanquet, 'The Home Arts and Industries Association', *The Charity Organisation Review*, No. 40, 1888, p. 135.
112. B. Bosanquet, *Essays and Addresses*, p. 26.
113. Ibid., p. 28.
114. B. Bosanquet, *Social and International Ideals*, p. 249.
115. Ibid., p. 320.

116. See G. D. H. Cole, 'A Retrospect of the History of Voluntary Social Service' in A. F. C. Bourdillon (ed.), *Voluntary Social Services* p. 20.
117. See B. Bosanquet, *Social and International Ideals*, especially lecture on 'Ownership and Management'.
118. See B. Bosanquet, *Essays and Addresses*, pp. 44–7.
119. B. Webb, *Our Partnership*, p. 432.
120. B. Bosanquet, 'Charity Organisation and the Majority Report', *International Journal of Ethics*, 20, 1910, p. 395.
121. B. Webb, *Our Partnership*, p. 452.
122. B. Bosanquet 'The Reports of the Poor Law Commission', *The Sociological Review*, 2, No. 2, 1909.
123. U. Cormack, *The Welfare State, The Formative Years 1905–9*, the Loch Memorial Lecture, London, 1953, p. 17.
124. B. Bosanquet, *Sociological Review*, p. 117.
125. B. Bosanquet, *International Journal of Ethics*, p. 397.
126. Ibid., p. 405.
127. S. Webb, 'The End of the Poor Law', *The Sociological Review*, 2, No. 2, 1909, pp. 131–2.
128. Sidney and Beatrice Webb, *English Poor Law Policy*, New York, reprint 1963, p. 275.
129. Sidney and Beatrice Webb, *The Prevention of Destitution*, London, 1911, p. 9.
130. S. and B. Webb, *English Poor Law Policy*, p. 351.
131. Ibid., p. 360.
132. B. Webb, *Our Partnership*, p. 403.
133. S. and B. Webb, *Prevention of Destitution*, p. 293.
134. J. H. Muirhead, *By What Authority?*, London, 1909, p. 32.
135. B. Webb, *Our Partnership*, p. 97.
136. S. and B. Webb, *Prevention of Destitution*, p. 320.
137. S. and B. Webb, *English Poor Law Policy*, p. 358.
138. U. Cormack, *The Welfare State*, p. 16.

CHAPTER 7 *Toynbee Hall: The Settlement and Civic Idealism*

1. B. Bosanquet, *The Philosophical Theory of the State*, p. 286.
2. For a contemporary discussion of this see R. Plant, *Community and Ideology*, London, 1974.
3. J. A. R. Pimlott, *Toynbee Hall: Fifty Years of Social Progress*, London, 1935, p. 23.
4. Quoted in Mrs H. Barnett, *Canon Barnett*, Vol. 1, p. 309.
5. Ibid., p. 303, where Lewis Nettleship asked Barnett why the poor were poor.
6. Canon & Mrs H. Barnett, *Practicable Socialism*, London, 1888, p. 158.
7. Ibid., p. 169.

8. W. Picht, *Toynbee Hall and the English Settlement Movement*, London, 1914, p. 1.
9. Sir John Gorst, 'Settlements in England and America', in J. Knapp, *The Universities and the Social Problem*, London, 1895, p. 3.
10. W. H. Beveridge, *Power and Influence*, London, 1953, p. 21.
11. E. Macadam, *The New Philanthropy*, London, 1934, p. 44.
12. A. Milner, *Arnold Toynbee: A Reminiscence*, London, 1895, p. 15.
13. Ibid., p. 27.
14. See A. Toynbee, 'The Education of Co-operators', in *Industrial Revolution*, p. 226.
15. J. H. Muirhead and H. J. W. Hetherington, *Social Purpose*, pp. 291–2.
16. A. Milner, *Arnold Toynbee*, p. 37.
17. See Mrs H. Ward, *Robert Elsmere*, London, 1888.
18. D. O. Wagner, *The Church of England and Social Reform Since 1854*, Columbia, 1930, p. 179.
19. K. S. Inglis, *Churhes and the Working Classes in Victorian England*, London, 1964, p. 156.
20. W. Picht, *Toynbee Hall*, p. 27.
21. E. Macadam, *The New Philanthropy*, pp. 202–3.
22. K. S. Inglis, *Churches and the Working Class*, p. 155; W. Picht, *Toynbee Hall*, pp. 12–13; J. A. R. Pilmott, *Toynbee Hall*, p. 23.
23. K. S. Inglis, *Churches and the Working Class*, p. 156.
24. A. Milner, *Arnold Toynbee*, pp. 31–2.
25. G. Toynbee, *Reminiscences and Letters of Joseph and Arnold Toynbee*, London, 1911, pp. 161–2.
26. J. H. Muirhead, *Reflections of a Journeyman in Philosophy*, pp. 159–160.
27. K. S. Inglis, *Churches and the Working Class*, p. 148.
28. Ibid., p. 151.
29. Quoted in W. Picht, *Toynbee Hall*, pp. 22–3.
30. Sir H. Jones and J. H. Muirhead, *The Life and Philosophy of Edward Caird*, Glasgow, 1921, pp. 113–16.
31. C. R. Attlee, *The Social Worker*, London, 1920, pp. 191–2.
32. Ibid.
33. Canon & Mrs H. Barnett, *Towards Social Reform*, London, 1901, pp. 249, 256.
34. Mrs H. Ward, *A Writer's Recollections 1856–1900*, London, 1918, p. 289.
35. Ibid., p. 261.
36. K. S. Inglis, *Churches and the Working Class*, p. 158.
37. W. Picht, *Toynbee Hall*, p. 126.
38. To be found in Canon and Mrs H. Barnett, *Practicable Socialism*.
39. Ibid., p. 101.
40. Ibid., p. 103.
41. Ibid., p. 106.
42. Ibid., p. 108.

43. W. Picht, *Toynbee Hall*, pp. 24–6.
44. Mrs H. Barnett, *Canon Barnett*, p. 307.
45. W. H. Beveridge, *Voluntary Action*, p. 131.
46. W. Picht, *Toynbee Hall*, pp. 27–30.
47. A. F. Young and E. T. Ashton, *British Social Work in the Nineteenth Century*, p. 227.
48. E. Macadam, *The New Philanthropy*, p. 203.
49. See K. S. Inglis, *Churches and the Working Class*, pp. 172–3.
50. W. Besant, 'On University Settlements', in W. Reason, *University and Social Settlements*, London, 1898, p. 4.
51. Mrs H. Ward, *A Writer's Recollections*, p. 133.
52. C. R. Attlee, *The Social Worker*, p. 187.
53. Mrs H. Barnett, *Canon Barnett*, p. 13.
54. E. Urwick, 'The Settlement Ideal', *The Charity Organisation Review*, No. 63, March 1902, p. 124.
55. Canon Barnett, 'Hospitalities', in J. Knapp (ed.), p. 53.
56. See J. S. Mackenzie, *An Outline of Social Philosophy*, London, 1918.
57. See W. Picht, *Toynbee Hall*, p. 50.
58. Ibid., p. 63.
59. Canon Barnett in *Toynbee Record*, 1893, quoted in Mrs H. Barnett, *Canon Barnett*, Vol. I, pp. 340–41.
60. W. Picht, *Toynbee Hall*, p. 64.
61. K. Woodroofe, *From Charity to Social Work*, London, 1962, p. 73.
62. Ibid.
63. Canon and Mrs Barnett, *Towards Social Reform*, p. 269.
64. P. Alden, 'University Settlements in Relation to Local Administration', in J. Knapp (ed.).
65. Ibid., p. 70.
66. Ibid., p. 74.
67. Ibid., p. 84.
68. D. O. Wagner, *The Church of England and Social Reform*, p. 186.
69. W. H. Beveridge, *Power and Influence*, pp. 29–30.
70. W. F. Wells and W. H. Beveridge, *The Evidence For Voluntary Action*, London, 1949, p. 123.
71. B. B. Gilbert, *The Evolution of National Insurance*, p. 44.
72. Ibid.
73. Canon & Mrs Barnett, *Practicable Socialism*, p. 143.
74. Canon Barnett, *Vision and Service*, London, 1917, p. 64.
75. See Mrs Barnett, *Canon Barnett*, p. 307.

CHAPTER 8 *Education and Citizenship*

1. E. Ashby and M. Anderson, *Portrait of Haldane*, London, 1974, p. xv.
2. T. H. Green, *Collected Works*, Vol. 3, p. 409

3. W. G. Addison 'Academic Reform at Balliol 1854–1882', *The Church Quarterly Review*, Jan. 1952. The scheme for University Extension was piloted by Jowett and Green in premises at St Giles to be called Balliol Hall, later to be the first home of Ruskin College, Oxford.
4. E. Ashby and M. Anderson, *Portrait of Haldane*, p. 173.
5. H. H. Asquith Papers, Bodleian Library, Vol. 18; 69, 16 Jan. 1922.
6. R. B. Haldane, *Autobiography*, p. 213.
7. H. H. Asquith to R. B. Haldane, Haldane Papers, National Library of Scotland, 5915/136, 22 Jan. 1922.
8. Ibid., 4915/143.
9. E. Ashby and M. Anderson, *Portrait of Haldane*, p. 112.
10. R. B. Haldane, *Autobiography*, p. 295.
11. R. B. Haldane, *The University and the Welsh Democracy*, Oxford, 1921, p. 15.
12. E. Ashby and M. Anderson, *Portrait of Haldane*, p. 126.
13. R. B. Haldane's Preface to G. Kerchensteiner, *The Schools and the Nation*, London, 1914, p. xvi.
14. R. B. Haldane, *The Conduct of Life and Other Addresses*, London, 1914, p. 77.
15. R. B. Haldane, *Autobiography*, p. 301.
16. Ibid.
17. Ibid., p. 295.
18. F. Maurice, *Haldane 1856–1915*, Vol. 2, London, 1939, pp. 24–38.
19. R. B. Haldane, *The Conduct of Life*, p. 75–6.
20. R. B. Haldane, *The Student and the Nation*, University of London Union Society Foundation Oration, London, 1916, p. 4.
21. Ibid.
22. G. Kerschensteiner, *The Schools and the Nation*.
23. R. B. Haldane, 'The Ideal of the University', Address given to the Court of the University of Wales, Llandridnod, 25 Nov. 1920, pp. 9–10.
24. Ibid., pp. 10–11.
25. R. B. Haldane, *The Nationalisation of the Universities*, London, 1920, p. 8.
26. E. Ashby and M. Anderson, *Portrait of Haldane*, p. 130.
27. R. B. Haldane, Introduction to N. Lockyer, *Education and National Progress Essays and Addresses 1870–1905*, London, 1906, p. v.
28. Ibid., pp. v–vi.
29. R. B. Haldane, *Universities and National Life*, p. 31.
30. R. B. Haldane, *The Conduct of Life*, p. 20.
31. R. B. Haldane, *Army Reform and Other Essays*, London, 1917, pp. 296–7.
32. R. B. Haldane, *Universities and National Life*, p. 14.
33. E. Ashby and M. Anderson, *Portrait of Haldane*, p. 12.
34. R. B. Haldane, *The National Education*, p. 13.
35. R. B. Haldane, *The Conduct of Life*, p. 72.
36. R. B. Haldane, *Education and Empire*, p. viii.

37. Ibid., p. x.
38. Ibid.
39. R. B. Haldane, *Education After the War*, London, 1916, p. 3.
40. R. B. Haldane, *The Nationalisation of the Universities*, pp. 4–5.
41. E. Haldane, *From One Century to Another*, Glasgow, 1937, p. 222.
42. R. B. Haldane, *Education and Empire*, pp. 39–40.
43. B. Webb, *Our Partnership*, p. 99.
44. R. B. Haldane, 'The Eight Hours Question', *Contemporary Review*, 1890, pp. 249–50.
45. Ibid., pp. 250–51.
46. R. B. Haldane, 'The New Liberalism', *The Progressive Review*, Vol. 1, No. 2, 1896, p. 135.
47. Ibid., p. 136.
48. E. Haldane, *From One Century to Another*, p. 107.
49. R. B. Haldane, speech to the Eighty Club, London, 1892.
50. J. H. Muirhead, *Reflections of a Journeyman in Philosophy*, pp. 146–7.

CHAPTER 9   *Citizenship, Human Nature and the State*

1. See A. MacIntyre, *Secularisation and Moral Change*.
2. See R. Plant, 'Community Concept, Conception and Ideology', *Politics and Society*, Vol. 8, 1978.
3. T. H. Green, *Prolegomena*, p. 393–4.
4. These theories are subjected to precise scrutiny in G. B. Parry, *Political Elites*, London, 1969.
5. R. H. S. Crossman, *Planning for Freedom: Essays in Socialism*, London, 1965, p. 27.
6. A. Downs, *An Economic Theory of Democracy*, New York, 1957.
7. J. Buchanan and G. Tullock, *The Calculus of Consent*, Michigan, 1965.
8. R. Dworkin, 'Liberalism' in S. N. Hampshire (ed.) *Public and Private Morality*, Cambridge, 1978, p. 127.
9. Hayek, who holds this view, does not wish to use the term.
10. Some have argued that Rawls' maxim in procedure adopted by the contracting parties in the original position is not just a purely formal rational procedure for behaviour in uncertainty, but embodies psychological assumptions about aversion to risk-taking.
11. See Iris Murdoch, *The Sovereignty of Good*, London, 1970, Ch. 1; Alasdair MacIntyre, *A Short History of Ethics*, London, 1967, p. 204 ff.
12. S. Hampshire, *Thought and Action*, London, 1959.
13. A. J. Ayer, *Metaphysics and Commonsense*, London, 1959.
14. P. F. Strawson, *Individuals: An Essay in Descriptive Metaphysics*, London, 1959, p. 9.
15. See W. H. Walsh, *Metaphysics*, London, 1963.
16. S. Hampshire, *Thought and Action*, p. 234.

17. G. W. F. Hegel, quoted in Raymond Plant, *Hegel*, London, 1973, p. 205.
18. T. H. Green, *Collected Works*, Vol. 3, p. 239.
19. C. B. Macpherson *Democratic Theory*, Oxford, 1973, p. 201.
20. See R. Plant 'Hegel and Political Economy', *New Left Review*, 1977, pp. 103–4.
21. G. W. F. Hegel, *Phenomenology of Spirit*, trans. Miller, Oxford, 1977, p. 213.
22. G. W. F. Hegel, *Philosophy of Right*, trans. Knox, Oxford, 1952, para. 199.
23. J. MacCunn, *Ethics of Citizenship*, London, 1894, p. 42.
24. For further discussion of these points see ch. 10 of R. Plant, H. Lesser and P. Taylor-Gooby, *Political Philosophy and Social Welfare*, London, 1980.
25. See R. Titmuss, *The Gift Relationship*, London, 1970; and K. E. Boulding, 'The Boundaries of Social Policy', *Social Work*, Vol. 12, 1967.
26. See F. Hirsch, *The Social Limits to Growth*, London, 1976.
27. C. B. Macpherson, *The Political Theory of Possessive Individualism*, Oxford, 1962, p. 2; and A. MacIntyre, *Against the Self Images of the Age*, London, 1971, p. 201.
28. R. Nisbet, *Twilight of Authority*, New York, 1975, passim.
29. G. A. Kelly, *Hegel's Retreat from Eleusis*, Princeton, 1978, p. 108.
30. Ibid., p. 109.
31. P. Clarke, *Liberals and Social Democrats*.
32. See R. Plant, 'Hirsch, Hayek and Habermas on Dilemmas of Distribution', in *Dilemmas of Liberal Democracies*, K. Kumar and A. Ellis (eds), London, 1983.
33. D. Harris, 'Returning the Social to Democracy', in *Democratic Theory and Practice*, G. Duncan (ed.), Cambridge, 1983. Similar points are to be found in V. Bogdanor, *Multi-Party Politics and the Constitution*, Cambridge, 1983; and D. Owen, *Face the Future*, Oxford, 1981, p. 189.
34. See R. Plant, *Social and Moral Theory in Casework*, London, 1970.
35. See A. MacIntyre, *After Virtue*, London, 1981.
36. See R. Plant, H. Lesser and P. Taylor-Gooby, *Political Philosophy and Social Welfare*.
37. For the difficulty here, see A. MacIntyre, *After Virtue*.
38. S. Collini, *Liberalism and Sociology, L. T. Hobhouse and Political Argument in England 1880–1914*, Cambridge, 1979, p. 253.

Bibliography

Addison, W.G. (1952) 'Academic Reform at Balliol 1854–1882, T. H. Green and Benjamin Jowett', *Church Quarterly Review*, January.

Alden, P. (1912) *Democratic England*. London: Macmillan.

Allett, J. (1981) *New Liberalism, The Political Economy of J. A. Hobson*. Toronto: Toronto University Press.

Ashby, E. and Anderson, M. (1974) *Portrait of Haldane at Work on Education*. London: Macmillan.

Asquith, H.H. (1919) *Memories and Reflections of the Earl of Oxford and Asquith*. London: Cassell.

Asquith, H.H. (1908) *Speeches 1892–1908*. London: The Times Printing House.

Attlee, C. (1920) *The Social Worker*. London: G. Bell and Son.

Avineri, S. (1974) *Hegel's Theory of the Modern State*. Cambridge: Cambridge University Press.

Ayer, A.J. (1959) *Metaphysics and Commonsense*. London: Macmillan.

Barker, E. (1951) *Political Thought in England 1848–1914*. Oxford: Oxford University Press.

Barker, M. (1975) *Gladstone and Radicalism, The Reconstruction of Liberal Policy in Britain 1885–94*. Sussex: Harvester Press.

Barnett, Canon (1917) *Vision and Service*. London: privately printed.

Barnett, H.O. (1918) *Canon Barnett, His Life, Work and Friends,* in two volumes. London: John Murray.

Barnett, Canon and Barnett, H.O. (1888) *Practicable Socialism*. London: Longmans.

Barnett, Canon and Barnett, H.O. (1909) *Towards Social Reform*. London: T. Fisher Unwin.

Baur, F.C. (1847) *Lehrbuch der Dogmengeschichte*. Tübingen.

Belloc, H. (1912) *The Servile State*. London: T. N. Foulis.

Beveridge, W.H. (1953) *Power and Influence*. London: Hodder and Stoughton.

Beveridge, W.H. (1912) *Unemployment: A Problem of Industry*. London: Longmans.

Beveridge, W.H. (1948) *Voluntary Action*. London: George Allen and Unwin.

Beveridge, W.H. and Wells, A.F. (1949) *The Evidence for Voluntary Action*. London: George Allen and Unwin.

Birch, A.H. (1969) *Representative and Responsible Government*. London: George Allen and Unwin.

Bogdanor, V. (1983) *Multi-Party Politics and the Constitution*. Cambridge: Cambridge University Press.

Boulding, K.E. (1967) 'The Boundaries of Social Policy', *Social Work*, volume 12.

Bosanquet, B. (ed) (1895) *Aspects of the Social Problem*. London: Macmillan.

Bosanquet, B. (1889) *Essays and Addresses*. London: Swan Sonnenschein.

Bosanquet, B. (1917) *Social and International Ideals, Being Studies in Patriotism*. London: Macmillan.

Bosanquet, B. (1927) *Science and Philosophy and Other Essays*. London: George Allen and Unwin.

Bosanquet, B. (1918) *Some Suggestions in Ethics*. London: Macmillan.

Bosanquet, B. (1899) *The Civilisation of Christendom*. London: Swan Sonnenschein.

Bosanquet, B. (1899) *The Philosophical Theory of the State*. London: Macmillan.

Bosanquet, B. (1912) *The Principle of Individuality and Value*. London: Macmillan.

Bosanquet, B. (1920) *What Religion Is*. London: Macmillan.

Bosanquet, B. (1910) 'Charity Organisation and the Majority Report', *International Journal of Ethics*, volume 20.

Bosanquet, B. (1898) 'Idealism in Social Work', *Charity Organisation Review*, no. 15.

Bosanquet, B. (1915) 'Patriotism in the Perfect State' in *International Crisis, lectures delivered at Bedford College*. Oxford: Oxford University Press.

Bosanquet, B. (1888) 'The Home Arts and Industries Association', *The Charity Organisation Review*, no. 40.

Bosanquet, B. (1920) 'The Notion of the General Will', *Mind*, volume XXIX.

Bosanquet, B. (1890) 'The Antithesis Between Individualism and Socialism Philosophically Considered', *The Charity Organisation Review*, no. 69.

Bosanquet, B. (1909) 'The Reports of the Poor Law Commission', *The Sociological Review*, volume 2.

Bosanquet, B. and Bosanquet, H. (1897) 'Charity Organisation, A Reply' *The Contemporary Review*, volume LXXI.

Bosanquet, C.B.P. (1868) *London: Some Account of its Growth, Charitable Agencies and Wants*. London: Hatchard.

Bosanquet, H. (1924) *Bernard Bosanquet, A Short Account of His Life*. London: Macmillan.

Bosanquet, H. (1906) *The Family*. London: Macmillan.

Bosanquet, H. (1898) *Rich and Poor*. London: Macmillan.

Bosanquet, H. (1898) *The Standard of Life and Other Essays*. London: Macmillan.

Bosanquet, H. (1914) *Social Work in London 1869–1912*. London: John Murray. Reprint, Sussex: Harvester 1973.

Bosanquet, H. (1909) *The Poor Law Report of 1909*. London: Macmillan.

Bosanquet, H. (1902) *The Strength of the People, A Study in Economics*. London: Macmillan.

Bosanquet, H. (1900) 'Methods of Training', *The Charity Organisation Review*, no. 44.

Bosanquet, H. (1893) 'Thorough Charity', *The Charity Organisation Review*, no. 101.

Bourdillon, A.F.C. (ed) (1945) *Voluntary Social Services: Their Place in the Modern State*. London: Methuen.

Bowle, J. (1957) *Viscount Samuel*. London: Gollancz.

Bradley, F.H. (1876) *Ethical Studies*. Oxford: Clarendon Press.

Brailsford, H.N. (1948) *The Life Work of J. A. Hobson*. Oxford: Oxford University Press.

Braithwaite, W.J. (1957) *Lloyd George's Ambulance Wagon: Memoirs of W. J. Braithwaite 1911–12* edited by Sir Henry Bunbury. London: Methuen.

Briggs, A. (1961) *Social Thought and Social Action, A Study of the Work of Seebohm Rowntree 1871–1954*. London: Longmans.

Brown, K.D. (1971) *Labour and Unemployment 1900–14*. Newton Abbott, Devon: David and Charles.

Bruce, M. (1966) *The Coming of the Welfare State*. London: B. T. Batsford.

Buchanan, J. and Tullock, T. (1965) *The Calculus of Consent*. Michigan: Ann Arbor.

Buckley, J. (1951) *The Victorian Temper*. New York: Alfred Knopf and Random House.

Bullock, A. and Shock, M. (1967) *The Liberal Tradition from Fox to Keynes*. Oxford: Oxford University Press.

Caird, E. (1883) *Hegel*. London: William Blackwood.

Caird, E. (1907) *Lay Sermons Delivered in Balliol College*. Glasgow: James Maclehose.

Chesterton, G.K. (1936) *Autobiography*. London: Hutchinson.

Churchill, W. (1909) *Liberalism and the Social Problem*. London: Hodder and Stoughton.

Churchill, W. (1909) *The People's Rights*. London: Hodder and Stoughton. Reprint, London: Cape 1970.

Clarke, P.F. (1971) *Lancashire and the New Liberalism*. Cambridge: Cambridge University Press.

Clarke, P.F. (1978) *Liberals and Social Democrats*. Cambridge: Cambridge University Press.

Colletti, L. (1973) *Marxism and Hegel*. London: Verso.

Collini, S. (1979) *Liberalism and Sociology: L. T. Hobhouse and Political Argument in England, 1880–1915*. Cambridge: Cambridge University Press.

Collini, S. (1976) 'Hobhouse, Bosanquet and the state: philosophical idealism and political argument in England 1880–1914', *Past and Present*, August.

Collini, S. (1980) 'Political theory and the "Science of Society" in Victorian Britain', *Historical Journal*, volume XXIII.

Cormack, U. (1953) *The Welfare State, The Formative Years 1905–9 The Loch Memorial Lecture*. London: Family Welfare Association.

Cross, C. (1963) *The Liberals in Power 1905–14*. London: Barrie and Rockcliff and Pall Mall.

Crossman, R.H.S. (1965) *Planning for Freedom: Essays in Socialism*. London: Hamish Hamilton.

Dangerfield, G. (1936) *The Strange Death of Liberal England*. London: MacGibbon and Kee.

Downs, A. (1957) *An Economic Theory of Democracy*. New York: Harper and Row.

Duncan, G. (ed) (1983) *Democratic Theory and Practice*. Cambridge: Cambridge University Press.

Dyson, K.H.F. (1980) *The State Tradition in Western Europe: A Study of an Idea and Institution*. Oxford: Martin Robertson.

Emy, H.V. (1973) *Liberals, Radicals and Social Politics, 1892–1914*. Cambridge: Cambridge University Press.

Fairbrother, W.H. (1896) *The Philosophy of T. H. Green*. London: Methuen.

Freeden, M. (1978) *The New Liberalism: An Ideology of Social Reform*. Oxford: Oxford University Press.

Freeden, M. (1976) 'Biological and Evolutionary Roots of the New Liberalism in England', *Political Theory*, November.

Friedman, M. (1962) *Capitalism and Freedom*. Chicago: Chicago University Press.

Gilbert, B.B. (1966) *The Evolution of National Insurance in Great Britain, The Origins of the Welfare State*. London: Michael Joseph.

Gordon, P. and White, J. (1979) *Philosophers as Educational Reformers: The Influence of idealism on British educational thought and practice*. London: Routledge and Kegan Paul.

Gore, C. (ed) (1915) *Property: Its Duties and Rights, Historically Philosophically and Religiously Considered*. London: Macmillan.

Green, T.H. (1895) *Lectures on the Principles of Political Obligation*. Reprint 1963, London: Longmans.

Green, T.H. (1883) *The 'Witness of God' and 'Faith': Two Lay Sermons*, London: Longmans.

Green, T.H. (1885–8) *Works*, (ed) R. L. Nettleship, 3 vols. London: Longmans.

Green, T.H. (1883) *Prolegomena to Ethics*, (ed) by A. C. Bradley. Oxford: Clarendon Press. Fifth edition 1906.

Greengarten, I.M. (1981) *Thomas Hill Green and the Development of Liberal-Democratic Thought*. Toronto: University of Toronto Press.

Haldane E. (1937) *From One Century to Another, The Reminiscences of E. S. Haldane*. Glasgow: Maclehose.

Haldane, R.B. (1887) *The Life of Adam Smith*, London: Walter Scott.

Haldane, R.B. (1892) *Social Problems*. London: Eighty Club Publications.

Haldane, R.B. (1902) *Education and Empire*. London: John Murray.

Haldane, R.B. (1903–4) *The Pathway to Reality*, Gifford Lectures for 1902–4 in 2 vols. London: John Murray.

Haldane, R.B. (1910) *Universities and National Life, Three Addresses to Students*. London: John Murray.

Haldane, R.B. (1914) *The Conduct of Life and Other Addresses*. London: John Murray.

Haldane, R.B. (1914) *The Inwardness of the Budget*. London: Liberal Publications.

Haldane, R.B. (1914) *National Education*. London: Liberal Publications.

Haldane, R.B. (1916) *Education after the War, with special reference to technical instruction*. London: Imperial College.

Haldane, R.B. (1916) *The Student and the Nation*. London.

Haldane, R.B. (1921) *The Problem of Nationalisation, evidence to the Royal Commission on Coal Mines*. London: George Allen and Unwin.

Haldane, R.B. (1921) *The University and the Welsh Democracy*. Oxford: Oxford University Press.

Haldane, R.B. (1929) *An Autobiography*. London: Hodder and Stoughton.

Haldane, R.B. (1890) 'The Eight Hours Question', *The Contemporary Review*, volume LVII.

Haldane, R.B. (1888) 'The Liberal Party and its Prospects', *The Contemporary Review*, volume LIII.

Haldane, R.B. (1896) 'The New Liberalism', *The Progressive Review*, vol I.

Haldane, R.B. (1920) 'The Ideal of the University', Address delivered at the University Court, Llandridnod Wells, November 25th.

Haldane, R.B. (1920) *The Nationalisation of the Universities*. London.

Halevy, E. (1961) *Imperialism and the Rise of Labour 1895–1905*, trans. E. I. Watkins. London: Ernest Benn.

Halevy, E. (1961) *The Rule of Democracy 1905–14*, trans. E. I. Watkins. London: Ernest Benn.

Halsey, A.H. (ed) (1976) *Traditions of Social Policy: Essays in Honour of Violet Butler*. Oxford: Blackwell.

Hamer, D.A. (1972) *Liberal Politics in the Age of Gladstone and Rosebery: A Study in Leadership and Policy*. Oxford: Clarendon Press.

Hampshire, S. (1959) *Thought and Action*. London: Chatto and Windus.

Hampshire, S. (ed) (1978) *Public and Private Morality*. Cambridge: Cambridge University Press.

Harris, J. (1972) *Unemployment and Politics: A Study in English Social Policy 1886–1914*. Oxford: Clarendon Press.

Hay, J.R. (1975) *The Origins of the Liberal Welfare Reforms 1906–14*. London: Macmillan.

Havinghurst, A.F. (1974) *Radical Journalist: H. W. Massingham*. Cambridge: Cambridge University Press.

Hayek, F.A. (1976) *Law Legislation and Liberty: The Mirage of Social Justice*, volume 2. London: Routledge and Kegan Paul.

Hegel, G.W.F. (1927–30) *Sämtliche Werke*, vols I–XX, (ed) H. Glockner. Stuttgart.

Hegel, G.W.F. (1907) *Theologische Jugendschriften*, (ed) H. Nohl. Tübingen.

Hegel, G.W.F. (1952) *Philosophy of Right*, trans. T. M. Knox. Oxford: Oxford University Press.

Hegel, G.W.F. (1977) *Phenomenology of Spirit*, trans. A. V. Miller. Oxford: Oxford University Press.

Hetherington, H.J.W. (1924) *The Life and Letters of Sir Henry Jones*. London: Hodder and Stoughton.

Hirsch, F. (1976) *The Social Limits to Growth*. London: Routledge and Kegan Paul.

Hobhouse, L.T. (1904) *Democracy and Reaction*. London: T. Fisher Unwin.

Hobhouse, L.T. (1911) *Liberalism*. London: Thornton Butterworth.

Hobhouse, L.T. (1918) *The Metaphysical Theory of the State*. London: George Allen and Unwin.

Hobhouse, L.T. (1898) 'The Ethical Basis of Collectivism', *The International Journal of Ethics*, volume 8.

Hobson, J.A. (1909) *The Crisis of Liberalism: New Issues of Democracy*. London: P. S. King.

Hobson, J.A. (1911) *The Science of Wealth*. London: Williams and Norgate.

Hobson, J.A. (1902) *Imperialism: A Study*. London: Nisbet.

Hobson, J.A. (1909) *The Industrial System*. London: Longmans.

Hobson, J.A. (1894) *The Evolution of Modern Capitalism*, revised edition 1926. London: Walter Scott.

Hobson, J.A. (1938) *Confessions of an Economic Heretic*. London: George Allen and Unwin. Reprint 1976, Harvester Press, with an introduction by Michael Freeden.

Hobson, J.A. (1896) 'The Social Philosophy of Charity Organisation', *The Contemporary Review*, volume LXX.

Hobson, J.A. (1902) 'The Restatement of Democracy', *The Contemporary Review*, volume LXXXI.

Hobson, J.A. and Ginsberg, M. (1931) *L. T. Hobhouse: His Life and Work*. London: George Allen and Unwin.

Houghton, W.E. (1957) *The Victorian Frame of Mind 1830 to 1870*. New Haven: Yale University Press.

Inglis, F. (1982) *Radical Earnestness: English Social Theory 1880–1980*. Oxford: Martin Robertson.

Inglis, K.S. (1964) *Churches and the Working Classes in Victorian England*. London: Routledge and Kegan Paul.

Jones, H. (1905) *The Function of the University in the State*. Aberystwyth.

Jones, H. (1909) *Idealism as a Practical Creed*. Glasgow: Maclehose.

Jones, H. (1910) *The Working Faith of a Social Reformer*. London: Macmillan.

Jones, H. (1913) *Social Powers*. Glasgow: Maclehose.

Jones, H. (1919) *The Idealism of Jesus*. London: Lindsay Press.

Jones, H. (1919) *The Principles of Citizenship*. London: Macmillan.

Jones, H. (1922) *A Faith that Enquires*. London: Macmillan.

Jones, H. (1923) *Old Memories*, (ed) Thomas Jones. London: Hodder and Stoughton.

Jones, H. (1911–12) 'The Corruption of the Citizenship of the Working Man', *Hibbert Journal*, volume 10.

Jones, H. (1917) 'The Education of the Citizen', *The Round Table*, volume 7.

Jones, H. and Muirhead, J.H. (1921) *The Life and Philosophy of Edward Caird*. Glasgow: Maclehose.

Jones, Thomas. (1951) *Lloyd George*. Oxford: Oxford University Press.

Kelly, G.A. (1978) *Hegel's Retreat from Eleusis*. Princeton, N.J.: Princeton University Press.

Kerschensteiner, G. (1914) *The Schools and the Nation*. London: Macmillan.

Knapp, J.M. (1895) *The Universities and the Social Problem*. London: Rivington.

Lichtheim, G. (1967) *Marxism*. London: Routledge and Kegan Paul.

Liddon, H.P. (1875) *The Divinity of our Lord and Saviour Jesus Christ*. London: Rivington.

Lockyer, N. (1906) *Education and National Progress: Essays and Addresses*. London: Macmillan.

Loch, C.S. (1892) *Old Age Pensions and Pauperism*. London: Swan Sonnenschein.

Loch, C.S. (ed) (1904) *Methods of Social Advance*. London: Macmillan.

Loch, C.S. (1905) *Charity Organisation*. London: Swan Sonnenschein.

Loch, C.S. (1910) *Charity Organisation and Social Life*. London: Macmillan.

Loch, C.S. (1897) 'Dr. Chalmers and Charity Organisation', *The Charity Organisation Review*, no. 2.

Loch, C.S. (1902) 'Christianity and Social Questions', *The Charity Organisation Review*, no. 71.

Loch, C.S. (1904) 'The Development of Charity Organisation', *The Charity Organisation Review*, no. 86.

Loch, C.S. (1906) 'The Problem of the Unemployed', *The Charity Organisation Review*, no. 119.

Loch, C.S. (1909) 'Solidarity Considered as a Test of Social Conditions in England' *The Charity Organisation Review*, no. 154.

Loch, C.S. (1909) 'The Development of the Charity Organisation Society', *The Charity Organisation Review*, no. 154.

Loch, C.S. (1910) 'The Programme of the Charity Organisation Society', *The Charity Organisation Review*, no. 163.

Lyon Blease, W. (1913) *A Short History of English Liberalism.* London: T. Fisher Unwin.

Macadam, E. (1934) *The New Philanthropy.* London: George Allen and Unwin.

MacCunn, J. (1894) *The Ethics of Citizenship.* Glasgow: Maclehose.

MacCunn, J. (1907) *Six Radical Thinkers.* London: Arnold.

MacDonagh, O. (1977) *Early Victorian Government 1830–1870.* London: Weidenfeld and Nicolson.

MacDonald, R. (1911–12) 'A Reply to Henry Jones', *Hibbert Journal,* volume 10.

MacIntyre, A. (1972) *Secularisation and Moral Change.* Oxford: Oxford University Press.

MacIntyre, A. (1967) *A Short History of Ethics.* London: Routledge and Kegan Paul.

MacIntyre, A. (1981) *After Virtue: A Study in Moral Theory.* London: Duckworth.

Mackenzie, J.S. (1895) *An Introduction to Social Philosophy.* Glasgow: Maclehose.

Mackenzie, J.S. (1897) *A Manual of Ethics.* London: W. B. Clive.

Mackenzie, J.S. (1918) *Outlines of a Social Philosophy.* London: George Allen and Unwin.

Macpherson, C.B. (1962) *The Political Theory of Possessive Individualism: Hobbes to Locke.* Oxford: Oxford University Press.

Macpherson, C.B. (1973) *Democratic Theory: Essays in Retrieval.* Oxford: Oxford University Press.

Marquand, D. (ed) (1982) *John P. Mackintosh: on Parliament and Social Democracy.* London: Longmans.

Marshall, T.H. (1950) *Citizenship and Social Class.* Cambridge: Cambridge University Press.

Marshall, T.H. (1967) *Social Policy in the Twentieth Century.* London: Hutchinson.

Martin, E.W. (ed) (1972) *Comparative Developments in Social Welfare.* London: George Allen and Unwin.

Massingham, H.J. (ed) (1925) *H.W.M.: A Selection from the Writings of H. W. Massingham.* London: Cape.

Masterman, C.F.G. (1909) *The Condition of England.* London: Methuen.

Masterman, C.F.G. (1920) *The New Liberalism.* London: Leonard Parsons.

Masterman, C.F.G. (1921) *How England is Governed.* London: Selwyn and Blount.

Masterman, C.F.G. (ed) (1901) *The Heart of the Empire.* London: T. Fisher Unwin. Reprint Sussex: Harvester, 1973.

Masterman, C.F.G. (1902) 'The Social Abyss', *The Contemporary Review,* volume LXXXI.

Masterman, L. (1939) *C. F. G. Masterman: A Biography.* London: Nicholson and Watson.

Matthew, H.C.G. (1973) *The Liberal Imperialists: The Ideas and Politics of a Post-Gladstonian Elite.* Oxford: Oxford University Press.

Maurice, J.F. (1937–9) *Haldane 1856–1915*, in two volumes. London: Faber and Faber.

Maurice, J.F. (1902) 'Where to Get Men?', *The Contemporary Review*, volume LXXXI.

McBriar, A.M. (1962) *Fabian Socialism and English Politics 1884–1918*. Cambridge: Cambridge University Press.

McCallum, R.B. (1963) *The Liberal Party from Earl Grey to Asquith*. London: Gollancz.

Milne, A.J.M. (1962) *The Social Philosophy of English Idealism*. London: George Allen and Unwin.

Milner, A. (1895) *Arnold Toynbee: A Reminiscence*. London: Arnold.

Moberly Bell, E. (1942) *Octavia Hill*. London: Constable.

Morgan, K.O. (ed) (1971) *The Age of Lloyd George*. London: George Allen and Unwin.

Morris, C. (ed) (1954) *Social Casework in Great Britain*. London: Faber and Faber.

Mowat, C.L. (1961) *The Charity Organisation Society 1869–1913: It's Ideas and Work*. London: Methuen.

Muir, R. (1920) *Liberalism and Industry*. London: Constable.

Muirhead, J.H. (1908) *The Service of the State*. London: John Murray.

Muirhead, J.H. (1909) *By What Authority*. London: P. S. King.

Muirhead, J.H. (1942) *Reflections by a Journeyman in Philosophy on the Movements of Thought and Practice in his Time*. London: George Allen and Unwin.

Muirhead, J.H. (ed) (1911) *Birmingham Institutions, Lectures at the University*. Birmingham: Cornish Brothers.

Muirhead, J.H. (1935) *Bernard Bosanquet and His Friends*. London: George Allen and Unwin.

Muirhead, J.H. (ed) *Contemporary British Philosophy*. London: George Allen and Unwin.

Muirhead, J.H. (1904) 'Foundations of Social Interest' *The Charity Organisation Review*, no. 98.

Muirhead, J.H. and Hetherington, H.J.W. (1922) *Social Purpose: A Contribution to a Philosophy of Civic Society*. London: George Allen and Unwin.

Murdoch, I. (1970) *The Sovereignty of the Good*. London: Routledge and Kegan Paul.

Nettleship, R.L. (1901) *Philosophical Remains*. London: Macmillan.

Nisbet, R. (1975) *Twilight of Authority*. Oxford: Oxford University Press.

Nowell-Smith, S. (1965) *Edwardian England 1901–1914*. Oxford: Oxford University Press.

Nozick, R. (1974) *Anarchy, State and Utopia*. Oxford: Blackwell.

Oakeshott, M. (1975) *On Human Conduct*. Oxford: Clarendon Press.

Owen, D. (1965) *English Philanthropy 1660–1960*. Oxford: Oxford University Press.

Owen, D. (1981) *Face the Future*. Oxford: Oxford University Press.

Paget, S. (ed) (1921) *Henry Scott Holland Memoir and Letters.* London: John Murray.

Pannenberg, W. (1968) *Jesus: God and Man.* London: S.C.M.

Parry, G. (1969) *Political Elites.* London: George Allen and Unwin.

Pelling, H. (1968) *Popular Politics and Society in Late Victorian Britain.* London: Macmillan.

Petter, M. (1973) 'The Progressive Alliance', *History,* volume 58.

Picht, W. (1914) *Toynbee Hall and the English Settlement Movement.* London: G. Bell and Son.

Pimlott, J.A.R. (1935) *Toynbee Hall: Fifty Years of Social Progress.* London: Dent.

Pinker, R. (1971) *Social Theory and Social Policy.* London: Heinemann.

Plant, R. (1970) *Social and Moral Theory in Casework.* London: Routledge and Kegan Paul.

Plant, R. (1973) *Hegel.* London: George Allen and Unwin.

Plant, R. (1974) *Community and Ideology.* London: Routledge and Kegan Paul.

Plant, R. (1978) 'Community Concept, Conception and Ideology', *Politics and Society,* volume 8.

Plant, R. (1977) 'Hegel and Political Economy', *New Left Review,* 103–4.

Plant, R., Lesser, H. and Taylor-Gooby, P. (1980) *Political Philosophy and Social Welfare.* London: Routledge and Kegan Paul.

Plant, R. (1983) 'Hirsch, Hayek and Habermas on Dilemmas of Distribution', in *Dilemmas of Liberal Democracies,* (ed) K. Kumar and A. Ellis. London: Tavistock.

Pugh, M. (1982) *The Making of Modern British Politics 1867–1939.* Oxford: Blackwell.

Rawls, J. (1973) *A Theory of Justice.* Oxford: Clarendon Press.

Reason, W. (ed) (1898) *University and Social Settlements.* London: Methuen.

Rimlinger, G.V. (1971) *Welfare Policy and Industrialisation in Europe America and Russia.* New York: John Wiley and Sons.

Richter, M. (1964) *The Politics of Conscience: T. H. Green and His Age.* London: Weidenfeld and Nicolson.

Ritchie, D.G. (1891) *The Principles of State Interference.* London: Swan Sonnenschein.

Ritchie, D.G. (1893) *Darwin and Hegel.* London: Swan Sonnenschein.

Robbins, P. (1982) *The British Hegelians 1875–1925.* New York: Garland Publishing, Inc.

Roof, M. (1972) *A Hundred Years of Family Welfare: A Study of the Family Welfare Association 1869–1970.* London: Michael Joseph.

Rose, M.E. (1974) *The Relief of Poverty 1834–1914.* London: Macmillan.

Rowland, P. (1971) *The Last Liberal Governments: Unfinished Business 1911–1914.* London: Barrie and Jenkins.

Rowntree, S. (1901) *The 'Poverty Line': a Reply.* London: Henry Good and Sons.

Rowntree, S. (1914) *Poverty: A Study of Town Life.* London: Thomas Nelson.
Samuel, H. (1902) *Liberalism: An Attempt to State the Principles of Contemporary Liberalism.* London: Grant Richards.
Samuel, H. (1945) *Memoirs.* London: Cresset Press.
Samuel, H. (1954) *The Good Citizen.* Liverpool: Liverpool University Press.
Scott Holland H. (1897) 'The Church of England and Social Reform', *The Progressive Review,* volume I.
Second Chambers (1911) *Second Chambers in Practice: Papers of the Rainbow Circle 1910–11.* London: P. S. King and Son.
Sennett, R. (1977) *The Fall of Public Man.* Cambridge: Cambridge University Press.
Seth, A. (1887) *Hegelianism and Personality.* London: William Blackwood.
Seth, A. and Haldane, R.B. (1883) *Essays in Philosophical Criticism.* London: Longmans.
Spillar, G. (1934) *The Ethical Movement in Great Britain.* London: Farleigh Press.
Stansky, P. *Ambitions and Strategies: The Struggle for Leadership in the Liberal Party in the 1890's.* Oxford: Oxford University Press.
Stedman Jones, G. (1976) *Outcast London.* Middlesex: Harmondsworth.
Strauss, D.F. (1973) *The Life of Jesus,* trans. George Eliot, edited with an introduction by P. C. Hodgson. London: S.C.M.
Strawson, P.F. (1959) *Individuals: An Essay in Descriptive Metaphysics.* London: Methuen.
Taylor, A.J.P. (ed) (1971) *Lloyd George: Twelve Essays.* London: Hamish Hamilton.
Terrill, R. (1974) *R. H. Tawney and His Times: Socialism as Fellowship.* London: Andre Deutsch.
Titmus, R. (1970) *The Gift Relationship.* Middlesex: Harmondsworth.
Thompson, P. (1967) *Socialists, Liberals and Labour: The Struggle for London 1885–1914.* London: Routledge and Kegan Paul.
Toynbee, A. (1884) *Industrial Revolution.* London: Rivington. Reprint Newton Abbot, Devon: David and Charles, 1969.
Toynbee, G. (1911) *Reminiscences and Letters of Joseph and Arnold Toynbee.* London: H. Glaisher.
Towards a Social Policy (n.d.) *Towards a Social Policy.* London: The Speaker Publishing House.
Urwick, E.J. (1902) 'The Settlement Ideal', *The Charity Organisation Review,* no. 63.
Ulam, A. (1951) *The Philosophical Foundations of English Socialism,* Harvard: Harvard University Press.
Verene, D.P. (ed) (1980) *Hegel's Social and Political Thought: The Philosophy of Objective Spirit.* Sussex: Harvester.
Vincent, A.W. (1984) 'The Poor Law Reports of 1909 and the Social Theory of the Charity Organisation Society', *Victorian Studies* (forthcoming).

Wagner, D.O. (1930) *The Church of England and Social Reform since 1854.* New York: Columbia University Press.

Wallace, W. (1898) *Lectures and Essays on Natural Theology and Ethics.* Oxford: Clarendon Press.

Walsh, W.H. (1963) *Metaphysics.* London: Hutchinson.

Warde, A. (1981) *Consensus and Beyond.* Manchester: Manchester University Press.

Ward, H. (1918) *A Writers Recollections 1856–1900.* London: Collins.

Webb, B. (1926) *My Apprenticeship.* London: Longmans.

Webb, B. (1948) *Our Partnership.* London: Longmans.

Webb, S. (1890) *Socialism in England.* London: Swan Sonnenschein.

Webb, S. (1909) 'The End of the Poor Law', *Sociological Review,* volume 2.

Webb, S. and Webb, B. (ed) *The Break-up of the Poor Law: Part I of the Minority Report of the Poor Law Commission.* London: Longmans.

Webb, S. and Webb, B. (ed) (1909) *The Public Organisation of the Labour Market: Part II of the Minority Report of the Poor Law Commission.* London: Longmans.

Webb, S. and Webb, B. (1911) *The Prevention of Destitution.* London: Longmans.

Webb, S. and Webb, B. (1911) *English Poor Law Policy.* London: Longmans.

Weiler, P. (1982) *The New Liberalism: Liberal Social Theory in Great Britain 1889–1914.* New York: Garland Publishing, Inc.

Wilson, T. (1968) *The Downfall of the Liberal Party 1914–1935.* London: Collins.

Woodroofe, K. (1962) *From Charity to Social Work.* London: Routledge and Kegan Paul.

Young, A.F. and Ashton, E.T. (1956) *British Social Work in the Nineteenth Century.* London: Routledge and Kegan Paul.

Younghusband, E. (1964) *Social Work and Social Change.* London: George Allen and Unwin.

Index